Motorbooks International Illustrated Buyer's Guide Series

Illustrated **BUYERS ★ GUIDE**™

HARLEY-DAVIDSON
Classics 1903-1965

D1569661

Jerry Hatfield

First published in 1997 by Motorbooks International Publishers & Wholesalers, 729 Prospect Avenue, PO Box 1, Osceola, WI 54020 USA

© Jerry Hatfield, 1997

All rights reserved. With the exception of quoting brief passages for the purpose of review no part of this publication may be reproduced without prior written permission from the Publisher

Motorbooks International is a certified trademark, registered with the United States Patent Office

The information in this book is true and complete to the best of our knowledge. All recommendations are made without any guarantee on the part of the author or Publisher, who also disclaim any liability incurred in connection with the use of this data or specific details

We recognize that some words, model names and designations, for example, mentioned herein are the property of the trademark holder. We use them for identification purposes only. This is not an official publication

Motorbooks International books are also available at discounts in bulk quantity for industrial or sales-promotional use. For details write to Special Sales Manager at the Publisher's address

Library of Congress Cataloging-in-Publication Data Available

ISBN 0-7603-0308-8

On the front cover: One of the most desirable Harley-Davidson motorcycles ever built, the Knucklehead is a milestone machine that brought overhead valves, the duplex frame, and dry-sump oiling to the HD line-up. This 1937 Knucklehead is owned by Bob Bishop.

On the back cover: Top: The street-legal 1959 Sportster CH was embraced with open arms by the motorcycling press. *Motor Cycling* gushed, "Breathtakingly fast....Shattering acceleration...." *Copyright H-D Michigan, Inc.* **Bottom:** A 1914 Twin with sidecar. The 1914 models were the first with foot boards and the "Step-starter," which permitted the rider to pedal-start the motorcycle without placing the bike on the rear stand. *Copyright H-D Michigan, Inc.*

Printed in the United States of America

Contents

Acknowledgments

I got a lot of help putting this book together. That's always the case when researching old motorcycles. To the following, I send an emphatic "Thank you!"

The Harley-Davidson Motor Company and its Harley-Davidson Archives permitted the use of more than 200 archival photos. Dr. Martin Jack Rosenblum of the archives supported my efforts in various ways. Archivist Susan Fariss processed my photo requests, which meant lots of work and much coordination. I've also used data contained in the official Harley-Davidson publication *The Legend Begins* and have cited that publication when appropriate.

Dale Walksler of Dale's Harley-Davidson in Mount Vernon, Illinois, gave special help. Dale operates the Wheels Through Time Museum, co-located with his motorcycle agency, and has assembled an extraordinary collection of Harley-Davidsons and other American-made motorcycles. Dale and his staff rolled out the red carpet and the motorcycles. Mark Dye, Dan McMahon, and Butch Wilson moved bikes and posed for photos. Museum visitor J. D. DeVries posed for photos. Most uncredited photos were produced with the assistance of Wheels Through Time.

The following people reviewed my draft, caught errors, and recommended improvements: Chris Haynes, Jeff Coffman, J. R. and Carolyn of JR Harleys & Classics, Michael Lange, Scott Lange, and Daniel Statnekov. Stan Brock came to my rescue with airbrushing equipment and advice.

Bruce Palmer, author *How to Restore Your Harley-Davidson*, helped identify photos. *Cycle World* provided a photo. I also used a photo taken by Sam Hotton.

George and Milli Yarocki hosted a visit to the extensive G. L. Yarocki Co. literature collection. A free bed for several nights, some free meals, complete access to the literature, and the use of their copying machine were great benefits.

The late Red Wolverton and the late Tom Sifton provided information and opinions. Others too numerous to mention have helped me in Harley-Davidson matters over the years, either stoking the fires of enthusiasm or rendering more specific assistance. Test rides taken long ago on their motorcycles, and bits of information from friendly conversations, now come into print. If you think you recognize your role somewhere, you're right. Thanks.

Introduction
What This Book Covers and How It's Organized

This book covers Harley-Davidsons made in the United States and Italy for model years 1903 through 1965. The book is organized by major Harley-Davidson types, such as Knuckleheads and Panheads.

The Star Rating System in This Book
The five ratings for each motorcycle are collectibility, smoothness of ride, passenger accommodations, reliability, and parts and service availability. Additionally, a maximum cruising speed is suggested.

Collectibility Ratings
Each of the 11 Harley-Davidson types rates from one to five stars. In most cases, the ratings aren't across the board for each model, but instead vary from year to year.

This rating system excludes the investment values. Also, prices are not rated. Some of the machines that rate two stars may cost more than some rated three stars. The ratings aren't a popularity contest, so the rank order of the star ratings isn't a rank order of the prices. What you get from me is similar to what you get from a movie critic. You get the opinion of somebody who has studied the matter more than most people, which doesn't make me right and the public wrong. You just stir my "expert" opinion in with yours and those of your buddies and the public, and use all of them as you wish.

Half of the weight in the collectibility rating comes from the model's history. In the case of competition motorcycles, the history of a specific machine may be considered. One-fourth of the collectibility rating weight is for technical features, and another fourth is for rarity.

What Are Five-Star Collectible Motorcycles?
The five-star motorcycles are the cream of the cream, the models so rare and historic that they never have to be advertised. Anyone looking for a five-star motorcycle, and who knows what they're looking for, will soon learn that a dozen or fewer people form their entire shopping network. Unless you have a net worth well beyond mere millionaire, there's little chance even an absurdly high (to you) offer is going to move the old motorcycle. The protocol goes like this: You make the owner aware of your interest; the owner more or less promises to give you a chance to bid if, for example, his widow is left with the bike, or if he becomes saddled with unbearable medical expenses, or if he loses his mind and comes to prefer money over passion. Make the offer anyway because it doesn't hurt to try even though a higher offer will be expected next time. Some five-star motorcycles will command a six-figure price.

Now in its 40th year, the Antique Motorcycle Club of America (AMCA) numbers some 7,000 members worldwide. The club's national calendar of events typically includes nine nationally sanctioned antique motorcycle shows and two nationally sanctioned road runs. Machines 35 years old and older qualify for judging. In addition, over a dozen regional chapters sponsor their own events. The network of personal contacts and friendships produces shared knowledge and help, as well as many an impromptu ride of two or more enthusiasts. The *Antique Motorcycle*, the quarterly journal of the AMCA, averages 56 pages and 75 photos, covering a wide variety of popular and occasionally, for the super enthusiasts, the obscure aspects of motorcycling history. To join the AMCA, write the author in care of the publisher, and the current procedure and address will be forwarded.

What to Buy

You buy an old Harley-Davidson because of what it does to your mind. You may be out to relive your youth or you may be nostalgic for reasons you don't understand. But for sure, you don't buy an old Harley-Davidson to get a better motorcycle. Vibration? You don't care. Performance? You don't care. What matters is your mind.

For instance, I want a 1951 or 1952 Model S 125 because my parents forced me onto a "safer" Cushman motorscooter. The 125 must be Persian Red like Tommy Nickell's. Sure, I could buy one a different color and then paint it, but if I'm to fall instantly in love with one of these popcorn poppers and maybe take a leap without worrying about being sensible, then the 125 has to be Persian Red. I also want a 1952 Model K, which has to be Rio Blue because that's the way Jackie Dean Anderson's was. The other old Harley on my wish list is a 45 WL, year unimportant, but the color must be bronze—Bob Lindsay had one of those. I intend to get even with those smart-ass Harley riders from my high school days.

In short, I can't tell you what old Harley-Davidson to buy because I don't know what's turning you on to old Harleys. If your game is combining motorcycling and investing, I'll give you some clues about market trends that may help you narrow your choices. But if you're entering the game with passion, you shouldn't worry about return on investment.

Basket Cases, Rolling Basket Cases, and Complete Bikes

A basket case has two things going for it. One, it gets you started for less money. Two, it quickly shows you the status of every part, so if your aim is a like-new restoration, you don't waste money for stuff that's working but not like-new. So a basket case has a certain honesty about it; you get junk, but you only pay for junk. But a basket case comes with its own problems, not the least being what that pile of parts may do to your enthusiasm. Even fanaticism can wither away in the seemingly endless search for the missing bits and pieces. Often the parts you need are missing because they're in short supply and somebody has already robbed your basket. Guess what. The same parts will be at least as hard for you to find as they were for the guy who robbed your basket 1, 2, or 10 years ago. There can be few situations more frustrating than having almost all the parts you need because the nearer you get to the end of the hunt, the slower the hunt goes. As you struggle to find the rarest of the missing items you are competing with others in the same predicament. You can spend years hunting; many have before you. Guys have been known to purchase a complete motorcycle, the kind they should've started with, just to get the one part needed to finish their seven-year-old basket case.

Generally, I don't recommend the basket cast approach. But do as I say, not as I do. I've started two restorations with basket cases. The first one, a 1947 Indian Chief, was undertaken without understanding the situation. The second one, a 1938 Indian Four, was undertaken because I couldn't find a complete example of this year and model. Of course, six months into the basket case restoration a complete 1938 Four showed up less than a hundred miles away. Anyway, if you're after something really rare, like a 1936 Knucklehead for example, you may have no choice but to start with a basket of parts. Onward, to the rolling basket case!

A rolling basket case is a cruel thing. There's no pretense on the part of the seller that the machine is complete. You can see for yourself that the roller is missing, say, the throttle mechanism, the clutch pedal, the front fender, and the instrument panel. The engine and tranny are dirty but in a dry way and the external oil seepage is covered with a thick layer of dust, meaning its been several presidential elections since the motor ran. But the thing looks like a motorcycle. You can push it around. Maybe you can sit on it and bounce up and down in the saddle. You can grip the bars and make motorcycle noises. But in the final analysis you just have a mobile basket case. You must take it apart to inventory what you have, which turns the roller back into a regular basket case. You then learn what an amazing array of parts are missing or completely worn out. A rolling basket case is like an old watch—you know, the kind with two hands like your grandpa had. On the outside you see the two hands, the face, and the case. So it doesn't go tick-tick-tick; you aren't worried because it sure looks like a watch. When you open the case you may find nothing at all, but more likely you'll see a lot of parts you don't understand, and you'll know you are a long way from having a watch.

When you open up a basket case motorcycle, roller or regular, you, being a smart, experienced motorcycle dude, may understand what every one of those rusty or bent or gouged or broken or cracked or mashed things is supposed to do. But where do you find the replacements? If they can't be replaced, can they be fixed? Do you know the answer? If you think they can be fixed, do you know who can do it? Can you? Or are you not the world's greatest machinist-welder-electrician as well as being the sexy devil that you are?

Which brings us to the school solution, the beloved complete old Harley, stowed in Mrs. Murphy's basement ever since her son, the owner, got killed in Korea. All it needs is a new battery, gas, and oil, and Mrs. Murphy, not being a motorcycle person, is ignorant of its value. Sure. While you're fantasizing, you might as well replay your clear memories of the Super Bowls you've won with a last-second touchdown.

Anyway, by all means try to find a complete or substantially here-and-now example. Your time is well spent in this search. Remember me, the guy who found a complete 1938 Indian six months too late. Your money is usually well spent, too. The seller, in the real world, knows what he's selling so the price will be high. Dicker; he expects you to.

Follow up. I remember 30 years ago a 1950 Harley 125 that I could have had for the seller's by-God-firm $100 asking price. I left. I followed up. The next day, I mailed a letter with a $60 counter offer I was afraid to make to the guy in person lest he beat the living snot out of me. In the letter was a stamped self-addressed return envelope and even a blank sheet of paper for his use. That envelope came back with a rude reply that reminded me his $100 was a firm price. A couple of weeks later, another letter arrived, this one in an envelope he bought. on it was a stamp he bought, and on the piece of paper he bought was a humble agreement to accept the $60. I should have accepted, of course, but it was too much fun to write him a wise-guy letter and kiss off the whole thing. Meanwhile, I'd still like a Harley 125, but they're all priced in the thousands now.

The Hired Gun versus Do It Yourself

The professional restorer is the hired gun of the antique motorcycle movement. You're probably uncomfortable around him because he knows so much more about old motorcycles than you do. He's carved his notches, so to speak. If the restorer you're considering has been doing this for several years, it's because he's honest. "Honest" doesn't mean cheap. "Honest" means the guy accurately represents what he sells, both in quantity (labor hours) and quality (repro versus new old stock).

Remember that although shop rates may be scary, the pro can probably do more in three hours than you can in a weekend. Or do you have a complete shop at home, plus all the little oddball parts you need so neatly housed in flagged containers and awaiting the favor of your touch. Did you catch that "weekend" term, when I compared your efforts to the pro? The work you do on your own will largely be done in your so-called spare time, which means weekends or nights (days if you work night shift). To the extent you enjoy this, okay. A few do-it-yourselfers I know really are in love with the process as much as the completed motorcycle. That ain't you, I suspect. By the way, there's no such thing as spare time.

So take stock of your situation. Realistically consider your skills, your tools, and the demands on your time. It is a rare bird who can do it all. That's why professional restoration shops either have on board a variety of craftsmen or the shops network with proven specialists such as painters. If you have a specialty or want to develop one, by all means consider doing an appropriate part of the restoration. But if you're like me and your favorite tools are the adjustable crescent wrench and the combination screw-driver/chisel/pry bar/scraper/fingernail cleaner, I recommend the hired gun. After all, specialized work is what got us out of the caves.

How Good Is Good Enough?

Maybe you mainly want to ride your old Harley on hundred-mile jaunts, radiusing out from your stomping ground. If so, and your new purchase is a runner, maybe you shouldn't buy a complete engine and tranny makeover. Enjoy. If you decide to get more serious, and/or if the bike starts to sag, you can spend those bucks later.

What about cosmetics? Depends. Is your game the restoration process itself, manifested in the pursuit of trophies and the esteem of your friends? That's a fine and honorable pursuit; a big part of the passion I have for old motorcycles I owe to the inspiration drawn from pristine restorations.

The differences between "excellent" and trophy-winning "sensational" are subtle. Many of the high-cost differences are known only within the lim-ited circle of the most knowledgeable. To the extent you treasure the esteem of the in-crowd, go for it. To the extent you want an attractive old bike that impresses people in everyday life, use some moderation. The AMCA doesn't penalize for evidence of use, like small amounts of oil residue, oil on the chain, carbon in the tailpipe, and so on. But to win a trophy in some organizations you almost need to keep your old Harley tied up in Saran Wrap, with a dehu-midifier underneath as well. Some people actually use pipe cleaners to finish off their detailing before showing a bike. What next? Dental floss?

In other words, an "excellent" bike can be one that was a "sensational" bike 5,000 miles ago. Now, being only "excellent," the bike has, maybe, tiny chips in the paint sprinkled in places so scattered and out of the way that you are the only one who sees them. Knowing about these little flaws, your eyes have a way of aiming right at them, but others don't see them. Really. The same thing holds true, in reverse, on a lot of the attributes of the "sensa-tional" restoration. Few people, if any, will share your pride in a genuine original trim item if the aftermarket equivalent looks either the same or as good. Few people, if any, will appreciate that the paint on the front fender is flawless because you had it painted a second time, thus eliminating an imperfection about the size of a postage stamp near the bottom trailing edge where it could only be seen by getting down on your knees. Of course, mind games are what old motorcycles are all about and that can be reason enough to pay the premium bucks for the absolute top-of-the-line restoration.

But in the case of the "sensational" restoration you can find yourself painted into a mental corner. You may have started out with the intention of riding your pride and joy, but now find yourself afraid to ride it because you don't want to lose the restoration edge you paid for so dearly. The months roll by. After the initial psychological surge of owning "the world's greatest restoration," one day while unloading your masterpiece from your truck, you figure something out. Your treasure has just spent the entire three-day weekend sitting as still as a Greek statue and it wasn't started even once, and that's why you aren't having the fun you thought you would have.

"Know thyself," said an ancient philosopher. Before restoring your old Harley you need to know how you intend to enjoy it. If you plan to be a rider instead of a shower, don't let yourself be trapped by piecemeal decisions to get better parts and better work. "Better" isn't always better.

1903–1929

F-Heads

The production history of Harley-Davidson began with the first successful 1903 prototype single-cylinder. The engine configuration was called "inlet-over-exhaust" or "IOE," also termed "pocket-valve" during the era and later taking on the name "F-head." F-head engines were the standard of the day, and derived from French-built DeDion-Bouton engines of the 1890s.

Starting out as a backyard company and the dream of young Bill Harley and Arthur Davidson, the venture was soon joined by brothers Walter (1905) and William Davidson (1907). Meanwhile, during this period Bill Harley was attending the University of Wisconsin, where he graduated with an engineering degree. The little firm adopted the wise policy of conservatism. While most motorcycle builders of the early twentieth century dissipated money, time, and energy in frenzies of experimentation with novel ideas, Harley-Davidson decided it had gotten it right the first time out. Therefore, they worked hard to achieve and maintain high quality in manufacturing, to make continual little motorcycle improvements that together increased reliability more than a little, and, not the least, to recruit and grow a network of competent dealers.

Twin and sidecar
The joys of spring! Catching the F-head mood is this 1920 Harley-Davidson sidecar rig. The motorcycle has new cylinders, inlet pushrods, and flywheels. © H-D Michigan, Inc.

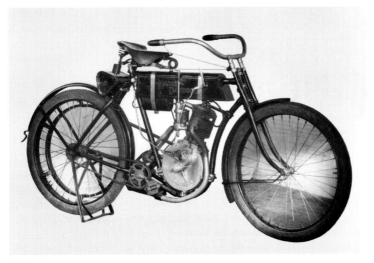

1903 (Simulated)
This simulated 1903 model is displayed at Harley-Davidson headquarters. The machine is a "1905 1/2" model, combining 1905 and later components. The oil tank is the thin section strapped to the tank top. The oil drip feeds through the needle valve under the saddle. The ignition system contact breaker cover is missing. © H-D Michigan, Inc.

1910
This 1910 model continued with the enclosed control wires introduced on 1909 models; 1903-1908 models used exposed control rods. Twist-grip controls were introduced on 1905 models; the throttle is on the right, and the ignition-timing control is on the left. Note how the upper-left-rear frame tube is bowed to clear the drive belt.

A key to Harley-Davidson's survival was unusually good management. Each of the four leaders was ideally suited to his task. The studious Bill Harley was the chief engineer. The outgoing Arthur Davidson developed the dealer network. The serious Walter Davidson brought to his presidency skills in engineering and riding, plus a strong will, good judgment, and tenacity. Production chief Bill Davidson was doubly skilled in manufacturing techniques and leadership.

The Harley-Davidson F-heads of the first decade were common-sense motorcycles. While rival brands stretched the limits of reliability by using undersized engines, Harley-Davidson used larger engines in their machines, producing both excellent power and slow-running long life. Lacking the "gee-whiz" features of a number of rivals, the early F-head Harley-Davidsons developed strong word-of-mouth support for their ability to run, and run, and run. The F-heads were important for what they weren't. They weren't headaches in the factory, in the parts department, and on the showroom floors. The F-heads didn't get in the way while the company was fully stressed in growing its dealer network and financial strength.

By 1914, the V-twin F-head Harley-Davidsons had added another attribute to the company's reputation—speed. The firm began to support racing, and after a tough first year shockingly emerged as the pre-eminent American racing motorcycle, ending the dominance of industry leader Indian. In 1921, Harley-Davidsons won every national championship race. In 1922, the company withdrew factory racing support, having proven its speed and reliability. For the balance of the F-head period, through 1929, the F-head Harleys were regarded (by Harley fans) as either the fastest American motorcycles or (by Indian fans) as

1910

All Harley-Davidson engines in this era had the inlet valve on the top and the exhaust valve on the side. The exposed valve spring closes the exhaust valve. The automatic inlet valve is sucked open on the inlet stroke and forced closed on the compression, power, and exhaust strokes. The motorcycle is from the Dale Walksler "Wheels Through Time" museum.

motorcycles that were just as fast as Indians. Meanwhile, Excelsior's Super-X was off in its own smaller 45-cubic-inch (750 cc) world, and the expensive four-cylinder Henderson wasn't around in enough numbers to get in the way of the Harley-versus-Indian rivalry.

The F-heads, which at first had been good but plain motorcycles, had evolved into good and fast motorcycles. With a sound product backed up by the company's shrewd management, and aided by Indian's mismanagement, the Milwaukee company was the American production leader by the end of the 1920s. But in the late 1920s the F-head line ran into some sales resistance and dealer complaints. Improving roads had brought reliability problems when running for long periods at high speeds. There was no crisis, and most riders weren't daring enough to experience the problems, but the ever-attentive Harley-Davidson management decided the F-heads had been pushed to the limit.

As a whole, the F-heads were the most important of all Harley-Davidsons. They put Milwaukee on the motorcycle map and helped Harley-Davidson become America's largest-selling motorcycle.

1903–1929 F-Head Development

The original 1903 Harley-Davidson had ideal specifications for the era. A standout feature was the 24.7-cubic inch (405-cc) F-head engine, which, being larger than almost all rivals, was never faulted for lack of power. Otherwise, the motor specifications placed Harley-Davidson squarely in the middle of convention at a time when numerous motorcycle makers experimented with "suck it and see" (i.e., sweet or sour) designs that failed in the marketplace. The motor was lubricated through the total loss system in which all oil delivered to the crankcase was consumed—the oil didn't circulate, in other words. The oil arrived at the crankcase by a drip-feed system.

Although in retrospect one might be critical of the belt drive, this system had lots of appeal in the earliest days of motorcycling. Chain drive was said by many to be too harsh for reliable use.

1910

The 1910 engine displaced 30.2 cubic inches (494 cc), enough power to move the motorcycle up to 45 miles per hour. Engines of this layout were referred to as inlet-over-exhaust, IOE, or pocket-valve motors. Later, the term F-head came into vogue. The long lever acts as a clutch. When the lever is pushed forward, the small idler pulley under the belt is raised, which increases belt tension, and the bike chuffs away.

The original loop frame showed perhaps the most important of all the early Harley-Davidson attributes, that the Harley-Davidson was designed as a motorcycle from the ground up. There was minimal connection between Harley-Davidsons and pedal bicycles, other than that both used two wheels and had pedals. This may have cost some sales to conservative buyers for

Starting a 1910
Owner Dale Walksler fires up his 1910 Harley by pedaling. The belt has been adjusted for no tension, so that the rear wheel won't start turning when the engine starts. If the bike doesn't fire quickly, Dale gets his daily required exercise. Neat, huh?

Setting up oiling on a 1910
With the engine running, Walksler confirms correct setting of the oiler drip-feed (no pump, just gravity through the needle valve). His right hand is on the twist-control for the needle valve.

Muffler cutout on 1910
Walksler's right hand has pulled up on a control rod, opening the muffler cutout. An open cutout produced a noisy thumping but gave extra power for fast riding on country roads, for long hills, and for heavy going through mud or sand. A closed cutout produced a silent chuffing, so the Harleys lived up to their nickname, "The Silent Grey Fellow."

1903–1908 F-Head Standard Road Models

Collectibility	★★★★★
Comfortable cruising speed	30 mph
Smoothness of ride	★☆☆☆☆
Passenger accommodations	★☆☆☆☆
Reliability	★☆☆☆☆
Parts/service availability	★☆☆☆☆

These models all shared the same styling and layout of the first successful 1903 prototype, and all are about equally rare. Technical features were typical of the era. As for history, this type established Harley-Davidson as a successful business, so a five-star rating is assigned. Models in this range are eligible for pre-1916 events sanctioned by the Horseless Carriage Club of America.

Engine............................One cylinder, automatic (suction) inlet valve disposed over two-piece exhaust valve in side pocket (termed pocket valve in the United States, inlet-over-exhaust or IOE in Europe)*

Bore and stroke ....3 1/8x3 1/2 in

Displacement..................26.8 ci (440 cc)

Bore design ....Straight

Piston Solid skirt, three evenly spaced rings

Connecting rod..............Automotive style with detachable big-end cap, big-end bushing, little-end bushing

Lubrication ....Oil metered through an oil-tank needle valve and consumed in the crankcase (total loss)

Starting ....Bicycle pedal action, provision for optional hand crank

Drive ....Single-speed belt drive from engine pulley to rear wheel, 1-1/4 -inch endless flat belt, leather-lined front pulley in optional sizes of 4 1/2, 5 1/4, and 6 in

Clutch............................No separate clutch, gradual power takeup provided by belt tensioning lever

Throttle ....Right-hand twistgrip

Brake control ....Backward pedaling

Wheelbase......................51 in

Tires ....Clincher, 2 1/4-in cross section

Weight ....185 lb (estimated)

Suspension......................None

Fuel capacity...................1 1/2 gal

Oil capacity.....................2 qt

Fuel consumption ....67–100 mpg

Speed..............................5–45 mph

Finish ....Black with gold striping, or Renault gray with carmine striping

Price $200

* Later American verbiage referred to both the side-valve and IOE designs as pocket-valve engines, so to avoid confusion, the author uses the term F-head, which was later popularized in American automotive circles.

1912 Single
A new frame with a sloping top tube and lower saddle position made the Harley-Davidson look less like a bicycle. Also, 1912 was the first year for seat post saddle suspension. The lower handlebar lever controls the hub clutch, termed a "free wheel" in factory literature. The pedals are eccentrically mounted, so the pedal chain can be adjusted independently of the drive belt. © H-D Michigan, Inc.

1914 Twin with sidecar
The 1914 models were the first with foot boards. Another first was the "Step-starter," which permitted the rider to pedal-start the motorcycle without placing the bike on the rear stand. It was the last year for the under-seat oil tank. The large canister supplies gas for the lights. © H-D Michigan, Inc.

Speedometer on 1914
Shown on Dale Walksler's 1914 single is this Stewart-Warner Police Special speedometer. Speedometers were optional on all models until 1936.

Oil pump on 1914
A close look at the Walksler 1914 single shows the long lever for control of the rear-wheel-mounted clutch or "free wheel." At the bottom of the seat mast is an auxiliary oil hand pump, which was first offered on some 1912 models. Primary lubrication remained the adjustable gravity drip-feed.

whom the bicycle look spelled familiarity and safety. But in the crucial early years the "real motor-cycle" philosophy helped Harley-Davidson outlive dozens of rivals that used Indian-like bicycle-rooted designs. The Harley-Davidson frame was copied from one of Milwaukee's other motor-cycles, the Merkel. This was done because Bill Harley and the Davidson brothers had their hands full with engine design. The simplicity and ruggedness of the frame were apparent to potential buyers, and the frame and motor combination appeared graceful.

By 1905 the company bragged that its machine was the fastest sin-gle-cylinder motorcycle on the market. Technical changes continued continuously in the early years, but although collectively these changes spelled substantial and successful evolution, no single change stood out.

A 1907 technical benchmark was the first Sager-Cushion spring front fork. The "springer" fork, as it came to be known, remained in prin-cipal the Harley-Davidson front fork through 1948 on most models, and through 1957 on one model. A 1907 prototype V-twin was built, but in typical company fashion, Harley and the Davidsons decided not to mar-ket the twin until further engineering development could be accom-plished. No technical advances were announced for the 1908 season.

In 1909 the factory built a few prototype V-twins for dealer evalu-ation. These first Harley-Davidson twins were unsuccessful because the automatic (suction) inlet valves used in these engines didn't work well when combined with a single intake manifold feeding two cylinders—conflicting pressure waves, in other words. The year 1909 also saw the use of wire controls in lieu of the former system of rods and bellcranks. The bore of the 1909 single was increased from 3 1/8 inches to 3 5/16 inches, and with the 3-1/2-inch stroke displacement grew to 30.2 cubic inches (494 cc). This was the first year of optional magneto ignition; the magneto was spun by a train of drive gears mounted between the magneto drivecase and the magneto cover.

In 1910 (as in 1909) no production V-twin was offered. A belt idler debuted, consisting of a long hand lever that rotated a small idler pulley to or from contact with the lower run of the drive belt. For the first time, Harley-Davidson riders could bring their motorcycles to a complete stop without killing the engine.

Harley-Davidson turned a corner in 1911 with the first successful production V-twin, with a displacement of 49.5 cubic inches (811 cc).

Using cylinder primers

Walksler is priming the front cylinder with gasoline, using the fuel injector that's integral with the (removed) fuel cap. The fuel is injected through the priming cup, which has been unscrewed from the seat against the cylinder. The main reason for priming was cold-weather starting, so that the fuel would thin the cold and gummy oil on the piston and cylinder, which made kick starting easier. A secondary benefit was an enriched mixture.

Two-speed control, 1914–1915

A two-speed, rear-hub transmission was offered for the 1914 and 1915 seasons. The two-speed control is seen just forward of the fuel and oil caps on this unrestored 1915 twin. It was the last year for the slab-sided tank. Unrestored motorcycles, like Dale Walksler's 1915 twin, are highly coveted.

1915, wavy striping

So you want a perfect restoration? Here's wavy striping that proves the factory was far from perfect.

The twin featured mechanical inlet valves but the singles kept automatic inlet valves. This was the last year in which power transmission was limited to single-speed belt drive. On all 1911 models, the frame front down tube was changed from curved to straight.

The 1912 season saw the greatest engineering changes of any single year up to then. The 1912 twin was available in two engine sizes, 49.5 cubic inches (811 cc) or 60.3 cubic inches (988 cc). The larger twin, the Model 8E, was the first Harley-Davidson with chain drive. The Model 8E was also the first to have connecting rods with a roller-bearing big end and the first Harley-Davidson with a ball-bearing mainshaft. Both twins were the first models to provide an auxiliary oil hand pump to supplement the main drip-feed oiling system. The hand pump was for use during heavy running such as up hills or through deep sand or mud. Signal advances for 1912 were the first seat-post springing and the first clutch of Harley-Davidson manufacture, which was mounted in the rear hub. The leather drive belt turned a separate spoked belt rim, which drove the rear wheel through the hub-contained clutch.

When the 1913 lineup appeared, Harley-Davidson showed it was phasing out belt drive. Only one single-cylinder model was belt equipped. The single's bore remained 3 5/16 inches, but the stroke was increased from 3 1/2 inches to 4 inches, so displacement grew to 34.5 cubic inches (565 cc). The singles were dubbed the 5-35, denoting 5 horsepower from 35 cubic inches. Larger inlet and exhaust chambers on the 5-35 singles were later built into the twin-cylinder range. All 1913 singles featured mechanical inlet valves, a feature introduced on 1911 twins.

The 1914 models were the first with the so-called step-starter, featuring an arrangement of pawls and cams to prevent the motor from backfiring through the bicycle-style pedals. A rider could stand on one foot while using the other to start up, and it wasn't necessary to place the motorcycle on the rear stand. The step-starter was forward acting through the bicycle-style pedals. The first footboards made the scene. The first clutch pedal and the first brake pedal completed the rider's new controls. Prior to 1914, the exhaust valves were exposed; the new models featured a telescoping two-piece enclosure. Prior to 1914, the company bought most of its wheel hubs from Eclipse, Thor, or Corbin, and most brakes were bought from Thor. Beginning with the 1914 models, Harley-Davidson made its own hubs and brakes except for those used on the Model 10A belt-drive single, which was being phased out.

Four major improvements graced the 1915 lineup: a three-speed transmission was introduced, a two-unit electrical system was offered as an alternative to acetylene (gas) lighting, motor power was increased, and oiling was improved. With these changes, the concept of the F-head motorcycle was essentially complete. The remainder of F-head history would be a process of refinement.

Several 1915 motor changes combined to produce more power and improved reliability. Harley-Davidson boasted it was the only motorcycle company to guarantee a power output. The factory guaranteed 11

1916 transmission
This is the "sliding-gear" three-speed transmission layout used from 1915 through 1935. The double-gear is moved along the splined shaft to shift gears. When you change ratios, you can feel the gear teeth come out of mesh and go back into mesh. Smooth shifting is an acquired skill; sloppy shifting can break off a gear tooth. © H-D Michigan, Inc.

1909–1915 F-Head Standard Road Models

Collectibility	★★★★☆
Comfortable cruising speed	40 mph
Smoothness of ride	★★☆☆☆
Passenger accommodations	★☆☆☆☆
Reliability	★☆☆☆☆
Parts/service availability	★☆☆☆☆

Some models for these years are only slightly less rare than the pre-1909 range. The 1909 and 1910 models with horizontal cooling fins on the cylinder head are arguably five-star models. The 1915 three-speed models are also strong favorites among collectors and are thus near the border between four stars and five stars. These models are all eligible for pre-1916 events sanctioned by the Horseless Carriage Club of America.

1915 Model 11J Specifications

Engine . . . . .45-degree F-head
    V-twin
Bore and stroke . . . . . . .3 5/16x3 1/2 in
    (8.41x8.89 cm)
Displacement . . . . .60.33 ci (987.7 cc)
Bore design . . . . .Tapered
Connecting rods . . . . . .Male-and-female
    (knife-and-fork) type, big-end roller
    bearings, little-end bushings
Lubrication . . . . .Total-loss system, oil
    pumped by integral drivecase cover
    and oiler, supplemental hand pump
Starting . . . . .Bicycle pedal action
Drive Chain primary, chain final
Clutch . . . . .Dry, multiple plates
Throttle . . . . .Right-side twistgrip
Brake control . . . . .Right-side foot pedal
Wheelbase . . . . .59 1/2 in
Tires . . . . .28x3 in (diameter
    includes tire) or 22x3 in (diameter
    includes wheel only)
Weight . . . . .325 lb
Suspension
Front . . . . .Leading-link fork
Rear . . . . .None
Fuel capacity . . . . .11 1/2 pt (1 7/16
    gal) in main section
Oil capacity . . . . .5 pt (5/8 gallon)
Fuel consumption . . . . .50 mpg (estimated)
Speed . . . . .60 mph (estimated)

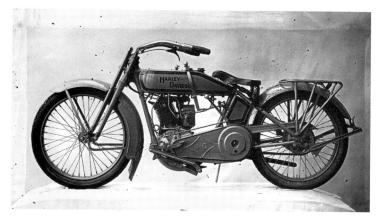

1916 F-head single
By 1916, relatively few single-cylinder Harley-Davidsons were produced because of the popularity of V-twins. Road-model singles accounted for only 7 percent of total 1916 production. This is the three-speed Model 16C. The 1916 models were the first to have tanks with rounded outlines. © *H-D Michigan, Inc.*

horsepower on the twins but mentioned that dynamometer tests produced up to 16.7 horsepower. A claimed 31 percent power gain was produced by new cylinders with larger inlet ports and mating with a larger Y-shaped inlet manifold and larger carburetor. The connecting rod big ends on the 1915 twins rode on new four-row roller bearings, two rows for each rod. The new roller bearings were the first of Harley-Davidson manufacture. The 1915 models were fitted with the first Harley-Davidson automatic (engine-driven) oil pump.

For the 1916 models, no significant technical changes were made. The 1917 F-heads got a new four-lobe cam configuration. There was still only one camshaft, but the camshaft carried four separate narrow

Ca 1919 twin
For the 1919 season, three-speed twins were the only offering. *George Yarocki*

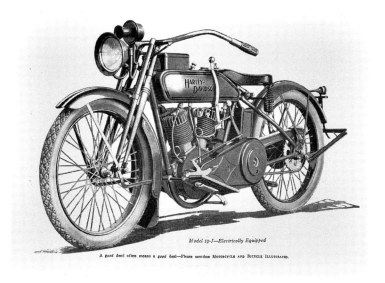

Model 19-J—Electrically Equipped

A good deed often means a good deal—Please mention MOTORCYCLE AND BICYCLE ILLUSTRATED.

lobes instead of two wide lobes. The additional lobes provided more precise valve timing.

A running change to the 1918 models replaced the vacuum-operated circuit breaker with a switch that was mechanically operated by a centrifugal switch. No technical changes were made to the 1919 F-heads because the company was concentrating on military production.

Substantial motor changes were made to the 1920 models, including new cylinders, new inlet pushrods previously used only on racing models, the first pushrod spring covers, and new flywheels. Some 1920 models were delivered with a compression plate under either the front or rear cylinder, but other new V-twins were shipped without it. The factory installed one of these

1920 F-head twin motor
From the 1920 catalog comes this picture (but actual 1920 engines differed in details). Installed are the one central camshaft and the exhaust valve lifters. Removed and shown in the foreground are the cam gear with cams and the inlet valve lifters. © H-D Michigan, Inc.

1916–1929 F-Head Standard Road Models	
Collectibility	★★★☆☆
Comfortable cruising speed	40–50 mph
Smoothness of ride	
1916–1924	★★☆☆☆
1925–1929	★★⯪☆☆
Passenger accommodations	★☆☆☆☆
Reliability	
1916–1924	★☆☆☆☆
1925–1929	★★☆☆☆
Parts/service availability	★☆☆☆☆

These standard models were the ones that made most of the money, while less common types explored different technical features for smaller customer groups. The F-head road models had typical design features and performance. Rideability: Top cruising speed of about 50 miles per hour, poor ride due to small tires, poor passenger accommodations, below-average reliability if used continuously at speeds of 50 miles per hour or faster, better reliability at slower speeds, no mainstream dealer support.

1921 F-head twin
This may be the first Harley-Davidson Seventy-four. The 1921 front fender valance is extended along the front section. The beefier front fender has concave sections to fit around the narrow fork. © H-D Michigan, Inc.

plates when necessary to equalize the compression in both cylinders, because the casting process produced irregular results.

History was made in the 1921 lineup, with the inclusion of the first 74-cubic inch (1,200-cc) model, an engine size that was to remain in the Harley-Davidson range through 1980. The increased capacity was achieved by increasing the bore from 3 5/16 inches to 3.424 inches (advertised as 3 7/16 inches) and the stroke from 3 1/2 inches to 4 inches. To handle the fueling of the new Seventy-four, the Schebler carburetor throat diameter was enlarged from 1 to 1 1/4 inches. Because of the longer stroke on the Seventy-four, the factory advised riders to use the hand pump at speeds above 35 miles per hour. A 1/3 stroke of the hand pump was recommended every few miles.

In the middle of the 1922 V-twin production run, the centrifugal cutout switch was replaced by a manual switch with a buzzer. As soon as the switch was turned on, the buzzer activated. After the motor started, generator current deactivated the buzzer. Late 1922 V-twins were fitted with a new double-plunger oil pump. New inlet and exhaust valve springs were claimed to have longer life. The sidecar wheel design was changed to keep dirt out of the hubs. In midseason the Seventy-four road models were available with DCA motors that featured aluminum pistons and drilled connecting rods; previously, these features were limited to racing engines. New rings were also used on the DCA motors.

The 1923 V-twins had a roller-bearing rear hub instead of a ball-bearing hub. New cylinder barrels on the Seventy-four featured more squarish cylinder-head cooling fins and seven fins on the exhaust manifold instead of five fins.

The 1924 74-cubic inch (1,200-cc) V-twins could be fitted with either of two types of piston-and-rings combinations, signifying the company was using customers as road testers. Buyers of 1924 models could choose the standard Schebler Model H carburetor, or they could specify the Schebler DeLuxe or the Zenith. Harley-Davidson wanted two carburetor suppliers in order to obtain lower bids for future orders. A new larger battery had four plates instead of two plates, was secured by two wing nuts, and had the terminals on the outside of the box. A larger box-shaped muffler was fitted, and late in the year brackets were designed so riders of 1915-and-later models could retrofit the new muffler to their machines. Lubrication of the running gear was now by Alemite gun, eliminating the need to disassemble anything for lubrication. Other new parts included new flywheels with different balance factors for the aluminum pistons and drilled connecting rods on models so equipped, front exhaust pipe on the Sixty-one, and front and rear exhaust pipes on the Seventy-four. A one-year-only JDCA-series motor featured the spark plugs in the combustion chamber proper, instead of off to the side in the valve pocket (correction to caption, page 25 of *Inside Harley-Davidson*).

For 1925, the F-head V-twins were entirely made over. The biggest change was a new frame, which lowered saddle height 3 inches and permitted the use of tanks that were more streamlined. The new front down tube terminated at its lower end instead of wrapping underneath the motor. Under the motor was a new steel channel. The battery was lowered and stood upright instead of being tilted. The new look added 25 pounds, raising the unserviced weight to 405 pounds. The wider 1925 frame allowed wider 27x3-1/2-inch tires in place of the former 28x3-inch tires. Both wheel-and-tire combinations listed were based on the outside diameter of the tires; wheel sizes from rim to rim were 22 inches through 1924 and 20 inches from 1925. New tube valves were of the same size as those used on automobile tubes (which made servicing easier), instead of the smaller type. With the wider frame and an offset rear sprocket, tire chains could be used in snow or mud.

Up front, the 1925 fork had softer cushion and recoil springs. Handlebars were newly shaped, and the gearshift lever was moved forward. Tank filler caps were larger. Sixteen Alemite fittings were provided instead of twelve. A new saddle was called the "bucket type" because it had a concave shape instead of the old, nearly flat-topped bicycle saddle. The muffler was changed to a long one-piece tubular-shaped speedster type with internal baffles for quieter operation. A muffler cutout was maintained and was foot-operated. Sales literature claimed a "fine tone" for the muffler, although not clarifying if that was with the muffler in the muffled or cutout mode!

Aluminum pistons had proven unreliable on the 1924 models, so for 1925 iron-alloy pistons were fitted to 61- and 74-cubic inch motors. The new pistons were claimed to be only slightly heavier than the old aluminum pistons, and all were fitted with bevel-joint rings that had previously been optional on certain models. A new foot-operated compression release replaced the former twist-grip release, which had been combined with ignition timing. Now riders could retard the spark timing to the maximum for slow running without bringing the compression release into effect.

As would be expected following the completely new 1925 Big Twins, changes to the 1926 twins were minimal. Harley-Davidson redesigned the clutch actuation on the 1926 V-twins, with the clutch-arm motion changed from vertical to horizontal. With the new clutch-arm layout there was no provision for a transmission lockout to prevent gear shifting without declutching. A new gearbox filler plug was mounted on the front side of the gearbox for easier access.

The year 1927 was another case of minimal changes. The most important change concerned the ignition system. Harley-Davidson discarded

1922 Twin
For 1922 and 1923, Harley-Davidson used the darker Brewster green. Brewster green proved unpopular, so olive drab returned on the 1924 models. © *H-D Michigan, Inc.*

1926 F-head
New styling keynoted the 1925 models. A new frame, new tanks, and lower saddle defined the biggest set of changes ever introduced in one year. Note that the crankcase is painted, which was standard practice on 1917–1927 V-twins. © *H-D Michigan, Inc.*

Circa 1924 F-head twin
In the early 1920s Harley-Davidson built one sidecar for every two motorcycles. This rig cost more than $400, about the same as a new Ford Model T. © *H-D Michigan, Inc.*

1928–1929 Two Cam Road Models

Collectibility	★★★★✦
Comfortable cruising speed	40–50 mph
Smoothness of ride	★★✦☆☆
Passenger accommodations	★☆☆☆☆
Reliability	★★☆☆☆
Parts/service availability	★☆☆☆☆

These were the hot-rod bikes of the day. If you were a Harley fan, these were the ultimate motorcycles. They had an image akin to the contemporary Harley-Davidson XR1000, the dirt-tracker with lights.

the distributor in favor of a wasted-spark system, in which both spark plugs fired on every motor revolution. This was claimed to enhance reliability. The wasted-spark system became a hallmark Harley-Davidson feature through 1959.

The new Two Cam Sixty-ones and Seventy-fours were the big news for 1928. The Two Cam concept had been used previously only on racers and hillclimbers. The Two Cam motors had two camshafts, each with two cam lobes. The use of two camshafts had previously meant the valve lifters (Harley called them cam followers) could be made shorter, hence, reducing the reciprocating weight and increasing maximum rpm before valve float occurred. For the 1928 Two Cam roadsters, the design was further improved by operating the valves directly through tappets instead of through pivoted lifters. The 1928 Two Cam roadster configuration was the current racing configuration used since 1924. Two Cam roadsters were fitted with Dow-metal (magnesium-alloy) domed pistons.

The 1928 models included several variants. Riders not wishing to go to the expense of buying a Two Cam Sixty-one or Seventy-four could opt for the 74-cubic inch (1,200-cc) JDL or the 61-cubic inch (1,000-cc) JL Special Sport Solo models. These had the conventional "one-cam" valve-gear configuration but had larger-than-standard inlet valves and valve cages. As with the Two Cams, both the "one-cam" 61- and 74-cubic inch Special Sport Solos came with Dow-metal pistons. The Two Cam models and the 74-cubic inch (1,200-cc) JDL Special Sport Solo had cylinders with uniform-outside-diameter cooling fins—they looked like normal "one-cam" cylinders in other words. The 61-cubic inch (1,000 cc) JL Special Sport Solo had cylinders that mimicked the factory racers by having the cooling fins graduated in size from the top to the bottom.

A new throttle-controlled oil pump ensured that extra oil was pumped at higher throttle settings; previously, only engine speed controlled oil output. This setup was a safeguard for heavy going up long grades or through deep sand or mud. However, riders were still cautioned to use the oil hand pump in such circumstances.

On all V-twins was a front brake, the first ever for Harley-Davidson road models. Also used throughout the V-twin range was the

1928 F-head
The 1928 models were the first equipped with a front brake, and the first V-twins since 1916 to have unpainted crankcases. © H-D Michigan, Inc.

1925 F-head
This new motorcycle wouldn't stay clean long because most roads were either dirt or gravel. Riders were grateful for dust, as otherwise they got mud. To make matters worse, designers of the era made no attempt to achieve smooth surfaces and reduce the number of places where filth could cling. © H-D Michigan, Inc.

gearshift lock gate on top of the gearbox, which reappeared after a two-year absence.

By the time the 1929 range debuted, the factory was heavily involved in the design of a new side-valve range that would constitute a new Harley-Davidson era. Consequently, there were relatively few technical updates to the 1929 F-heads. All Big Twins got new inlet rocker arms with larger bushings—these had been phased in beginning with late 1928 Two Cam models. Inlet-housing caps, the fulcrums for the rockers, were beefed up on the standard twins. An oiler cover made its official debut on the 1929 standard twins, although this had been phased in with late 1928 motors.

F-Head Rideability
The 1903–1908 models are at the bottom of the practicality scale. Cruising speeds would be 30 miles per hour or lower. The earliest models have no front suspension. Passenger suitability is slight, even if you could find period passenger accessories. For passengers, the exposed belt drive is a safety concern. These models would be limited to specialized use, such as organized pre-1916 rides and special appearances, as well as the occasional ride around the block. Consequently, reliability would be a direct function of the quality of the restoration effort and the amount of owner attention. Surprises could be few or many. Total-loss oiling wouldn't be a problem on short rides and in organized rallies where support vehicles are on hand. Longer and unmonitored rides would require you to take along some extra oil. There is no dealer support.

Later F-heads are only slightly more practical. The biggest change to this range

1928/29 F-head Two-cam
The company offered the Two Cam twins for 1928 and 1929. This design, previously used only on racers, had two camshafts instead of one. Shorter and lighter valve lifters were possible, which enabled these engines to spin faster than standard engines. © H-D Michigan, Inc.

occurred on the 1925 models when the saddle was improved in shape, lowered, and placed farther from the rear axle. These factors increased comfort.

Overalls and Raccoon Coats

Starting out as the "silent grey fellows," the F-head singles were anything but flashy. They were machines for commuters, mail carriers, farmers, delivery boys, and a rising crop of motorcycle sports enthusiasts. In the main, the F-head singles had no image apart from the uses in which they were placed. They were tools, in other words. Typical riding gear was a pair of overalls.

In 1911, along came the first successful Harley-Davidson V-twin, and with it, a brand new image. Harleys were fast and, increasingly, had the records to prove it. By 1925, if you were conservative you were an even bet to pick an Indian, Excelsior, or Henderson. But if you were a macho guy, you likely would head for a Harley shop to do your shopping. The F-heads, especially the 1928–1929 Two Cams, were the go-fast bikes of the era. Riding a 1920s F-head V-twin evokes images of raccoon coats, Harvard-Yale games, and speakeasies.

1928/29 Two-cam
The Two Cam twins were the ultimate road-going Harley-Davidsons of their time, but their time lasted only two model years. Although the Two Cams were fast, their exposed inlet valve gear was noisy and wore rapidly. On long, fast runs they tended to overheat. © H-D Michigan, Inc.

1919–1934

Lightweights and Middleweights

Harley-Davidson found out early in the game that its destiny was tied up with big V-twins, but along the way the company tried other concepts, partly to experiment and partly to chase after a few extra dollars on the market fringes. In the United States, the main market was for big, fast motorcycles, while the fringe market consisted of practical, ride-to-work machines. This was quite the opposite of the rest of the motorcycling world.

The original F-head Harley-Davidsons had been utilitarian motorcycles. But in those pre-1910 days, even practical ride-to-work motorcycles were also exciting creatures. The balance between practicality and excitement gradually shifted, as the motorcycle market evolved to its domination by the go-fast crowd. Racing helped Indian and Excelsior squeeze out the smaller brands, but racing hurt overall motorcycle sales because of several highly publicized racing accidents. Harley-Davidson didn't even get into the racing game until 1914, by which time the Milwaukee company was drawing near sales leader Indian and bypassing Excelsior. So by the time the racing age reached its zenith in the United States, Harley-Davidson was well experienced in making motorcycles that were conservative, practical, and reliable, motorcycles that had no pretense of racing glory.

The company continued to cater to practical-minded riders even after moving the emphasis to sport and speed. After all, the sporting V-twin had started as simply a double-up of existing single-cylinder models, so Milwaukee just kept making the one-lung versions for as long as they could sell them. From 1915 on, about 90 percent of new Harleys were twins, yet the company could continue to efficiently make utility models because they were simply "half-twins"—variations on the main theme.

This combined sport/utility approach worked with decreasing success through the 1918 season, the last year in which the big singles were offered. By this time, most riders had concluded that the big singles were nearly as heavy and just as bulky as the twins, while offering decidedly inferior performance.

To reinvigorate the utility market, Harley-Davidson designed a radically new motorcycle, the Model W Sport. They hoped this smaller, more refined, and more advanced machine would make a dramatic breakthrough, to reach citizens who were turned off by loud and fast motorcycles. Something dramatic was needed because of the alarming failure of the American motorcycle industry to grow at a time when automobile sales were skyrocketing.

The 1919 Sport was unlike anything Harley-Davidson had ever built. For openers, it was powered by the company's first side-valve or flat-head engine. The Sport had helical-gear primary drive linking the engine to the transmission. This was a year before Indian came out with helical gears on the 1920 Scout. The Sport had the engine and transmission enclosed in a single bolted-up pair of large castings, making it a true unit-construction design. This was a near first, as only obscure brands such as Minneapolis and the moderately selling Cleveland lightweight two-stroke had used unit construction up to this time.

Sport sales for 1919 were only 753, 3 percent of company totals, because of the model's midseason debut. For 1920 the magneto-ignition, lightless model designation was changed from W to WF, and a battery-ignition Model WJ with electrical lights joined the lineup. With a full sales year under its belt, Sport sales totaled 5,269, about 20 percent of company totals. This was the only good year for Sport sales. Incidentally, 84 percent of the Sports were the bare bones WFs.

Either there simply weren't many Harley-Davidson customers interested in a smaller and more refined model or the Sport didn't compare well against the Indian Scout that debuted as a 1920 model. Both factors probably applied. The year 1921 saw total Harley-Davidson sales fall drastically to less than half of 1920 totals. The Sport fared slightly worse, with 1,923 units representing less than 17 percent of total company sales.

Sales of Sports plummeted again in the 1922 model year, with the Sport total of 843 units representing less than 8 percent of total sales. This was probably when plans were begun to drop the model. The Sport continued

1919–1923 Sport, Models W, WF, and WJ Specifications

Engine ....Horizontally opposed side-valve twin
Bore and stroke..............2 3/4x3 in
Displacement ....35.6 ci (584 cc)
Compression ratio..........4:1 (estimated)
Power ....6 hp (rpm not specified) Ignition
1919 Model W and 1920–1923
Model WF ....Magneto
1920–1923 Model WJ.....Battery and coil
Electrical equipment
Models W and WF ....None
Model WJ........................Battery and lights
Transmission ....Three-speed, sliding-gear type, unit construction with motor
Shift ....Left hand
Primary drive ....Helical gears
Clutch ....Wet, multiple plates, actuated by left foot
Wheelbase......................57 in
Wheels and tires ....Clincher rims, 26x3 in (26-in outside tire diameter; in modern terminology this would by 20x3)
Suspension
Front ....Trailing-link, coil-spring fork
Rear ....Rigid
Weight............................250 lb (fully serviced)
Saddle height.................29 1/2 in without load, 28 1/2 in with 140-pound rider
Fuel consumption............70 mpg (claimed)
Top speed ....50 mph (estimated)

1920 Sport
The Sport was intended as a breakaway model that would appeal to the public at large. Despite design excellence and good performance, the model was a commercial failure.
© H-D Michigan, Inc.

1920 Sport

The Sport's top speed of about 50 miles per hour (maximum cruising speed of about 40 miles per hour) was more than adequate for most of the roads of that era. Electric lights were available on 1920–1923 Sports, but some riders preferred the old acetylene gas lamp shown here. © *H-D Michigan, Inc.*

1919–1923 Model W Sport

Collectibility	★★★☆☆
Comfortable cruising speed	40 mph
Smoothness of ride	★☆☆☆☆
Passenger accommodations	★☆☆☆☆
Reliability	★★☆☆☆
Parts/service availability	★☆☆☆☆

Technically, these were (and are) interesting motorcycles. But they failed in the market and they failed to affect the mainstream of Harley-Davidson engineering. The short production run makes them rare, but this also means the Sport models didn't contribute much to the Harley-Davidson success story.

during the 1923 model year, reaching 1,095 sales, but its share of the company total was less than 7 percent. With no sales growth in sight, Harley-Davidson pulled the plug, and no Sports were offered for the 1924 season.

Old timers say the Sport didn't catch on because it didn't have the power and speed of the rival Indian Scout. One observer of the scene also thinks the Sport didn't sound right. He's probably right. The V-twin was the standard American design, and motorcycles were supposed to sound a certain way. The Harley-Davidson Sport didn't have the "correct" *lumpety-lump* sound of the V-twin Indian Scout.

Harley-Davidson could have logically given up on the utility market after the flop of the Sport. But at this time, the company had a substantial export market that was particularly strong in Australia and New Zealand. Although Americans weren't turned on by small motorcycles, the company still needed a good-selling small model to sustain foreign sales. So in April 1924, only four months after the last Sports were sold, company executives toured Europe to look at motorcycle designs and get ideas. In Europe, the executives saw a lot of 21.35-cubic inch (350-cc) side-valve single-cylinder motorcycles. They concluded that Harley-Davidson should build such a model for export sales. The single would also be sold in the United States, but the company didn't expect large domestic sales. The single's success or failure would be driven by the export market.

Circa 1920 Sport motor
The inlet and exhaust manifolds were housed in a single casting, the idea being to preheat the inlet charge for quicker warm up and to promote better fuel economy. However, preheating diluted the inlet charge and reduced power.

Two versions of the 21.35-cubic inch (350-cc) side-valve "New Harley-Davidson Single" came on the market in the late summer of 1925 as 1926 models. The side-valve singles were designated the Model A (with magneto ignition) and Model B (with lights and a battery). Companion overhead-valve models were also offered, the Model AA (with magneto ignition) and Model BA (with lights and a battery). All variants were termed 21-cubic inch or 350-cc machines in company literature and press releases. For domestic sales, five single-cylinder road models were offered, four of these being road models and the other one a stripped-down race model, the Model S. It is discussed in the chapter on racers and hillclimbers. For export markets, there were side-valve and overhead-valve models with additional equipment, such as front stands and luggage racks. These were also the defined 1927 models.

Incidentally, Indian also brought out 21.35-cubic inch side-valve and overhead-valve singles in parallel with Harley-Davidson. Based on the frequencies of observed models in the antique motorcycle movement, it appears that Harley-Davidson sold more of its singles than did Indian.

For the 1928 season, the magneto option was dropped, leaving only two domestic choices, either side-valve (Model B) or overhead-valve configuration (Model BA), both with battery ignition and lights. Also absent from the dealer order blanks was the Model S racer, but it may still have been available, as there was a lot of under-the-table racing activity. The 1929 single-cylinder range included two overhead-valve models, both with battery ignition and electric lights, but differing in that one had a single exhaust port and the other had two. These were primarily for export, as evidenced by the domestic catalog, which listed only the twin-

1926 Models A, B, AA, and BA Specifications

Engine
Models AA and BA ....Overhead-valve
    single
Models A and B ....Side-valve single
Bore and stroke..............2 7/8x3 1/4 in
Displacement ....21.10 ci (346 cc)
Power
Models AA and BA ....10 bhp (estimated)
Models A and B ....8 bhp at 4,000 rpm
    (factory power curves)
Transmission ....Three-speed, sliding-
    gear type
Shift ....Left hand
Clutch ....Dry, multiple disks
Clutch operation ....Left foot
Ignition
Models A and AA...........Magneto
Models B and BA ....Battery and coil
Electric lighting
Models A and AA...........None
Models B and BA ....Yes
Wheelbase.......................56 1/2 in
Wheels...........................Clincher
Tires 26x3.30 in (3.30x20 in by modern
    terminology)
Suspension
Front ....Leading-link fork
Rear ....Rigid
Weight
Model AA.......................245 lb
Model A ....251 lb
Model BA ....263 lb
Model B..........................269 lb
Saddle height..................28 1/2 in
Fuel consumption............50 mpg (estimated,
    for all-around use), 80 mpg (advertised)
Top speed
Models AA and BA ....60 mph (estimated)
Models A and B ....55 mph (estimated)

1923 Sport
This 1923 model is the last of the breed. The dark Brewster green was used on the 1922 and 1923 Sports, along with the open chain guard. The flywheel was covered with a pressed steel jacket. © H-D Michigan, Inc.

cylinder models. Another new 1929 model was a 30.50-cubic inch (500-cc) side-valve single, the Model C, with battery ignition and lights.

The single-cylinder range was trimmed to just two domestic models for 1930, the Model B side-valve 21-cubic inch and the Model C 30.50-cubic inch domestic models. No 1930 export models were offered because tariffs and exchange rates made the Harley singles too expensive. The Model C was the only single offered as a 1931 model, but for the 1932 through 1934 seasons both the Model B and Model C were available. In the 1933 and 1934 model years there was also a model with the 30.50 single-cylinder engine in the same smaller frame used for the 21-cubic inch single, the Model CB.

Although Harley-Davidson stuck with the singles through the 1934 model year, Indian bowed out after the 1928 season. Harley's single-cylinder program in its last three or four years was probably to some extent a matter of assembling overstocked components left over from prior years. In such a situation, positive cash flow could have been generated despite

1926 Single
This is a single, but the Harley twins looked about the same to the rider. The left switch controls the ignition, and the right switch sets the lights off, on (bright), or dim. The front two filler caps are for fuel, and the rear cap is for oil. Behind the oil cap is the auxiliary oil hand pump. © H-D Michigan, Inc.

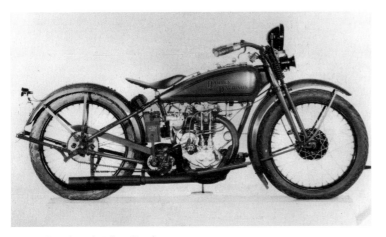

1928 Overhead Valve Single
In the 1928 model year, front brakes arrived on all models of Harley-Davidsons, Indians, Excelsiors, and Hendersons. Previously, the factories had argued that a front brake was dangerous on America's mostly unpaved roads. © H-D Michigan, Inc.

1930 Model C Specifications

Engine	Side-valve single
Bore and stroke	3 3/32x4 in
Displacement	30.1 ci (493 cc)
Compression ratio	5:1 (estimated)
Power	10 1/2 bhp @ 3,600 rpm
Transmission	Three-speed, sliding-gear type, mounted remotely to frame, positive gear locking
Shift	Left hand
Primary drive	Double-row chain, oil-mist lubricated
Clutch	Dry, fiber and metal disks
Clutch operation	
Standard	Left foot
Optional	Right hand
Wheelbase	57 1/2 in
Wheels and tires	Drop-center rims, quickly detachable, interchangeable, 18x4 in (18-inch wheel diameter), clincher tires
Suspension	
Front	Leading-link, drop-forged fork
Rear	Rigid
Weight	365 lb (fully serviced, estimated)
Saddle height	26 1/2 in
Fuel consumption	45 mpg (estimated)
Top speed	60 mph (estimated)

the models' failure to carry their share of factory overhead. Building a few and losing a little money on paper may have made more sense than scrapping the stock, laying off workers, and possibly losing even more money.

Middleweight Rideability

Maximum cruising speed of 40 miles per hour, specialized use, rough riding, poor passenger accommodations, and no mainstream dealer support, all add up to impractical riding. The total-loss oiling merits close attention; be sure to carry extra oil for long rides.

1926–1934 Side-valve and Overhead-valve Singles

Collectibility	★★★☆☆
Comfortable cruising speed	40 mph
Smoothness of ride	★★☆☆☆
Passenger accommodations	★☆☆☆☆
Reliability	★★☆☆☆
Parts/service availability	★☆☆☆☆

The story of these "Peashooters" is similar to that of the Sport—interesting, but not trendsetters. Since some of the singles were raced, they have a stronger history than the Sport model. This is counterbalanced by less-interesting technical specifications. The overhead-valve models would be the most coveted. For export only, an attractive 1930 overhead-valve road model was built with twin exhaust ports. A two-port road model would be prestigious, as none are known to have survived.

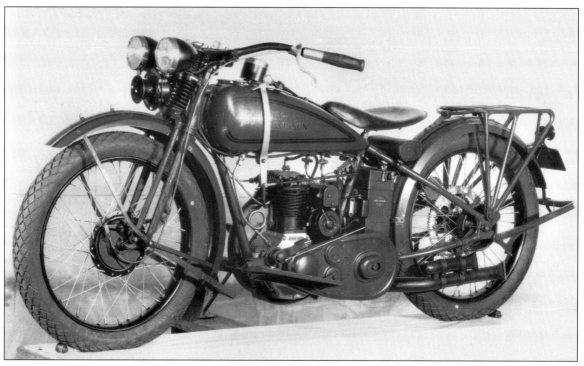

1928/29 Side Valve Single
About 80 percent of the single-cylinder models were fitted with side-valve engines. The four-tube muffler (two tubes on each side) was on the 1929 models only. © *H-D Michigan, Inc.*

Prehistoric Nerds

The Sport opposed twin had only one good selling season, as a 1920 model, so it likely never built any kind of image. *Poof*, and it was gone. As for the 1926–1934 singles, a few dealers such as Milwaukee's Knuth emphasized the singles during the late 1920s. The word "nerd" hadn't been invented, but a lot of singles riders were probably nerdish. As nerds, they either were unaware of or were uncaring about their second-class status in the eyes of many around them. Virtually none of the singles riders stayed on the singles if they held the view that motorcycling is a sport. That was true even if you were weak in the wallet and had been captured by the low prices of the singles. You could buy a lot more performance with a used Forty-five than you could with a new single. You could even get a pretty good used Seventy-four for the price of a new single. So new singles were one-time purchases because if you came back to the trough, you came back for a V-twin. The singles were tolerated, not coveted. If you rode one and you weren't embarrassed, you were a nerd. If you rode one and were embarrassed, and if you showed the proper envy of your V-twin riding buddies, you were granted non-nerd status until you could swing a deal for a V-twin. A single was like kissing your sister.

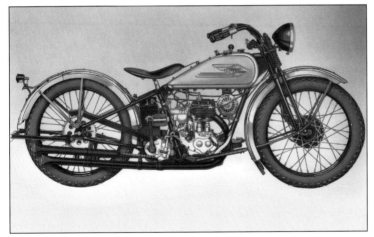

1929/30 Overhead Valve Single
Harley exported leftover 1929 two-port overhead-valve 21.35-cubic inch (350-cc) Singles as 1930 models. © H-D Michigan, Inc.

1934 21 Single
The last of the 21-cubic inch (350-cc) "Peashooters" were built for the 1934 model year, as were the last of the 30.50-cubic inch (500-cc) singles. The 1933 and 1934 single-cylinder models were assembled from leftover stock. © H-D Michigan, Inc.

Forty-Fives

As the "roaring twenties" drew to a close, even Harley-Davidson was beginning to admit that the era of the F-head motor had ended. The company had earlier produced the side-valve Sport, and side-valve singles had been in the lineup for a number of years. But the company's bread and butter, the V-twins, had always featured F-head design. In 1929, Harley-Davidson entered the side-valve V-twin era with the release of new small twins, the Models D and DL. Both were powered by all-new side-valve motors, with the D featuring mild tuning and the DL featuring a high-compression variant of the same design. The 1929 Harley-Davidson Model D was the company's answer to the V-twin Scout, launched by Indian in the spring of 1927. Both the Harley and Indian mid-sized V-twins had a nominal displacement of 45 cubic inches, and as such, they were referred to as "Forty-fives" verbally and as "a 45" or "the 45" in writing. They were never called "four-fives" during the production years.

Harley-Davidson chose the side-valve configuration because of the success of the side-valve or "flat-head" configuration used by Indian and, in the car world, by Ford. The side-valve design, in short, had become the automotive industry standard. To protect itself against possible patent infringements, as well as to save engineering development time and money, Harley-Davidson contracted with Englishman Harry Ricardo for the design of the Forty-five cylinder heads. As Ricardo already had a high reputation internationally, Harley-Davidson emphasized the Ricardo connection in advertisements.

To save money, the company mounted the Forty-five motor in the same frame used by the 21-cubic inch (350-cc) Model B single. Because the frame had a straight front down tube, the Forty-five generator was mounted vertically on the left side of the motor. Indian riders scornfully referred to the new model as the "three-cylinder Harley."

Indian's most popular model was the 45-cubic inch Scout, so Harley-Davidson had a rough time competing in this field. Harley's main interests were to provide an alternative lighter model for new riders and, later, to provide a model suitable for racing under American rules.

Manufacturing costs were driven by the number of parts instead of the size of the parts. For example, there was little difference in the manufacturing costs of Forty-five and Seventy-four cylinders. Consequently, the manufacturing cost of the complete Forty-five was close to that of the complete Seventy-four and Eighty side-valve twins. In most years, the price gap between the Forty-five and the top-of-the-line Big Twins was about $50 or 16 percent.

The Forty-five started its sales history with a bang, but soon fell within the shadow of Harley-Davidson's bread and butter, the Big Twins. According to the book *The Legend Begins*, sales of Forty-fives peaked in 1929, when about 6,856 were bought. You don't want to peak in your first year. Incidentally *The Legend Begins* draws its information from both production and sales reports, and from reports that parallel calendar, business (company fiscal), fiscal (government fiscal), and model years, so we're dealing with a mixture of eight kinds of information. As the book notes, the cited production data is approximate. Further references to a "year" of "production" should be considered with this caveat in mind.

The year 1930 was also strong, but thereafter, sales of the Forty-five dropped steadily, as did sales of other models. In the late 1930s, Forty-five annual sales hovered around 2,000 and, because Big Twin sales were rising, the Forty-five accounted for a smaller and smaller percentage of total motorcycle sales.

1929 45s
From *The Enthusiast*, "Lookit 'em go, these 1929 Harley-Davidson whoopees!" Harley-Davidson reached out to a new group with the new 1929 Forty-fives. Anybody know the way to the nearest speakeasy? © *H-D Michigan, Inc.*

In its entire civilian sales history (discounting questionable 1941 and 1942 numbers), the Forty-five two-wheelers amounted to 20 percent of total company sales. However, much of the Forty-five design was carried over in the three-wheeled Servi-Car, of which a few hundred were sold in most model years. The Servi-Car was in production from mid-1932 through 1973, officially, and in 1974 the last units (with 1973 serial numbers) were built and delivered to honor contracts with the cities of New York, Chicago, and Los Angeles. The Forty-five racers buttressed the company's advertising theme that Harley-Davidsons were superior motorcycles with proven performance. Above all, the military Forty-five was responsible for seeing the company through the trying World War II years, and in fine fashion, with over 88,000 units produced, according to company press releases. As a result, Harley-Davidson emerged from the war even more dominant over its old rival Indian. So the Forty-fives were big players in the Harley-Davidson saga. In my opinion, the Forty-five is the most under-rated of all Harley-Davidsons.

1929 45

The toggle switch on the right handlebar was used to select either both headlamps or to extinguish the right lamp while dimming the left. The generator wasn't capable of keeping the battery charged if both lights were used for prolonged low-speed running. © H-D Michigan, Inc.

1930 45

The new 1930 frame lowered the saddle height 2 1/2 inches but increased the ground clearance. A right-side-only twin-tube muffler was used on all 1930 V-twins. Another new feature was the I-beam front fork. © H-D Michigan, Inc.

1929 45

The 1929 Forty-fives used the same frame as the 21.35-cubic inch (350-cc) singles, so the generator was necessarily vertically situated. Some riders and dealers had problems with the low-slung frame grounding. A four-tube muffler (two tubes on each side) was fitted to all 1929 Harley-Davidsons. © H-D Michigan, Inc.

1929 D Series

Collectibility	★★★✦☆
Comfortable cruising speed	50 mph
Smoothness of ride	
Stock tires	★★✦☆☆
Retrofitted 5.00x16-inch tires	★★★☆☆
Passenger accommodations	
Period tandem seat	★☆☆☆☆
Retrofitted buddy seat	★★★☆☆
Reliability	★★☆☆☆
Parts/service availability	★☆☆☆☆

Rarity, sire of a long line of 45-cubic-inch models, and aesthetics are strengths. Practicality and technical features are weaknesses. Expect a seller's market as there are probably fewer than five of these in existence.

1930 Models D, DL, DLD, and DS Specifications

Engine ....45-degree side-valve V-twin
Bore and stroke..............2 3/4x3 13/16 in
Displacement ....45.32 ci (747 cc)
Compression ratio
Models D and DS............4.3:1
Model DL 5:1
Model DLD......................6:1
Power
Models D and DS............15 bhp @ 3900 rpm
Model DL ....18.5 bhp @ 4000 rpm
Model DLD......................20 bhp @ 4000 rpm
Transmission ....Three-speed, sliding-gear type, mounted remotely to frame, positive gear locking
Shift ....Left hand
Primary drive ....Double-row chain, oil-mist lubricated
Clutch ....Dry, fiber and metal disks
Clutch operation
Standard.........................Left foot
Optional ....Right hand
Wheelbase......................57 1/2 in
Wheels and tires ....Drop-center rims, quickly detachable, interchangeable, 25x4 in (4.00x19 in modern terminology)*
Suspension
Front ....Leading-link, drop-forged fork
Rear ....Rigid
Weight...........................390 lb (fully serviced)
Saddle height..................26 1/2 in
Fuel consumption............60–75 mpg
Top speed (estimated figures)
Model D ....55–60 mph
Model DL ....60–65 mph
Model DLD.....................65–70 mph
* The factory referred to the Forty-five wheels as having an 18-inch diameter, but termed the tires 25x4-inch; their math

Forty-Five Development

The Forty-five experienced several problems in its original 1929 configuration. Idling and low-speed running were poor with the original Ricardo cylinder heads. This was cured by redesigning the heads to include a "dam" between the valve area and the area above the pistons. Oil-pump output was too low at high speeds, which again called for a redesign. Complaints were received about inadequate ground clearance; this was due to the use of the Model B frame. The frame problem wasn't solved on the 1929 Forty-five. Another problem was inadequate primary-chain lubrication, for although riders were instructed to manually oil the chain, most of them relied on the air-oil-mist lubrication provided. This was another problem deferred to the 1930 range. Early 1929 Forty-fives used the same 4 3/8-gallon tank as the Model B single; late 1929 Forty-fives used the same 5 1/4-gallon tank as the Model C single introduced in midseason.

For the 1930 season, four versions of the Forty-five were offered: the standard D, the DS with sidecar gearing, the high-compression DL, and the DLD Special Sport Solo with a larger carburetor and a 6:1 compression ratio. Chief among 1930 improvements was a new frame built especially for the Forty-five. The new frame provided needed increased ground clearance, yet lowered the saddle height 2 1/2 inches. The factory pipeline of motors in the building process prevented a switch to a conventional horizontally mounted generator. Consequently, the new frame retained a straight down tube. Another noteworthy improvement was a larger clutch, the new unit in fact being the same size as the big-twin clutch.

The 1931 Forty-five got a new larger brake, the same as that used on the 1929 F-head Big Twins. A gear lock was put on the transmission

1930–1931 D Series	
Collectibility	★★★☆☆
Comfortable cruising speed	50 mph
Smoothness of ride	
4.75-inch or smaller tires	★★✦ ☆☆
Retrofitted 5.00x16-inch tires	★★★☆☆
Passenger accommodations	
Period tandem seat	★☆☆☆☆
Retrofitted buddy seat	★★★☆☆
Reliability	★★☆☆☆
Parts/service availability	★☆☆☆☆

These were lackluster models, struggling on with the weird vertically mounted generator. In fact, only rarity saves them from a two-star rating. Aesthetically, these models weren't much—that's my opinion, but opinions about styling differ. My objection is the shape of the tanks, rather hump-backed and I think less graceful than the 1929 tanks.

1932 45
With a bent front down tube and a horizontal generator, the 1932 R-series took on the appearance of the 74-ci twin. All Harley-Davidson side-valve V-twins were built in this basic cam-gear layout, with four cam gears and a separate cam for each valve. © H-D Michigan, Inc.

to prevent shifting without the clutch disengaged. The top-of-the-line DLD model got a new clutch, while other Forty-fives continued with the old clutch. Both the new brake and the new DLD clutch illustrate Harley-Davidson's practical factory management, which emphasized using up old parts whenever possible. The toolbox was changed to a wedge shape and a disk horn replaced the Klaxon horn. A 7-inch headlamp with a flat (nonconvex) diffusing lens replaced the dual headlamps used on 1929 and 1930 models.

The 1932 Forty-five was the most changed model in the Harley-Davidson lineup, with the R series replacing the D series. The R models got a new frame with a curved down tube, at last permitting a conventional horizontal generator mounting. The new generator was the same as used on the Seventy-four and featured larger brushes to produce more uniform output and cooler running.

The top of the 1932 line was the RLD with a 6:1 compression ratio; the R and RS (sidecar model, "S" not in motor number) had 4.3:1 compression ratios. The RLD used a 1 1/4-inch carburetor and the other R models used a 1-inch carburetor. All R models were fitted with larger flywheels and the necessarily larger crankcases. New cylinders provided an airspace between the exhaust ports and the barrels. Aluminum pistons replaced the former Lynite variety. Longer connecting rods had bronze-bush upper bearings; previously there were no upper bearings. Stronger valve springs and an improved crankcase breathing design were introduced. The Servi-Car made its debut as a midseason offering.

The new 1932 Forty-five oil pump with redesigned internals also had a different mounting so the pump could be removed without

1933 45
Art deco styling, which came into vogue in the early 1930s, featured geometric shapes and angular representations of animals and people. The 1933 Harley-Davidsons ushered in this popular style, which had lately adorned new buildings. This was the first year of standard colors other than olive drab. © H-D Michigan, Inc.

1934 ride control
The accessory "ride control" became available in late 1933. The rider tightened the adjuster for a stiffer ride. The device offered equal resistance in rebound and compression, so a stiffer setting reduced fork travel. Although of doubtful worth, the device was popular. © H-D Michigan, Inc.

1932–1936 R Series

Collectibility	★★★☆☆
Comfortable cruising speed	50 mph
Smoothness of ride	
4.75-inch or smaller tires	★★✦☆☆
Retrofitted 5.00x16-inch tires	★★★☆☆
Passenger accommodations	
1932–1936 tandem saddles	★☆☆☆☆
1933–1936 buddy seat	★★★☆☆
Reliability	★★☆☆☆
Parts/service availability	★☆☆☆☆

The 1932 model was the first with the horizontally mounted generator and curved front down tube, so I think it's the strongest of the range. The 1933–1936 models continued with total-loss (noncirculating) lubrication, a deficiency compared to Indian's dry-sump (circulating) oiling introduced in 1933. The constant-mesh transmission debuted on the 1935 models (1933, on the Servi-Car), which put them forever ahead of Indian on this point. The 1934–1936 models had an art deco look because of the colorful tank panels, and if art deco turns you on, be my guest. I still don't like the tank's shape.

1934 45
The 1934 Forty-five rear fender was unique in that the valance didn't extend below the chain guard. A 1934-only upturned tailpipe was also used on the Seventy-four side-valve twin. © H-D Michigan, Inc.

removing the new gear-case cover. The oil pump body was reinforced to prevent distortion, and the gear-case cover was redesigned to accommodate the new pump. The new gear-case cover also featured an air venting section designed to work with the new combined generator drive gear and oil slinger. The oil slinger spun in the air-oil mist and by centrifugal force pushed the oil out through holes in the periphery of the slinger. A new four-plate clutch was used on the 1932 Forty-five.

On the 1933 Forty-fives, there were only three notable technical changes. Magnesium-alloy pistons were fitted instead of aluminum-alloy pistons. Late 1933 models were fitted with Schebler die-cast brass carburetors instead of Schebler pot-metal carburetors. The third change was to the three-speed-and-reverse transmission fitted only on the three-wheeled Servi-Car. Signaling a forthcoming change to the two-wheelers, the new Servi-Car gearbox was of the constant-mesh design. This was a major improvement because instead of sliding gears into mesh, with the inevitable chipping and wear on the gear teeth, the gears were changed by the movement of sliding dogs (Harley called them clutches) in the middle of each gear. The gear teeth remained constantly in mesh so that they weren't banged up by the shifting process.

For 1934 the Forty-five was equipped with a new oil pump, in response to Indian's introduction of dry-sump (circulating) lubrication a year earlier. However, the new Harley-Davidsons still used a total-loss system. The new pump was supposed to have better oil control over a wide speed range. A Linkert die-cast brass-bodied carburetor was fitted instead of the Schebler die-cast unit, with the sporty RLD continuing to have a 1-

1935 45
Some of the major controls on Dale Walksler's 1935 Model RL, left to right, are left-handgrip ignition control, left-bar-mounted front brake lever (out of sight), horn button, gear shift lever, auxiliary oil hand pump, ignition key, press-and-twist instrument panel light, lights key, ride-control adjusting wheel, speedometer maximum-speed-hand set/release button, odometer reset button, dimmer switch, and right-handgrip throttle. Check out the fork; it's fun to watch the springs work while you're riding.

1935 45
Girls found the lighter Forty-five friendlier than the Seventy-four side-valve Big Twin. The company featured a lot of lady riders in their ads, but this was probably a matter of drawing male attention more than selling to the few women who rode. © H-D Michigan, Inc.

1/4-inch mixer and the other R models continuing with a 1-inch carbure-tor. New low-expansion aluminum-alloy pistons replaced the 1933-only magnesium-alloy pistons, this change being made to improve reliability. A new 14-spring clutch replaced the former 12-spring clutch, and the new clutch featured several other changes. Elsewhere, additional changes to the Forty-five involved engineering processes such as heat treating.

Like other 1935 models, the 1935 Forty-five featured cylinders with a straight bore instead of the time-honored tapered bore unique to Harley from 1914–1934. Although the new cylinders were advertised as a 1935 improvement, some late 1934 models got them. The change to a straight bore simplified maintenance. Along with the new straight-bore cylinders

1935 45

Walksler shows the technique for hard riding. The rider supplemented the engine-driven oil pump with this auxiliary hand pump. The pump will pull up about 6 inches, as shown here, but generally a half-stroke or less was used in heavy going. Riders from time to time backed off the throttle, and if they saw heavy smoke, the motor was okay. A no-smoke condition called for the hand pump.

1936 45

This 1936 Forty-five shows off the last use of art deco tank styling. Another last-year feature was total-loss (noncirculating) lubrication. A Y-shaped inlet manifold and angled inlet ports improved appearance and offered the promise of more power. Cylinder cooling fins were larger and wrapped around the inlet ports. © H-D Michigan, Inc.

came cam-ground pistons in lieu of round pistons. Another major change was the incorporation of a constant-mesh transmission on the two-wheeled models; Indian never got around to this improvement. A new RLDR model was listed for Class C racing and hillclimbing. Because Class C riders were required to ride their motorcycles to the events, full road equipment was included with the RLDR.

The 1936 Forty-fives were fitted with new cylinders, which featured a Y-shaped inlet manifold. The medium- and high-performance RL and RLD had inlet ports increased from 1 inch to 1 1/4 inches, and carburetor venturis were enlarged from 7/8 inch to 1 1/16 inches. Detail changes were made to the clutch and transmission. The fork rake

was reduced about 2 degrees to lighten the handling. These were the last Forty-fives of the early 1930s style.

For 1937 the Forty-five, as well as the Seventy-four and Eighty side-valve models, benefited from the engineering development of the Knucklehead. As with the 1936 Knucklehead, a new dry-sump (circulating) lubrication system on the 1937 side-valve models replaced the historic total-loss setup. A new vane-type dry-sump oil pump was fitted. The pump and its location behind the timing cover were similar to the setup on the Seventy-four and Eighty side-valve twins. Although other Forty-five changes were in the details, the new dry-sump lubrication plus the complete cosmetic makeover of the model amounted to a major redesign. Signifying the major update, the Forty-fives were all listed in the W series. As things turned out, the 1937 models were the last major update of the Forty-five.

For 1938, the Forty-five transmission was equipped with a big-twin-style slotted drum shifter cam, and a positive locking device was added. On the 1939 Forty-fives, new valve springs were fitted, the crankcases were lapped straight through both cases at the same time to improve accuracy, and new piston rings were incorporated.

In mid-1939 the WLD Special was announced as the new top-of-the-line model ready to go racing; some factory documentation referred to this model as the WLDD. The new name "WLD Special" highlighted the fact that, unlike the previous WLDR, the new model had new larger aluminum cylinder heads. Naturally, most owners of the previous WLDRs soon retrofitted their bikes with the new aluminum cylinder heads, and soon the factory reinstated the WLDR designation for the sporting configuration. The inlet ports were enlarged from 1 5/16 to 1 7/16 inches (nonracing W series models still had 1-1/4-inch

1937 45
The 1937 Forty-five joined the styling revolution launched by the 1936 61 OHV (Knucklehead), with tear drop tanks and tank top instrument panel. Functionally, the big news was dry-sump (circulating) lubrication, which doubled oil mileage. © H-D Michigan, Inc.

1938 45
Stylish riders of the 1930s preferred the military look. All of his garb was for sale by Harley-Davidson dealers. The ribbed timing cover and aft-mounted oil pump were introduced on the 1937 models. The 1938 Forty-five benefited from several transmission improvements aimed at greater reliability. © H-D Michigan, Inc.

1937–1940 W Series	
Collectibility	★★★☆☆
Comfortable cruising speed	50 mph
Smoothness of ride	
4.75-inch or smaller tires	★★✫☆☆
Retrofitted 5.00x16-inch tires	★★★☆☆
Passenger accommodations	★★★☆☆
Reliability	★★★☆☆
Parts/service availability	★★★☆☆

Strongest of the range is the 1937 model, which introduced the new Knucklehead styling to the Forty-five range. The 1937–1940 models are terrific-looking bikes, and with dry-sump (circulating) lubrication were thoroughly up to date. Least attractive of the era were the 1938 models with striping that separated the upper and lower tank halves, thus detracting from the natural beauty of the tank curves. The 1940 D-shaped footboards were better looking than the earlier rectangular footboards. The 1940 tank striping was tastefully applied, that is, without excess and with the striping harmonizing with the tanks profiles.

inlet ports). Later parts books referred to all 1939 racers as WLDR models, with both types of cylinders listed.

The 1940 model year saw additional refinements. A new tubular fork (as on the Big Twins) replaced the I-beam fork. The setup for piston rings, rods, and baffles was changed to the big-twin style (see big-twin development section). Shifting of the Forty-five was made faster by the use of a ball lock with an adjustable spring load instead of a fixed pin lock. Positions on the tank-side shifter guide were placed farther apart to allow for extra shifting motion, which further reduced shifting effort. Other transmission and clutch changes were also made.

The 1940 WLDR racers had new highly polished combustion chambers plus new cylinders and redesigned valve gear. The new cylinders had 1 9/16-inch inlet ports (formerly 1 7/16 inches). The valves were brought in closer to the cylinder bore by angling in the valves. In other words, when viewed from the front the valves were inclined toward the cylinder instead of parallel to the cylinder. The tilted valves rode on valve lifters or shoes that were angled on the top side to provide a straight thrust against the valves. Although outfitted with full road gear, the 1940 WLDR models had in fact become pure racers.

Most changes to the 1941 Forty-five concerned the clutch and transmission details. On the clutch, a larger hub permitted the spring load to be reduced from 500 pounds to 300 pounds. Transmission gears were strengthened and increased in diameter. The shifting dogs (Harley called them clutches) were heavier and had larger diameters. Easier

1939 45
For 1939, the Forty-five ride control (accessory) was relocated to the underside of the headlamp. The new location was more attractive, but the rider could no longer easily adjust the fork stiffness while under way. © H-D Michigan, Inc.

1939 Servi-Car
The Servi-Car first came on the scene as a mid-1932 model. The model was never a big seller during the 1930s because of the Depression and the fact that Harley-Davidson and Indian were dividing the police and commercial markets. Every motorcycle sale was vital to the survival of the two companies. © H-D Michigan, Inc.

shifting was achieved by redesign of the transmission cam and shift-lever gear—the ratio of the shifter lever was increased and the track of the shifter cam lengthened. The gearbox was made 7/16 inch wider to accommodate the increased spacing between the gears. The gearbox was mounted to the frame with three studs instead of two. The transmission oil filler plug was lengthened and relocated for improved access. These were the last major changes to the Forty-five transmission, which had been modified frequently.

1940 45
For 1940, a tubular front fork was fitted to the Forty-five. The Knucklehead had a tubular fork since 1936 and the big side-valve twins since 1937. The deep-finned aluminum cylinder heads were optional. © *H-D Michigan, Inc.*

1941 45
A new oil pump had a centrifugally controlled bypass valve. © *H-D Michigan, Inc.*

The 1941 WR, a brake-less flat-tracker, and WRTT, a brake-equipped road and TT (forerunner of motocross) racer, were milestone motorcycles as the first Class C racers sold without the formality of lights, battery, and fenders. These models are detailed Chapter 11.

The 1941 model year closed out the last significant engineering updates to the civilian Forty-five because in the postwar era Harley-Davidson was preoccupied with overhead-valve big-twin production and engineering matters. But before commenting on the postwar models, a brief summary of the military Forty-fives is in order. According to company press releases more than 88,000 military motorcycles were produced during World War II, the majority of these being Forty-fives.

There were two large "families" of military Forty-fives, the WLA series for the United States and other allied nations, and the WLC series for Canadian forces. A bewildering array of subtypes was produced with the configurations

Military Models

Collectibility	★★★☆☆
Comfortable cruising speed	50 mph
Smoothness of ride	
4.75-inch or smaller tires	★★✦☆☆
5.00x16-inch tires	★★★☆☆
Passenger accommodations	
Tandem saddles	★☆☆☆☆
Buddy seat	★★★☆☆
Reliability	★★★☆☆
Parts/service availability: WLs	★★★☆☆
XAs	★

These were mainly the WLA for the United States and the WLC for Canada, but there were various configurations within each category. The WLC differed mainly in the use of a big-twin front wheel and brake, which made front and rear wheels interchangeable. The military Forty-fives are extremely important motorcycles because they kept the company prosperous during the challenging war years. However, military finish is a turnoff for most enthusiasts. There are also too many of them around to put them in the rare category. So the collectibility rating is a strong three stars.

1941–1949 WL Series

Collectibility	★★★☆☆
Comfortable cruising speed	50 mph
Smoothness of ride	
4.75-inch or smaller tires	★★✦☆☆
5.00x16-inch tires	★★★☆☆
Passenger accommodations	★★★☆☆
Reliability	★★★☆☆
Parts/service availability	★★★☆☆

In 1941, a new, more robust transmission with longer shafts marked the final major technical change for the Forty-five series. As for styling, there was a plus and there was a minus on the 1941, '42, and '46 models. The plus was the highly stylized speedometer. The minus was the stainless steel strip that separated the upper and lower tank halves, which in my opinion detracted from the natural beauty of the curved tank lines as did the 1938 paint scheme. By 1949, we see the weakest of the range, due to the beginning slide in relative status caused by the newly imported British middleweights.

15850

1942 XA

To meet a hurry-up Army request for a shaft-drive design, Harley-Davidson copied the German BMW to produce the Model XA. The throttle was on the left in compliance with Army specifications which envisioned right-handed men passing messages back and forth between bike and Jeep. So the hand clutch was on the right. © H-D Michigan, Inc.

1942 XA

Shifting was by the left foot (a first for Harley-Davidson). The channel steel luggage rack was designed to carry a 40-pound radio considered too heavy for the traditional Harley rack. © H-D Michigan, Inc.

15848

frequently changing in details, due to new requirements and changes to different subcontracted suppliers. Most of the WLA series were produced in two editions; I'll call them early and late editions. WLA early editions were fitted with a green-painted standard air cleaner, but some may have been fitted with the later long rubber carburetor inlet hose and canister air cleaner. Early-edition WLA models had a fork that was lengthened by 2 3/8 inches (compared to the civilian fork) to increase ground clearance about 2 inches. Late-edition WLA models were fitted with at least two different canister air cleaners, as well as a standard-length fork. The WLC models differed mainly in using the big-twin wheel and brake, which made the front and rear wheels interchangeable. The brake wasn't integral with the hub but was attached with lug screws. The WLC also was fitted with big-twin fork rockers and fender braces, and with a fender mounted toolbox. This information is courtesy of Bruce Palmer, who has studied this history of American military motorcycles for a number of years. As stated earlier, there were many other variances in details, which space doesn't permit listing.

After World War II there were few technical changes to the Forty-five, which was recognized as being near the end of its production life. Large numbers of British motorcycles were being imported, more with each passing year, and the Forty-five had become noncompetitive in both specifications and price. The 1947 Forty-five was equipped with rubber fittings on both ends of the gas lines. By now, the Forty-five had become something of an embarrassment in the Harley-Davidson line. From front to rear, its engineering was rooted in the 1930s. Sales of the functionally unchanged 1948 and 1949 Forty-fives were about 7 and 10 percent, respectively, of total Harley-Davidson sales. Comparing this to the Panhead's roughly 70 percent sales share, shows just how uncompetitive the Forty-five had become.

The 1950 model got a new Linkert M-54 big-twin-style carburetor with a fixed jet. On the 1951 model, the cylinder heads were secured

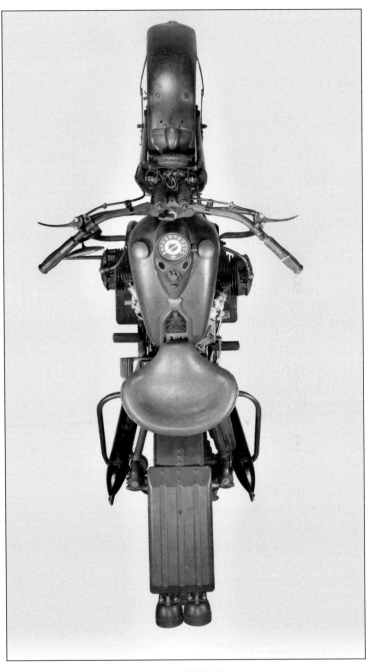

1942 XA
The front brake was operated by the left-hand lever. The dual taillights came out on 1941 WLAs as well as XAs. © H-D Michigan, Inc.

1947 45

The 1947 Forty-fives had a new shifter guide and instrument panel. The 1948 Forty-fives were identical in appearance except for a new instrument panel. No additional styling changes were made to the 1949 models. © H-D Michigan, Inc.

1948 45

By 1948, Forty-five production and sales were only about 7 percent of company totals, partly due to the growing popularity of British bikes. Another factor was that Harley-Davidson couldn't build enough big motorcycles to satisfy demand, so the new Panheads and One-twenty-fives naturally out-prioritized the Forty-fives. © H-D Michigan, Inc.

with cap screws instead of studs and nuts. Also, the 1951 Forty-five had the oil pump fitted with a longer, larger diameter, and stronger governor control spring to achieve more oiling at slow speeds. A new fixed-jet Linkert M-54 carburetor was put on the 1951 Forty-five. No technical changes were made on the 1952 Forty-five because the replacement Model K was nearing production. As can be seen from this overview, the Forty-five two-wheeler got as much engineering attention in its first six years, 1929–1934, as during its last eighteen years, 1935–1952.

The Servi-Car was fitted with a telescopic fork for the 1958 season. The 1964 model year saw the Servi-Car become the first Harley-Davidson equipped with 12-volt electrics and an electric starter. For model year 1966, an alternator replaced the generator. The 1967 Servi-Car introduced fiberglass construction of the load box. The last official model year was 1973, when the Electra-Glide front disc brake was fitted.

Forty-Five Rideability

All have a maximum cruising speed of 50 miles per hour. The 1929–1936 models would be best for specialized use such as displays and organized rides where support vehicles are on hand. The 1933-and-later models fitted with a buddy seat of the era offer surprising comfort for long solo rides if you feel like taking along some extra oil.

The 1941 and later models were available with 5.00x16-inch tires, which significantly softened the ride, while making the handling

1950–1952 WL Series

Collectibility	★★☆☆☆
Comfortable cruising speed	50 mph
Smoothness of ride	
4.75-inch or smaller tires	★★✦☆☆
5.00x16-inch tires	★★★☆☆
Passenger accommodations	★★★☆☆
Reliability	★★★☆☆
Parts/service availability	★★★☆☆

Hey, I like these. They make my short list of "wanna-have" Harleys. But I want one because of my lingering high-school inferiority complex (some say it was, and remains, not a complex but actual inferiority). In the cold, hard light of the times, the Forty-five became increasingly an embarrassment to Harley-Davidson. The Enthusiast offered not a single word of text about the Forty-five in its new-models issue for the 1952 model year. The same antique-ish funkiness that I like about them today was a big drawback in the showrooms when compared to the rising tide of British motorcycles. The styling tried to mimic the popular Hydra-Glides but the big-twin front fender didn't work in my opinion. Rival shops offered British bikes that were less costly, lighter, faster, and more comfortable. The 1950–1952 Forty-fives are really fun bikes, just as much as the earlier models, and it hurts to give them the two-star nod. But they were, and are, short in the status department compared to contemporary rivals.

a little mushy—take your pick, skinny or fat tires. If you have the retrofit philosophy you can fit the larger tires on the earlier models, as riders of the era did. But retrofitting could cost you points if the bike is to be judged. The same situation applies to the popular buddy seat, which was available beginning in late 1933 and often was retrofitted to earlier models.

The 1937 and later Forty-fives with dry-sump oiling are practical touring bikes if you can settle into the 50-mile-per-hour rhythm and enjoy back roads that permit this leisurely pace. Dealer support for 1937-and-later models is surprisingly good. That's because of two factors: one, more than 67,000 Forty-fives were made for the Army, so many of these motorcycles and spare parts are still in the system; and two, the Forty-five three-wheeler Servi-Car was made up through 1973.

Servi-Cars are as much driven as they are ridden. They are fine for around town or around the parking lot, but sluggish performance and meter-maid handling are unsuitable for fast highway riding.

Riding a 1947 Harley-Davidson Forty-five

I straddle the Forty-five, grasp the bars, and rock the motorcycle left and right. Compared to Harley Big Twins, the Forty-five feels light and reassuring. It seems odd to look down and see what looks like a Big Twin, but at the same time to feel the lightness under my shoe soles as I rock the Forty-five gently from side to side.

Harley gave you the choice of either a 5:1 or 6:1 compression ratio, not much either way, but the kicking is further eased by the small size of the cylinders. So, the Forty-five starts easily. I enjoy the slow galloping idle for a couple of minutes until the motor is warmed up.

I roll back on the left-hand grip, counter-clockwise when viewed from the grip end, to retard the ignition timing. I remind myself that the clutch is backwards from a car clutch. The Harley-Davidson clutch is disengaged by the heel instead of the toe. I push down on the heel pedal and move the shift lever swiftly forward into "1" (low). Clunk. The noise is normal and harmless, and is caused by the shifting-dogs engaging in the center of the selected-gear. I look down for the kickstand, and with my left foot sweep the long rod back into stow position.

I roll the left-hand ignition control grip fully back or clockwise when viewed from the grip's end, which sets the ignition for maximum advance. Then, I move the left-hand grip back about 1/8 turn. I roll on the throttle until I get a 30-mile-per-hour sound and simultaneously push smoothly down on the toe-for-go rocker clutch pedal. We're away!

Acceleration seems faster than it is because I'm used to a 1,200-cc V-twin. The Forty-five makes pretty much the same sounds as the larger motors, although putting out fewer decibels. I get to the shift speed about as fast as with a Big Twin, but with the higher (numerically) gear ratio I'm shifting at a slower speed. Shifting into second at about 15 miles per hour is like shifting into low; you do it swiftly. This time I pull the lever back toward me, through neutral, then smartly into second. I let the Forty-five pick up speed on half-throttle until about 25 miles per hour, then clunk into high or "3." I let the speed climb to 30 miles per hour and hold the gait. I'm in no hurry, savoring the V-twin rhythm.

We're on a winding paved road now, still chuffing along but with the ignition fully advanced

Adding oil to 45
Checking the oil on a Forty-five is a snap, as shown by Mark Dye of Dale's H-D; contrast this photo to the companion photo in the Panhead chapter. Another neat thing about post-1936 Forty-fives is the right-side oil tank, which is completely separate from the left-side fuel tank. Unlike rival Indian V-twins, the Forty-five will never have fuel leaking into the oil tank (a condition that can burn up a motor quickly).

and the cruising speed now up to 40 miles per hour. The Forty-five motor is busy but with a happy kind of noise. I slow down to about 30 miles per hour, also easing the left-hand ignition control grip back about halfway toward the fully retarded position, which ensures the smoothest possible slow-speed running.

We enter a tight left-hand turn. I'm an Indian-motorcycle enthusiast, so I'm brainwashed. I expect the handling to be inferior to that of an Indian Sport Scout. I'm surprised; the Forty-five has a lighter and more certain feel in the turns than a Sport Scout. I take on a few more corners and bends at faster and faster speeds and confirm my initial reaction. Apparently, this is caused by the Forty-five's upper fork

Rider's view of 45
Another charm of the post-1936 Forty-fives is the big-twin feel, which you get while saving a 100 pounds of heft. From the seat post forward, the Forty-five has a rider layout identical to that of the Big Twins. Saddle height and placement, position of tanks, steering head height, and position of bars relative to the saddle all match up with the Big Twins, inch for inch.

Riding position on 45 with buddy seat
An inch is a mile, so to speak. One of the great charms of the 1937–1952 Forty-fives, and companion Big Twins through 1948, is the riding position, demonstrated here by Butch Wilson of Dale's H-D. On all springer models, the handlegrips are 27 inches from the seat post, just one inch less than the 1949 and later Big Twins. But that all-important extra inch lets an average-sized solo rider comfortably hug the big back end of the buddy seat, for painless all-day cruising.

weight being carried close to the steering head, instead of sticking out in front, as with a Sport Scout.

We come upon a fast straight section of highway without a car in sight. I open the throttle. The speed climbs fast from 40 miles per hour to 50 miles per hour. This is a comfortable cruising speed that I could maintain indefinitely. I up the ante to 60 miles per hour, which takes several seconds to reach. Here, the Forty-five motor gets very much on the busy side and old man vibration makes his presence felt strongly through the footboards and handlebars. I could ride 60 miles per hour on the Forty-five for a few minutes, or zip up to 60 miles per hour now and then, but I wouldn't want to cruise at this pace—55 miles

per hour maybe, but not 60 miles per hour.

Now the handling becomes different. The Forty-five feels too light on the front end and I imagine—or do I feel?—that the bike would be happy to whip up some unwelcomed excitement. Still, I don't encounter the speed wobble my Indian-motorcycle friends had guaranteed. The whole thing probably comes down to a rider's experience on either a Harley or an Indian: Whichever was your brand, the other doesn't seem to match up.

Conclusions? Good looks. Good low-speed handling. Comfortable. Good for 50-mile-per-hour cruising on back roads. Good two-passenger bike. Hey—50 miles per hour on back roads is real living.

From Stepchild to Lovable Clunker

The Forty-five was an unusual combination of big-twin styling and comparatively light weight. People who didn't ride could scarcely tell the difference between a Forty-five and a Seventy-four side-valve. So, if you wanted to impress your nonmotorcycling friends, a Forty-five worked as well as a bigger Harley. Hey, it said Harley-Davidson on the tanks so it was a real he-man's motorcycle.

Within the motorcycling community, the Forty-five was viewed differently. The Forty-five was only 10–15 percent cheaper than the Seventy-four side-valve, so most Forty-five owners were penny pinchers. A few road models were sold to the tiny minority of off-road enthusiasts and, before the company built race-ready models, to aspiring racers who had to strip off the road gear. Harley-Davidson continually portrayed the Forty-five as a good motorcycle for beginners and ladies, which lessened its appeal to seasoned riders. The local Harley-shop sales pitch steered in the big-twin direction as much as possible, for in the Harley-Davidson realm bigger always meant better.

Harley-Davidson always emphasized the reliability of the Forty-five. Indian fans snickered that the middleweight Harley didn't have enough power to stress itself. In the words of the late Tom Sifton, longtime Harley dealer, "A Harley-Davidson dealer trying to use the Forty-five to compete with the Indian Scout had his work cut out for him. And a lot of them didn't make it." The Harley Forty-five was by and large a second-class motorcycle within the Harley agencies, whereas the Scouts and Sport Scouts were always pitched as connoisseur's motorcycles within the Indian shops. The most coveted Sports Scouts were the magneto-ignition jobs that were favored for Class C (stock) racing. These bore a higher price tag than the battery-ignition 74-cubic inch Indian Chief!

In summary, prior to World War II, the Harley-Davidson Forty-five had somewhat the character of a neglected stepchild. The Forty-five was a good racer, a good learner's bike, and a good girl's bike, but the sociology of the Harley shops made the middleweight mainly a transition bike while you were on your way to a real motorcycle, a Harley Big Twin.

After the war, the return of service men meant there was a sudden jump in the 20-something population, among whom were thousands who would've already become motorcyclists if it hadn't been for the war. No sales pitch was needed to put them on two wheels. Large numbers of surplus Army Forty-fives came on the market when the government auctioned them off. Franchised Harley dealers competed with unfranchised motorcycle shops, car dealers, and opportunistic

1951 45

The 1951 and 1952 Forty-fives were identical. The tank badge was the only change from the 1950 models. In the new-models edition of *The Enthusiast* not a single word was devoted to the 1952 Forty-five. No Forty-five development was under way, because behind the scenes the company was hip-deep in developing the forthcoming replacement, the 45-ci Model K. © H-D Michigan, Inc.

individuals. Retailers bought Forty-fives by the truckload. The sellers doubled or tripled or quadrupled their purchase price and still sold the Forty-fives cheap. To Harley-Davidson dealers these were sales that otherwise would've been lost. The factory couldn't meet the huge demand for new motorcycles and was rationing new bikes to dealers according to the dealers' prewar sales averages. The war-surplus Forty-fives were a godsend, keeping dealers busy when they might otherwise have folded. Some, like Chambless Harley-Davidson in Montgomery, Alabama, got started with surplus Forty-fives, a backyard shed, and plenty of enthusiasm. They couldn't have made it without the Forty-fives.

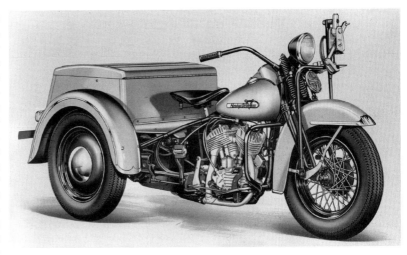

1955 Servi-Car
The two-wheeled Forty-five was last offered as an early 1952 model, but the Servi-Car stayed in the lineup through the 1973 season. © H-D Michigan, Inc.

A lot of these surplus Forty-fives were bought away from the franchised shops, and bought by self-sold young men whose interest hadn't been nurtured within the shops. They were a more open-minded lot, not so concerned with the model's lack of status as had been the case with the prewar in-crowd. The new riders could see that here was a real motorcycle—it had to be a real motorcycle because it was a Harley-Davidson. They could discover the pleasures of 50-mile-an-hour cruising. A lot of them had their six-month fling and went on to other things shortly after the first frost, while others stayed in the game by moving up to a Big Twin.

Whether transients or long-term riders, the postwar group felt an affection for the Forty-five. In their minds were images of indestructible Army Harleys bouncing over Africa's desert dunes and zig-zagging by Europe's shell holes, of Harleys flung to the ground to escape snipers' bullets, of Harleys that would then start and run no matter how deep the dents or how bent the bars. The funny thing is—the civilianized Forty-fives lived up to the image. For the August 1953 *Cycle* magazine, Edward C. Atkinson penned "Ode to an Antique," an affectionate tribute to his "clunker." "I love the old wench," confessed Atkinson. Atkinson talked about the Forty-five's performance, or rather the lack of it. ". . . I selected a nice long stretch of road with a few curves and mountains thrown in for good luck. I didn't pay too much attention to maximum in low, and second, but brother, in high, 40-45-50-55, and groan to 60 miles per hour. That's all, no dice, no faster, a bird flying over offered to give me a tow." Stamina, not speed, endeared the Forty-five to Atkinson. "For sheer guts and stamina, I take my hat off to the little darling. She has flipped the wife and me off on our heads while cow-trailing, bounced down gullies, rolled over boulders and skidded on ice and piled up in snow and come up fighting and ready to start again. . . . All in all, for my money, $250, my beat-up old Harley has been worth every cent of it."

Chapter 4

Seventy-Four and Eighty Side-Valves

The term "flat-head" came into vogue in the hot-rod world several years after the big side-valve twins weren't the leading Harley-Davidson models. I've used "flat-head" sparingly, preferring the era's term "side-valve."

Harley-Davidson flattered and flirted in 1929 and 1930 when they brought out the Forty-five and the Seventy-four. The flattery was directed to Indian, which had proven the merits of side-valve motorcycle engines in both street and track applications for over a decade. In the case of the Seventy-four, the flirting was with disaster, for, as was the case with the Forty-five, the new side-valve Seventy-four was not a good motorcycle in its original configuration. Ultimately, however, the Seventy-four proved to be a match for the Indian Big Twin, the Chief.

The move to side-valve configuration was for two reasons. First, the F-head V-twins were at the limit of development. Under the most stressful conditions and in the hands of the roughest riders, increasing breakdowns were occurring on improved highways that permitted ever-faster cruising. Second, the side-valve conversion was in response to the popularity of Indian's 74-cubic inch (1,200-cc) Chief and 45-cubic inch (750-cc) Scout.

The side-valve configuration was less radical than a switch to all overhead valves. Indeed, the all-important task of combustion-chamber design was farmed out to Englishman Harry Ricardo, whose success in the side-valve field had brought him international acclaim. With Harley-Davidson's two-to-one sales lead, there was no need to risk rejection by a conservative rider corps. The promise of Harley-Davidson side-valve engines was that they would deliver as much speed and reliability as the Indian models. The object wasn't to take chances and increase an already substantial sales lead, but to reaffirm the allegiance of Harley-Davidson riders by upgrading V-twin reliability and styling.

Initial customer and dealer reaction to the Seventy-four was favorable, but development problems (see the Development History section) soon gave the model a black eye. The economic downturn on mainstreet USA lagged the stock market crash by a few months, which is why over 10,000 1930 Seventy-four were sold.

Gradually, the Seventy-four gained acceptance because, after the initial troubles were overcome, the model proved reliable. There remained a few diehard F-head enthusiasts because the older models were about 100 pounds lighter and hence had better acceleration. Engineering updates over the next several years saw gradual power increases in the Seventy-four and improved high-rpm breathing, so that Seventy-four top speed proved superior to that of the old F-head Two Cam. Side-valve big-twin acceler-

1934 74
Representing the era of big flatheads is this happy couple on a 1934 Seventy-four. Unpaved roads got smoother and smoother in the 1930s. Road signs gained in numbers, and motels blossomed, so that uncertainty was removed from touring. The Harley-Davidson Buddy Seat arrived in late 1933, just in time for the new era of practical touring. © H-D Michigan, Inc.

ation, however, never got better than that of the Two Cam, if as good.

The role of the Seventy-fours and Eighties was a lot like the role of the earliest F-head singles. The big side-valve V-twins were meant to be reliable, low-risk motorcycles that would keep the company on its traditionally conservative path to success. In other words, the big side-valve twins were not to get in the way of company and dealer success, while Harley-Davidson's engineering efforts could sustain far-reaching development of an overhead-valve V-twin. Judged in this light, the Seventy-four and Eighty side-valve models were clearly successful.

1930–1948 Seventy-Four and Eighty Flathead Development

The 1930 Seventy-four twin featured a new motor, new clutch, new frame, and new front fork. Carryover parts from the F-head twins were limited to the air cleaner, spark plugs, piston pins, roller bearings, and other small parts. Four Seventy-four side-valve models were

Early 1930 V Series

Collectibility	★★★⯪☆
Comfortable cruising speed	60 mph
Smoothness of ride	★★★☆☆
Passenger accommodations	
Tandem saddles	★☆☆☆☆
Retrofitted buddy seat	★★★☆☆
Reliability	★★★☆☆
Parts/service availability	★★☆☆☆

Find one if you can. I know of only one. They're rare because all were supposed to be retrofitted with new frames, flywheels, and crankcases, and at no expense to the customer. In view of the retrofit program, I guess the early 1930 Seventy-four stunk. But their mere existence signaled a new Harley-Davidson era. I give them, or it (as in one-of-a-kind), a charitable 3 1/2 stars.

1930 74

The 1930 Seventy-four side-valve twin was new from the ground up. Nothing of the old F-head models was retained except bits and pieces like spark plugs and bearings. As with the F-head twins, the new Seventy-four side-valve frame had a double-butted (reinforced) front down tube. © *H-D Michigan, Inc.*

1930 74
The 1931 Seventy-four continued mid-1930 changes that were made in response to customer complaints. Chief among these were new larger and heavier flywheels, a change so fundamental that the late 1930 models required new crankcases and new frames. Dealers got the new parts free but had to absorb the cost of converting early 1930 Seventy-fours to the new configuration. © H-D Michigan, Inc.

1931 74
A new single-tube muffler was fitted to the 1931 Seventy-four side-valve. Other changes involved small details. © H-D Michigan, Inc.

offered. These were the low-performance V, the high-performance VL, and the magneto-equipped variants of each, the VM and VLM.

The new 1930 side-valve motor had cylinder heads with a built-in "dam" between the valve and piston areas, as did the late 1929 Forty-fives, to eliminate plug fouling. Instead of full crankcase baffling like the Forty-five engine, the Seventy-four side-valve retained the F-head setup of a full baffle (with six holes) under the front cylinder and a half-baffle under the rear cylinder. The Seventy-four had about the same power output as the former top-of-the-line F-head Two Cam JDH. However, the Seventy four side-valve weighed 529 pounds, and the Two Cam weighed only 408 pounds, so the Seventy-four side-valve's acceleration was well below that of the old Two Cam.

As with the 1929 Forty-five, linking the 1930 Seventy-four side-valve motor to the transmission was a double-row chain; the F-heads had used a single-row chain. For the first time on Big Twins, an effort was made to provide automatic lubrication to the front chain. The F-heads had featured a crankcase relief tube that sprayed oil mist onto the primary chain. The new side-valve Big Twins positively metered oil to the primary chain. The new Seventy-four clutch had six springs, as in the F-heads, but the Seventy-four clutch had almost four times the surface area of the F-head clutch. The larger clutch area was intended to facilitate an

Late 1930 and 1931 V Series

Collectibility	★★★☆☆
Comfortable cruising speed	60 mph
Smoothness of ride	★★★☆☆
Passenger accommodations	
Tandem saddles	★☆☆☆☆
Retrofitted buddy seat	★★★☆☆
Reliability	★★★☆☆
Parts/service availability	★★☆☆☆

The first-year status of the 1930s argues for a stronger rating, but the surviving late 1930 configurations are really second-generation bikes. The late 1930 and 1931 models were about the same as the rival Indian Chief Big Twin.

optional hand-operated clutch. The Seventy-four transmission housing was new, but most internals were carryovers from the F-heads.

The new front fork on the 1930 Seventy-four was of I-beam construction. Like the F-head twin frame, the frame on the new Seventy-four side-valve had a double-butted front down tube, but the Seventy-four frame was curved to clear the front-mounted generator.

Unfortunately, dealers were nearly unanimous in severely criticizing the new Seventy-four. The dealers may have been in part reacting emotionally to the lack of pep in the new heavyweights, but their other criticisms were valid. Chief among the complaints was inadequate flywheel momentum. The light flywheels were an attempt to provide a needed boost to acceleration. However, low speed running was rough. Dealers were told to instruct the riders to slip the clutch during low-speed running, a time-honored practice in American Big Twins. But slipping the clutch proved impractical because of the all-or-nothing action of the new fiber-plate clutch. Other Seventy-four problems

1932 74 SV
The 1932 Seventy-four got a new Burgess muffler that was longer and slimmer. © *H-D Michigan, Inc.*

1933 74 SV and 45
Right: Art Deco styling graced the 1933 models (the motorcycles, not the girls). This was the first year of no-extra-charge paint options. © H-D Michigan, Inc.

1934 74
Middle: The 1934 sidecar received the same fender and fender trim as the motorcycles. Out of sight is the new 1934 upturned tailpipe; see the earlier 1934 Forty-five photo for the general appearance. © H-D Michigan, Inc

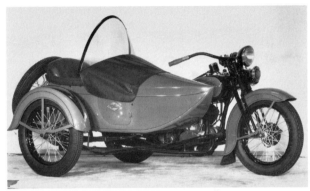

1935 74 SV
Below: Here we see the new 1935 tank panel. The longer rear chain guard was also new. The light-colored (probably cadmium-plated) foot pedals were first used on the 1934 models. © H-D Michigan, Inc.

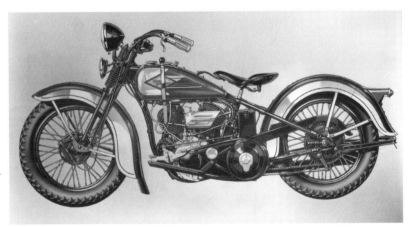

included broken or weak valve springs, broken brake operating shaft, and broken spokes caused by excessively loose splines on the new quick-detachable rear hub.

In mid-October, about six weeks after the Seventy-four debuted, the company had to halt production and reengineer the model. The most important change to the late 1930 Seventy four side-valve was the fitting of new, larger flywheels. This was a big deal, cost-wise, because the new flywheels called for new, larger crankcases. The "fun" didn't stop there. The larger crankcases required a new frame. Other new parts included valve springs and a new clutch with nine springs instead of six, the latter ending the possibility of an auxiliary hand clutch. The new parts were shipped free to dealers as a kit, but the dealers had to bear the large labor cost of the massive retrofit program. Later in the production year, the VM and VLM were replaced on dealer order

1935 74 SV
Harley-Davidson adopted "straight" (parallel) cylinder bores on the 1935 models. Dealers' order blanks listed an 80-ci (1,300-cc) model, although *The Enthusiast* and sales literature hadn't yet acknowledged the Eighty's existence.

1936 74/80
An optional four-speed transmission became available on the side-valve Big Twins. The four-speed had shifting action through a rotary plate or disk instead of a cylindrical cam. The board of directors considered the four-speed more a matter of marketing than a necessity. © *H-D Michigan, Inc.*

blanks by two new models, the VC commercial model and the VS side-car model ("S" not in motor number). (Note: the late 1930 debut of the VC and VS models is a correction to *Inside Harley-Davidson*.)

Two new 1931 models were introduced. These were the VCR road-marking model and the VMG with a magneto generator. With so many changes incorporated into the late 1930 Seventy-fours, predictably only a few noticeable changes were made to the 1931 models. A new single-tube muffler was fitted, as was a new die-cast Schebler carburetor. In mid-year, a three-speed-plus-reverse transmission was offered; this was advertised as a new 1932 feature. Another midseason change was a constant-mesh kickstarter mechanism that prevented jamming. Many other detail changes were made.

On the 1932 Seventy-fours, new cylinders provided an air space between the exhaust ports and the barrels, as on the Forty-five. Piston-pin lock rings were new, as was a longer muffler. The mid-1931 constant-mesh starter was advertised as a 1932 improvement. The transmission mounting was changed. The forward cast-in "ear" on the aluminum gearbox was replaced with a removable steel plate secured by the gearbox studs. This prevented an occasional problem, the breaking of the forward gearbox ear by a thrown and jammed rear chain.

1932 V Series

Collectibility	★★☆☆☆
Comfortable cruising speed	60 mph
Smoothness of ride	★★★☆☆
Passenger accommodations	
Tandem saddles	★☆☆☆☆
Retrofitted buddy seat	★★★☆☆
Reliability	★★★☆☆
Parts/service availability	★★☆☆☆

The 1932 Harley Big Twins suffered in the looks department when compared to the Indian Chiefs, the latter gaining better-looking tanks and general outline in 1932.

Two new 1933 Seventy-fours were offered. These were the VLE and the VLD. The VLE was basically a VL with magnesium-alloy (formerly called "Dow metal") pistons. The VLD was like a VLE but with a new Y-shaped inlet manifold and corresponding new Y-ported cylinders. The new VLD cylinders and heads produced a 5:1 compression ratio, compared to the other Seventy-four engines with either 4:1 or 4.5:1 compression ratios. Output of the new top-of-the-line VLD was 36 horsepower, which was a 20 percent increase over the 1930 VL output of 30 horsepower. Few other technical changes were made.

For 1934, Harley-Davidson fitted a "Y" inlet manifold to all Seventy-fours; previously only the top-of-the-line VLD had the "Y" manifold. Milwaukee upgraded the total-loss lubrication system with a new oil pump for the Seventy-four (and Forty-five) designed to provide better oil control over a wider rpm range. This move was in response to Indian, which in 1933 introduced dry-sump (circulating) lubrication. To signify the improved inlet manifold and oil pump, all Seventy-four motors were termed "TNT motors" in company advertising and on the dealer order blanks. New heat treating was used on all frames and forks. Linkert die-cast carburetors replaced the Schebler die-cast units; this was a running change made on late 1933 models. New low-expansion aluminum-alloy pistons promised better reliability than the previous magnesium-alloy pistons, while adding only a slight weight penalty.

The most significant engineering change for 1935 was the switch from tapered-bore cylinders and round pistons to straight-bore cylinders and cam-ground pistons. Although advertised as a 1935 improvement, these features were incorporated on late 1934 models. Harley-Davidson had been alone in the use of tapered cylinder bores from 1914–1934.

Nineteen thirty-five also brought an even larger Harley-Davidson Big Twin, the 80-cubic inch VDDS and VLDD, commonly called the "Eighty." According to the dealer order blanks for the 1935 models, the

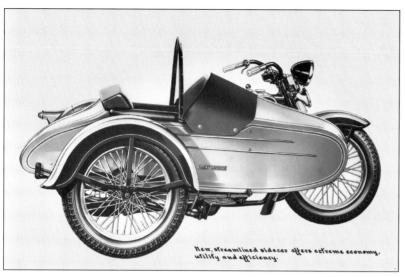

1936 Sidecar
The new 1936 sidecar body was used until the late 1960s. © H-D Michigan, Inc.

1937 74 SV
For 1937, all the side-valve models got the streamlined styling introduced on the 1936 Knuckleheads. Functionally, the big news was the incorporation of dry-sump (circulating) lubrication, also following the lead of the 1936 Knuckleheads. In standard trim, the oil tank was finished to match the fuel tanks and fenders on 1937 models. Color-matched oil tanks were never again standard. © H-D Michigan, Inc.

Eighty was offered as the VLDD "Sport Solo, Solo Bars" and the VDDS "Low Compression, Sidecar Gearing and Bars." A VLDJ "Twin, Competition Special, Solo Bars" was also offered, although never featured in new-model announcements or sales catalogs.

The 1936 season saw the introduction of the first cataloged 80-cubic inch side-valve twins, the VHS (low-compression motor and sidecar gearing) and VLH (high-compression motor), although the Eighty had been made in limited quantities for 1935. The Seventy-four and Eighty twins were available with a one-year-only optional four-speed, sliding-gear transmission. The big side-valves had new nine-bolt cylinder heads instead of eight-bolt heads. Cylinder and cylinder-head cooling fins were larger, and the cylinder fins wrapped around the inlet ports. Changes to the internal shapes of the cylinder heads improved combustion. The new Seventy-four and Eighty side-valve heads were available with two compression ratios, 5.3:1 and 5.5:1.

For 1937, the side-valve Big Twins underwent a mammoth remake. Dramatically new looks were the result of incorporating the new front fork, frame, fuel tanks, oil tanks, and four-speed, constant-mesh transmission of the Sixty-one overhead-valve twin. Henceforth, the same running gear changes, clutch changes, and transmission changes applied to the Sixty-one, Seventy-four, and Eighty. To avoid

1933–1936 V Series

Collectibility	★★★☆☆
Comfortable cruising speed	60 mph
Smoothness of ride	★★★☆☆
Passenger accommodations	
Tandem saddles	★☆☆☆☆
Buddy seat	★★★☆☆
Reliability	★★★☆☆
Parts/service availability	★★☆☆☆

The 1933–1936 models continued with total-loss (noncirculating) lubrication, a notable deficiency compared to Indian's dry-sump (circulating) lubrication. The transmissions of the rival brands were about the same, three-speed with sliding-gear shifting mechanism. Indian had a much superior oil-bath primary drive that didn't leak like the Harley drive covered with sheet metal. On the other hand, the 1933 models ushered in tanks with the art deco styling that was so characteristic of the era. The 1934 models got attractive standard two-color finishes (on some, three colors if you count the black frames). The 1935 and 1936 models were equally colorful. The 1933 models offer the strongest three-star rating because of rarity, followed by the 1934 models for both rarity and style. Weakest of the range are the 1936 models because they weren't competitive with either the new Harley Knuckleheads or the Indian Chiefs. The 1936 Seventy-fours and Eighties with the four-speed sliding-gear transmission are very rare. Frankly, I don't know if there's any external difference for this transmission, but even if there is, I don't think the rarity of this unsuccessful design would be worth the rarity of transmission parts, should you need them.

repetition, highlights of the shared changes of the 1937 and later models are listed in the Knucklehead development section as "big-twin" changes. The remainder of this discussion concerns technical changes that applied only to the Seventy-four and Eighty side-valve twins.

Like the Sixty-one, the 1937 Seventy-four and Eighty side-valve models got dry-sump (circulating) lubrication. But the oil pump used on the side-valve Big Twins differed from the oil pump used on the Sixty-one. On the side-valve Big Twins, the pump was of the vane type, was driven by the rear exhaust cam gear shaft, and was mounted on the outside of the gear-case cover. A new gear-case cover was shaped to assist in moving crankcase air-oil mist to the new oil slinger (centrifuge) on the generator drive gear. As part of the new lubrication setup, a full baf-

1938 74 SV
The 1938 frame had thicker tubing in the rear section (upper and lower rear forks). The clutch and transmission were modified for extra strength and improved reliability. © H-D Michigan, Inc.

1939 74 SV
The 1939 crankcase baffling system was revised and the connecting rods were reversed. The 1939 and later side-valve Big Twins had the forked rod connected to the rear piston and the plain rod connected to the front piston. Additionally, half of the slot on the lower boss of the forked rod was closed off. © H-D Michigan, Inc.

fle was placed under the rear cylinder instead of a half-baffle (note: not mentioned in the author's *Inside Harley-Davidson*). The Seventy-four and Eighty used the Sixty-one-style clutch. The pinion gear shaft was changed from a plain bearing to a roller bearing, so the side-valve Big Twins were now fully roller-bearing mounted.

The 1937 Seventy-four and Eighty flywheels were increased in diameter and the balancing factor was changed to provide smoother running at high speeds. The stroke of the Seventy-four was changed to the same as used on the Eighty, from 4 to 4 9/32 inches. The Seventy-four got a new, smaller bore, 3 5/16 inches in lieu of 3 7/16 inches. The same cylinder castings were used on the Seventy-four and Eighty, so the Seventy-four cylinder walls were 1/8 inch thicker. In the opinion of the late

1933–1936 V Series

Collectibility	★★★☆☆
Comfortable cruising speed	60 mph
Smoothness of ride	★★★☆☆
Passenger accommodations	
Tandem saddles	★☆☆☆☆
Buddy seat	★★★☆☆
Reliability	★★★☆☆
Parts/service availability	★★☆☆☆

The 1933–1936 models continued with total-loss (noncirculating) lubrication, a notable deficiency compared to Indian's dry-sump (circulating) lubrication. The transmissions of the rival brands were about the same, three-speed with sliding-gear shifting mechanism. Indian had a much superior oil-bath primary drive that didn't leak like the Harley drive covered with sheet metal. On the other hand, the 1933 models ushered in tanks with the art deco styling that was so characteristic of the era. The 1934 models got attractive standard two-color finishes (on some, three colors if you count the black frames). The 1935 and 1936 models were equally colorful. The 1933 models offer the strongest three-star rating because of rarity, followed by the 1934 models for both rarity and style. Weakest of the range are the 1936 models because they weren't competitive with either the new Harley Knuckleheads or the Indian Chiefs. The 1936 Seventy-fours and Eighties with the four-speed sliding-gear transmission are very rare. Frankly, I don't know if there's any external difference for this transmission, but even if there is, I don't think the rarity of this unsuccessful design would be worth the rarity of transmission parts, should you need them.

Charles "Red" Wolverton, a dealer from 1929 to 1958, the thicker Seventy-four cylinder walls were responsible for overheating problems not experienced by earlier Seventy-fours or the companion 1937 and later Eighties. The inlet and exhaust valves of the Seventy-four and Eighty were made 1/4 inch longer.

For 1938, all Seventy-four and Eighty side-valve changes were in common with the Sixty-one. These shared changes are highlighted in the Knucklehead development section.

The 1939 Seventy-four and Eighty received new steel-strutted, horizontally slotted pistons and new rings. Although advertised as 1939 improvements, the new pistons and rings were introduced on late 1938 models. The crankcase baffling system was changed on the 1939 Seventy-four and Eighty.

1937–1942 U Series

Collectibility	★★★☆☆
Comfortable cruising speed	60 mph
Smoothness of ride	★★★☆☆
Passenger accommodations	
Tandem saddles	★☆☆☆☆
Buddy seat	★★★☆☆
Reliability	★★★☆☆
Parts/service availability	★★☆☆☆

The 1937 models were the first big side-valvers with dry-sump (circulating) lubrication, which was introduced the previous season on the Knuckleheads. Coupled with the fantastic styling sired by the previous year's Knuckleheads, the 1937 Seventy-fours and Eighties were a big-time improvement on the 1936 side-valves. So why still three stars? Because even with the big improvements, the 1937 and later side-valve Big Twins were now second fiddle to the more advanced Knuckleheads. As usual, the earlier the better, so we have the range extending from a strong three rating for the 1937s to a weak three rating for the 1942s.

1940 80
The 1940 Eighty side-valve was the last of the line, due to the growing popularity of the Knucklehead. The deep-finned aluminum cylinders became standard on the 1940 Eighties and optional on the 1940 Seventy-four side-valves. Planning for the 1941 Seventy-four overhead-valve model was well under way, so development of the big side-valve models came to a halt. © H-D Michigan, Inc.

1947 74 SV
The 1947 Seventy-four side-valve got a new instrument panel and shifter guide in common with the rest of the range. © H-D Michigan, Inc.

There were no baffles under the rear cylinder, which was done to reduce the power-robbing air-compressor effect caused by the pistons pumping up the crankcase air pressure on the downstroke. To keep proper lubrication with the new baffle layout, the connecting-rod arrangement was reversed. The 1939 and later side-valve Big Twins featured the forked rod connected to the rear piston and the plain rod connected to the front piston. Additionally, half of the slot on the lower boss of the forked rod was closed off.

The inlet manifold on the 1939 Seventy-four and Eighty was lengthened 3/4 inch and a 1/8-inch asbestos-insulated bracket was placed between the carburetor and the manifold. These changes were made in order to keep heat from building up in the carburetor, thereby preventing vapor lock and eliminating occasional loping during low-speed running. New valve spring covers featured only two telescoping pieces instead of three pieces. On the Eighty, to better dissipate heat, the cylinder barrels were made thinner.

For 1940, deep-finned aluminum cylinder heads became standard on the Eighty and optional on the Seventy-four. These features were the last significant updates unique to the side-valve Big Twins because the new 1941 Seventy-four overhead-valve model removed any lingering thoughts that the Eighty side-valve was the power champion. In other words, the company planned to phase out the side-valve Big Twins. The Eighty side-valve was last produced as a 1940 model, and the Seventy-four side-valve was last offered as a 1948 model.

Seventy-Four and Eighty Side-Valve Rideability

A maximum cruising speed of 60 miles per hour makes the big side-valve twins better highway bikes than the 50-mile-per-hour Forty-fives. However, the big flat-heads have far less dealer support than the

1948 74 SV
Nineteen forty-eight saw the final offering of new side-valve Seventy-fours. A new touch was aluminum paint on the cylinders and heads. According to *The Legend Begins*, the model accounted for just 8 percent of total production. © *H-D Michigan, Inc.*

1943–1948 U Series	
Collectibility	★★☆☆☆
Comfortable cruising speed	60 mph
Smoothness of ride	★★★☆☆
Passenger accommodations	
Tandem saddles	★☆☆☆☆
Buddy seat	★★★☆☆
Reliability	★★★☆☆
Parts/service availability	★★☆☆☆

A few side-valve Big Twins were made for military use, so the 1943–1945 years are included. In this era, these were obsolete motorcycles.

Forty-fives. The 1930–1936 models have total loss oiling, so you will need to track oil consumption carefully and take extra oil on long trips. The 1937 and later models have dry-sump oiling, making them more suitable as touring bikes.

Bread and Butter

During the heyday of the Harley side-valve Big Twins, 1930–1936, they were the most popular American models on the road. They were the bread and butter of the factory and the dealerships. Racing wasn't as big a deal in these years as it had been in the old F-head and Eight-valve days, when Harley-Davidson, Indian, and Excelsior fielded factory teams on special racing models. Hence, the Harley Big Twins didn't suffer much in the image department despite Indian's successes in the newly emerging Class C (stock) racing events. The hallmarks of Harley-Davidson's success in the first half of the Great Depression were its superior dealers and good motorcycles. Indian fans had some good arguments about the relative merits of the opposing models, but in most cities, Indian dealerships were decidedly smaller and less attractive than Harley dealerships. Many Harley riders were sold on their dealer as much as they were sold on their brand. The Seventy-four and Eighty side-valve models were like the old F-head singles, in that they were motorcycles that didn't get in the way of success.

Even after the introduction of the revolutionary 1936 Sixty-one overhead-valve Knuckleheads, the Seventy-four and Eighty side-valve twins continued to outsell the Knuckleheads until the 1940 season. The side-valve Harley-Davidson Big Twins were well respected for their reliability, and conservative riders kept a wait-and-see attitude about the Knuckleheads.

The 1940 and 1941 Knuckleheads outsold the side-valve Big Twins, but only after World War II did the big flat-heads really fall from favor, with sales at less than 25 percent of the figure for overheads. In summary, the side-valve Big Twins were reliable motorcycles with plenty of performance for their touring role. They didn't arouse passion, but they were objects of affection.

Chapter 5

Knuckleheads

The Knuckleheads were the motorcycles that saved Harley-Davidson, in the opinion of some. That's a slight stretch because Indian was too sick to seriously threaten Harley with a knockout blow. Still, there's no denying that the Knucklehead was Harley-Davidson's first out-of-the-box success since the original 1903 single. Harley-Davidson was lucky, some say, to bring out its 61-cubic-inch (1,000-cc) E and EL overhead-valve V-twins at the same time that Indian brought out its unsuccessful "upside-down" Four. But Harley-Davidson made its so-called good luck, and Indian made its so-called bad luck. Luck had nothing to do with the success of the overhead-valve Harleys.

The Knuckleheads were instantly received with enthusiasm by the more knowledgeable Harley riders and dealers. More conservative Harley people needed three or four years of Knucklehead success to convince them to abandon the Harley side-valve Big Twins. But within five years the Knuckleheads ruled American motorcycling more than any previous Harleys had.

The E series was termed the "61 O.H.V." in Harley-Davidson literature of the era. In everyday terminology, riders called the model the "Sixty-one." Not until the advent of the 1948 redesigned "Panheads" did the term "Knucklehead" arise for the first generation of Harley-Davidson overhead-valve road models. The Knucklehead nickname arose from the resemblance to a closed fist that was presented by the covers that enclosed the valve stems, valve springs, and rocker arms. Hereafter, I'll use the term "rocker covers." I'll also use the term "Sixty-one" now and then as a reminder that nobody called the Harley overhead-valve models "Knuckleheads" during the era.

The Knucklehead was a sensation when it debuted as a midseason 1936 model. The overhead-valve engine was exciting because previously this configuration on American motorcycles was limited to special racers and hillclimbers campaigned by both Harley-Davidson and Indian. So the speed image was immediately established based solely on what the eye beheld.

Perhaps even more important was the superb styling of the Knucklehead. The fuel tanks and tank-top instrument panel were beautiful. All the space under the tanks was filled with the engine, which gave an impression of immense power.

During its fiscal year 1936 (October 1, 1935, through September 30, 1936) the company sold 1,836 Knuckleheads, according to company President Walter Davidson in his annual report to the stockholders (November 1937). Sales of the Sixty-one increased 10 percent for model year 1937, to 2,025. The year 1938 was a somewhat subtle affir-

1941 Knucklehead
This happy couple symbolizes the Knucklehead era, but touring was only one of the Knucklehead's many uses. The versatile overhead-valve twin could fit any need: track racing, dragracing, enduro-riding, record setting, police patrol, and, of course, touring. © *H-D Michigan, Inc.*

mation of the Knucklehead's future. *The Legend Begins* lists 2,478 Knuckleheads produced, which accounted for 30 percent of company totals, compared to the 1936 Knucklehead's 27 percent.

The Knucklehead became known for its versatility, and in so doing, carved out a unique niche in American motorcycling history. From 1940 on, it was the Harley-Davidson sales leader. After World War II, the demand for new Knuckleheads was so great that the company rationed new motorcycles to dealers on the basis of prewar sales. In its final model year of 1947, the Knucklehead accounted for nearly 60 percent of the more than 20,000 new Harley-Davidsons produced. It was the highest civilian production since 1920. All in all, the Knucklehead ranks alongside the early F-head singles for major contributions to Harley-Davidson success.

1936–1947 Knucklehead Development

On the 1936 Knucklehead, the astounding news was the overhead-valve configuration. Here was a motorcycle that even in its most docile form could be expected to outperform breathed-on Indian side-valve twins. In scattered and isolated cases, for several more years, a few but decreasing number of Indian diehards would make its side-valve redskins keep up with or even outrun the new Knucklehead Harleys. But Indian's days as highway front-runner for Joe Average were effectively ended with the Knucklehead.

Not only was the valve placement new, but the Knucklehead valve actuation differed from any other motorcycle engine. Elsewhere, even on racing and hillclimbing Harleys, the pushrods for overhead-valve motors were actuated by at least two different camshafts. Competition Harleys of recent design had used side-valve cases with four camshafts, so that each camshaft drove a dedicated valve. This was a good approach for rac-

1936 E Series

Collectibility	★★★★↙
Comfortable cruising speed	60 mph
Smoothness of ride	★★★☆☆
Passenger accommodations	★★★☆☆
Reliability	★★★★☆
Parts/service availability	★★★★☆

This is the model that brought Harley-Davidson technical leadership in the vitally important big-twin field. The 1936 61 O.H.V. scores high in every category—history, technical features, rarity, practicality, and aesthetics. But be very careful if you intend to buy a 1936 Knucklehead. These models differed in many ways from the 1937-and-later Knuckleheads. Some of these differences were frame, fork spring nuts, fork top plate, speedometer, speedometer light switch (1937), gearshift lever, shifter gate, timing-case cover, and oil tank. There are so-called 1936 Knuckleheads out there that have 1936 numbers and little if anything else that is correct. Before joining the quest for a 1936 Knucklehead, I recommend you join the 36 EL Registry, care of Gerry and Lisa Lyons, 160 South Highland Avenue, Winter Garden, FL 34787, ph. (407) 654-0230. The registry lists 138 1936 Knuckleheads, but some are crankcases only, and fewer than two dozen are complete originals. Now, if there remained fewer than two dozen complete original 1936 Knuckleheads, I'd be inclined to cast a five-star vote. But the potential is out there to see more than a hundred of these classics eventually completed with reproduced parts indistinguishable from the originals. Complete post-1936 Knucklehead frames are currently being built, and in my opinion, it's only a matter of time until faithfully copied 1936 frames and other 1936-only parts will be available. Buying my book Inside Harley-Davidson or Bruce Palmer's book How to Restore Your Harley-Davidson (both also published by Motorbooks International) would be a good idea.

ing and hillclimbing because it simplified tuning, minimized reciprocating weight for higher peak engine revolutions, and reduced costs.

But on a touring engine where maximum engine speed wasn't a goal, Harley-Davidson took the opportunity to tailor the new overhead-valve engine to normal road needs. The designers opted for a single centrally mounted camshaft with four lobes placed side by side along the length of the shaft. This layout reduced valve-gear noise at the outset,

1936 Knucklehead

The 1936 61 OHV Model E (low compression) and EL (high compression) ushered in a new era in American motorcycling with their overhead-valve configuration. Later to become known as "Knuckleheads," the new overhead-valve models were instantly accepted for their superb styling. The tank top instrument panel made all other Harleys and all the Indians look old-fashioned. © H-D Michigan, Inc.

and made for less variation in gear teeth clearances as the crankcases warmed up during operation, which further reduced wear and racket.

The overhead valves were actuated by solid pushrods as in all other overhead-valve motorcycle engines. The pushrods were contained within tubular covers. On the top of each cylinder a cast aluminum housing or "rocker box" accepted the pushrods and pushrod covers. Each rocker box supported the thrust end of two rocker arm shafts, the shafts extending sideways across the cylinder head, one to the inlet valve and the other to exhaust valve. The outboard or valve end of each rocker arm shaft was supported by a tab integral with the iron cylinder head.

Although stories exist about new 1936 Sixty-ones without enclosure of the valve springs, in my opinion these examples were limited to a few prototypes that were shipped to selected dealers. Harley-Davidson

1936 Knucklehead

The extruded tube forks used on the 1936 Knucklehead were more stylish and were probably cheaper than the drop forged I-beam forks of the 1936 side-valve models. The new fork was adapted to the side-valve Seventy-four and Eighty twins in 1937. Note: this example is a prototype and differs in small details from the production models. © H-D Michigan, Inc.

1947 Knucklehead
Although this is a 1947 engine, it's much the same as a 1936 unit. The single cam shaft is reminiscent of the early F-heads, but this concept actually has some advantages (see text). © H-D Michigan, Inc.

1936 Knucklehead
All four cams were on a single central shaft. This reduced dimensional variances, which in the side-valve layout caused noise and wear from cam gears that were either too tightly or too loosely engaged. © H-D Michigan, Inc.

often used dealers as engineering testers. As delivered to customers, a small "baby food jar" cover was placed over each valve spring and over the rocker arm where it acted against the valve stem. The two-piece cover, consisted of a small sheet-metal cylinder within which the valve stem and the inner and outer valve springs moved, and a companion top piece that also covered the rocker arm tip. The bottom piece around the valve attached to the cylinder head by the valve guide. The valve guide was pushed through a hole in the floor of the rocker cover until an annular ring on the valve guide—sort of a hat brim—bottomed out the rocker cover on the cylinder-head surface. The top and bot-

1936 Knucklehead motor closeup
The double-loop frame used on the Knucklehead was originally designed for the side-valve Big Twins. Unlike the earlier frames, there are no forgings at the bottom of the front down tubes, which simply bend to form one continuous tube on each side all the way to the rear axle. This was a 1936-only feature.

tom sections of the rocker cover had slightly different diameters and were press fitted together.

In retrospect, the rocker-cover design appears to have been an afterthought. This is especially clear when one considers that major manufacturers of British overhead-valve engines invariably left the valve springs, and in some cases the pushrod end of the rocker arms, totally exposed. The theory of the era was that the valve springs, particularly those of the exhaust valve, needed exposure to cooling air. Thus, in offering only rudimentary enclosure, the rocker covers were both an advancement over contemporary practice yet an inadequate approach by modern standards. You can make of the design what you will. While the rocker covers generally prevented gobs of oil from collecting, oil mist naturally settled over the cylinder heads. As the Sixty-one was a mount originally intended for the more sporting contingent, the situation wasn't very important to likely buyers.

Second in importance only to the new overhead-valve configuration was Harley-Davidson's first dry-sump (circulating) lubrication system. The system drew oil from the oil tank behind the rear cylinder,

1939 Big Twin transmission
The Knucklehead's four-speed layout was the first for an American motorcycle. The constant-mesh design, another American first, accomplished shifting by sliding notched gear shafts along the gear centers. The rider felt a pronounced but harmless clunk with each shift. Goodbye forever to broken gear teeth. © H-D Michigan, Inc.

Fork rocker
The rider of an old Harley should keep the fork rockers greased. Check the rockers periodically for wear. These are great handling forks when everything is right. But excessive wear produces looseness, and under this condition the leading-link design is dangerous.

1937 Knucklehead
The Knucklehead styling was so successful that the side-valve models got the treatment in 1937. The 1937 frame was strengthened with an 11-inch reinforcement between the seat post and seat bar connection. The rear section (upper and lower rear forks, or upper and lower chain stays) was made of heavier tubing. © H-D Michigan, Inc.

then provided oil under pressure to the mainshafts and crankshaft, and then to the valve rockers. The amount of oil delivered to the rockers was adjustable by rotating the rocker arm shaft, which had an eccentric groove. Oil returned from the overhead areas to the crankcase under vacuum draw. The gear-type oil pump was driven from the pinion shaft and mounted to the crankcase. As in earlier Harleys, the pistons and crankcase baffle plates worked together to further assist in the movement of oil. The downward motion of the pistons provided needed pressure, and the upward motion of the pistons drew oil through the baffle slots to be deposited on the cylinder walls. Also in line with previous Harley-Davidson practice was the use of a timed crankcase breather valve operated by one of the cam gears.

For 1936, the factory ushered in its first four-speed, constant-mesh transmission on the Knucklehead. The Knucklehead box joined the optional four-speed, sliding-gear transmission on the big side-valve twins. The fourth speed was important for highway cruising, where the taller top gear reduced vibration, and all the more so because rival Indian had come out in 1935 with an optional four-speed gearbox. The Harley-Davidson four-speeds, however, had a more practical set of gear ratios for solo road use, whereas the oddly chosen ratios of the Indian four-speed transmission made it suitable only for sidecar work.

No less important than the fourth speed was the constant-mesh design of the new Knucklehead transmission. Rider input to the transmission was translated into internal gearbox motion through a slotted cylindrical drum, or cam drum, mounted in the roof of the gearbox. The new transmission also had a spiral gear drive for the speedometer, which dispensed with the troublesome chore of aligning the rear-wheel-driven speedometer mechanism with the rear wheel hub when changing the rear tire.

The Sixty-one clutch was a new design along the lines of the clutches used on the singles and the Forty-fives. Mounted against clutch spring pressure, a single circular spring collar replaced the three spring-nut sectors used on side-valve Big Twins from 1912 through 1936. Ten evenly spaced springs replaced the previous nine springs, which had been dispersed in three sets of three springs.

Although the new 1936 instrument panel generally and rightfully is considered a styling touch, the panel did provide the new capability of oil-pressure monitoring. At zero oil pressure when starting up, the oil gauge showed a warning "flag." Upon start up, proper minimal oil pressure would cause the flag to move out of the viewing window. The instrument panel also included an ammeter and the speedometer.

The 1936 Knucklehead front fork and frame were entirely new. The fork was of drawn tubular construction. The frame had two front down tubes instead of the traditional single tube. The lower run of the tubes bent gradually at the bottom and then continued horizontally along each side of the crankcase. Although this frame debuted on the Sixty-one, the design was actually conceived for the Seventy-four and Eighty side-valve models.

In standard 1936 EL trim with a 7:1 compression ratio and mild cams the claimed output was 40 horsepower at 4,800 rpm. The bore and stroke of 3 5/16x3 1/2 inches were typical for 1936 motorcycle engines of this size such as the J. A. Prestwich (JAP) and Matchless engines used in the world-renowned Brough-Superior machines. As with all new motorcycles of the era, some Sixty-ones were faster than others. Out of the box most would top out in the low 90s, a few would hit 95 miles per hour, and very few would see 100 miles per hour. Still, they were faster than out-of-the-box Indians, and that's what mattered to Joe Average.

During the production of 1936 Knuckleheads, numerous changes were made. Many if not most of these take a trained eye to spot. Rather than detail these running changes here, they are highlighted in the table titled "1936 versus Later Knuckleheads"

1937 Knucklehead
The tank top instrument panel was immediately accepted. The concept is still with us today. For 1936 and 1937 an ammeter reported the electrical status, and a warning flag signified low oil pressure. © H-D Michigan, Inc.

1938 Knucklehead
For the 1938 model year, all Big Twin frames were again strengthened. The steering head was fitted with a self-aligning lower head cone. © H-D Michigan, Inc.

1936 Models E, EL, ELS, and ES Specifications

Engine ....45-degree overhead-
    valve V-twin
Bore and stroke...............3 5/16x3 1/2 in
Displacement ....60.33 ci (989 cc)
Compression ratio
Model E...........................6.5:1
Model EL........................7:1
Model ES........................5.5:1
Model ELS.......................6:1
Power
Model E...........................37 bhp @ 4,800 rpm
Model EL........................40 bhp @ 4,800 rpm
Transmission ....Four-speed, constant-
    mesh type, mounted remotely to frame,
    positive gear locking
Shift ....Left hand, indicator
    gate on tank
Primary drive ....Double-row chain, oil-
    mist lubricated
Clutch ....Dry, multiple-disk
    type, left-foot actuated
Wheelbase.......................59 1/2 in
Wheels and tires ....Drop-center rims,
    quickly detachable, interchangeable, 4
    1/2x18 in
Suspension
Front ....Leading-link, drop-
    forged fork
Rear ....Rigid
Weight............................515 lb (fully serviced,
    with standard solo group)
Saddle height..................26 in
Fuel consumption............35–50 mpg
Top speed
Model E...........................85–90 mph
Model EL........................90–95 mph

1936 Knucklehead versus Later Knuckleheads

Feature	1936 (all or early)	Late-1936 or 1937 and later
Frame front down tubes	1936: front down tube and lower horizontal tube are one continuous piece at intersections	1937: front down tube and lower horizontal tubes are separate pieces, joined by forgings
	1936: butted (double-diameter) section near sidecar loops	1937: not butted but double diameter throughout
Frame, upper rear	1936: turns gradually into backbone	1937: turns abruptly into backbone
Speedometer	1936: 100 mph	1937: 120 mph
Speedometer light	1936: none	1937: switch on instrument panel switch
Fork top plate	1936: chrome-plated steel with four holes	1937: stainless steel without the holes
Fork top nuts	Early-1936: parkerized	late-1936: chrome plated
Shift lever	1936: round in cross section, held in gear position by spring-loaded detent	1937: flat in cross section, held in gear position by shifter-gate notches
Shifter gate	1936: simple slot	1937: zig-zag slot
Safety guard	Early-1936: three-piece type, bolted at bottom to sidecar mounts	Late-1936: one-piece type, bolted at bottom to footboard mounts
Air intake horn	1936: somewhat rectangular	1937: tapered
Rocker-shaft end covers	Early 1936: domed cap, fastened by a screw to rocker shaft	Late 1936: large nut threaded onto end of rocker shaft
Oil tanks	Earliest 1936s: smooth tank tops with welded oil-line fittings	Later 1936s: some embossed tanks with welded oil-line fittings; some embossed tanks with swaged fittings
Rear chain guard mount	1936: hangs down from rear fender	1937: extends up from frame

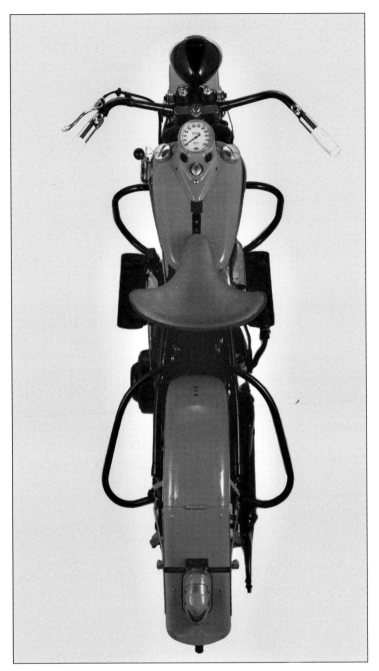

1938 Knucklehead
On the 1938 models this new
instrument panel had warning lights
in place of the former ammeter and
oil pressure warning flag. © H-D
Michigan, Inc.

Rider's view of Knucklehead
Here's the look enjoyed by tens of thousands of Knucklehead riders
over the years. For all-around performance and top quality dealer
support, the Knucklehead was hard to beat.

1937–1947 E and F Series

Collectibility	★★★★☆
Comfortable cruising speed	60 mph
Smoothness of ride	★★★☆☆
Passenger accommodations	★★★☆☆
Reliability	★★★★☆
Parts/service availability	★★★★☆

Lacking the special mystique and rarity of the 1936 Knuckleheads, these still rate four stars for their historical significance as sustainers and improvers of Harley-Davidson's sales lead over Indian. Most are harder to find than the later Panheads, but 1946 and 1947 Knuckleheads are more common than some years of Panheads. Several old timers told me they preferred the 1936–1940 Sixty-ones to the 1941 and later Sixty-ones and Seventy-fours. The pre-1941 Sixty-ones had more pep than the later ones because the later Sixty-ones used the same, heavier flywheel castings as the Seventy-fours. All of the Sixty-ones, they said, were smoother than the Seventy-fours. All of the 1937–1947 Knuckleheads are easier to restore than the 1936 Knuckleheads because the later ones don't have as many one-year-only features as did the first Knuckleheads. The 1940 Knuckleheads were optionally fitted with 5.00x16-inch tires, and all later Knuckleheads had these tires. Comfort is improved with the large tires, but the handling is less precise, so this is a matter of rider preference. If you opt for the large tires, be sure to keep them properly inflated. With underinflated 5.00x16-inch tires it's possible to ground the frame in a turn.

There were several 1937 Knucklehead changes. Running-gear changes made to the Sixty-one were also made to the 1937 side-valve Big Twins. Front frame members were made of heavier gauge steel with 6-inch reinforcements that tied into a drop forging at the bottom that could be used to attach a sidecar or a package truck. The top frame member was given an 11-inch "double-tubed" reinforcement between the seat post and the seat bar connection, and the rear stays were of heavier gauge steel. A stronger transmission mounting bracket and a hardened-steel stabilizer bushing rounded out the frame changes for both the Sixty-one and the side-valve Big Twins.

The 1937 oil tank differed from earlier and later tanks. On the 1936 tank, the supply (or takeoff) line was on the back of the tank. On the 1937 tank, the supply line exited the center of the drain plug. A check valve kept oil from immediately spilling when the supply line was

INSTRUMENT PANEL

Built-in instrument panel with large 4"
easily read aeroplane type speedometer
dial. Two-mile per hour calibrations. Precision instrument. Special electrical speed
recording device, handlebar controlled,
included in police accessory group.

1939 Knucklehead
The new 1939 instrument panel, later nicknamed the "cat's eye" panel, remains a popular customizing option on later models. © H-D Michigan, Inc.

1940 Knucklehead
The 1940 Knucklehead motors were unique for the short cooling ribs on the timing case cover. © H-D Michigan, Inc.

1939 Knucklehead
New parts on the 1939 Sixty-one engine included the pinion shaft, pump drive gear, pistons, rings, breather valve screen, and exhaust valve spring. © H-D Michigan, Inc.

1940 Knucklehead
Harley-Davidson promoted low pressure 5.00x16 tires, because Harleys so equipped rode about as smoothly as spring-frame Indians. Handling with the 5.00x16 was a bit vague. Underinflation, practiced by some riders, could cause a Harley to drag the ground in corners. © H-D Michigan, Inc.

disconnected. The reason for this change is unknown, and the new layout certainly complicated oil changes. Other oil-tank features were the same as on the late 1936 oil tanks.

The 1937 Knucklehead had a larger rear brake, the same as used on the side-valve Big Twins. The gearshift gate was changed to include positive stops. The gearshift lever was changed from a round cross-section to a flat-sided style to work with the new shifter gate. On the 1936 and early 1937 Sixty-ones, a single oil passage in each rocker arm fed the rocker pad, which actuated the valve. On the late 1937 Knuckleheads, a second passage was drilled in each rocker arm to channel oil to the ball stud, which received the pushrod thrust.

The 1938 Sixty-one was fitted with much-improved rocker covers that at last managed to keep the oil inside. This was accomplished by installing new sheet-metal rocker-cover assemblies that each enclosed a valve stem and valve spring, as the old covers had done, but also enclosed the rocker arm and shaft. Each new rocker-cover assembly consisted of upper and lower sheet-metal stampings and assorted gaskets, screws, and spacers. As with the old "baby food jar" rocker covers, the lower portion of each new rocker-cover was secured to the cylinder head by the valve guide. The illustration clarifies the construction.

The 1938 rocker-covers could be retrofitted to earlier models. Retrofitting required grinding of the cylinder-head cooling fins. Oil was now pumped through both the inlet and exhaust rocker arms via a drilled passage in each arm. Exiting the rocker arms, the oil bathed the head of each valve stem, then flowed over each stem into the applicable valve guide.

1941 Knucklehead
The 1941 Seventy-four overhead-valve twin was brought out mainly to satisfy the craving of police for more low-end power. A new styling touch was the metal strip that ran the full length of the tank sides. © H-D Michigan, Inc.

1941 Knucklehead
Model year 1941 saw the third instrument panel change in four years, with the debut of the "airplane-style" speedometer, later termed the "bull's eye" speedometer. Note the new fuel reserve control in front of the left filler cap. It was unlocked by twisting counter-clockwise, then raised about an inch where it stayed as a reminder that the motorcycle was running on reserve. © H-D Michigan, Inc.

The Sixty-one and side-valve Big Twins now shared the same front fork, frame, fuel tanks (although the frame-backbone side of the tanks differs slightly), oil tank, transmission, and other parts. Due to this commonality, many identical changes were made to all three of the large twins. These common changes are highlighted in this section, and from this point on the Sixty-one and the two large side-valve twins are all referred to as "Big Twins."

The 1938 big-twin frames were strengthened. Upper and lower stays were 14 gauge instead of 16 gauge; the upper left stay was reinforced to the bend; the lower right stay received a reinforcement. The transmission mounting bracket and rear support were made of thicker gauge steel, and the upper frame strut tube was 1 inch instead of 7/8 inch in diameter. The steering head was fitted with a self-aligning lower head cone.

On the 1938 Big Twins, larger oil vent pipes were installed. Big-twin clutches and transmissions were revamped, with changes including a stronger clutch releasing finger, a new thrust bearing, a new clutch pushrod with a larger end, and a new starter cover.

The 1938 big-twin oil tank had an embossed top with the supply (takeoff) line moved from the unpopular drain-plug location to

1947 Knucklehead
These were the last of the Knuckleheads. A new tank badge and shifter guide distinguished the 1947 models from the 1946 models. Postwar technical development of the Knuckleheads didn't happen because of the engineering work on the forthcoming 1948 Panheads. © H-D Michigan, Inc.

the rear of the tank as in the 1936 Knucklehead. The different features for 1938 were the compression-type fittings for the oil lines in lieu of the earlier lines with banjo fittings.

On the 1939 Big Twins, detail changes were made to the clutch and transmission. Riders raised on the old sliding-gear transmissions felt uneasy about the clunking feel and sound of the new constant-mesh transmission. To cater to this concern, the transmission incorporated a sliding-gear assembly, which gave a better feel to the shifting. On the four-speed transmission, the sliding gear action occurred when shifting into second gear. This was the only year for this combined sliding-gear and constant-mesh configuration on the four-speed transmission, and was also the only year in which neutral was located between second and third gears. With the optional three-speed-with-reverse transmission, first was a sliding gear. This transmission would remain the optional with-reverse transmission for several more decades.

The 1939 Big Twins received the sixth and final oil-tank configuration. The 1939-and-later oil tanks were reinforced by a seamed top with a wall or fence about 1/4 inch high around all edges. The oil tank plumbing was the same as in 1938, with male compression fittings and the supply (takeoff) line exiting from the back of the tank. Also new were the softer front fork cushion springs.

1947 shifter guide
A horizontal shifter guide was fitted to the 1947 models. © H-D Michigan, Inc.

The 1939 Sixty-one engine had a number of detail changes. Among these were a new one-piece pinion-gear shaft, spline-fitted oil-pump drive gear, reinforced pistons with different ring combinations, perforated cylindrical screen on the breather valve, and new inlet and exhaust valve springs to prevent bottoming out. Late 1939 Knuckle-heads had the oil-bypass-valve spring pressure reduced.

The 1940 Big Twins had a 1 1/4-inch crankpin instead of a 1 1/8-inch crankpin. The front brake drum was cast instead of stamped, and an integral stiffening ring was added—these changes being made to stop brake chatter. The heat treating of the front fork was changed. Detail changes were made to the clutch, and the four-speed transmission was changed to full constant-mesh.

The 1940 Sixty-one crankcases no longer had oil-control baffles, and new piston rings were fitted. The oil supply to the valve rockers was no longer adjustable; this feature was advertised as a 1940 change but late 1939 Knuckleheads were so fitted. The Sixty-one got a new Link-ert carburetor with a diameter of 1 1/2 inches (instead of 1 1/4 inches) and a 1 5/16-inch venturi (instead of 1 1/16 inches). The Sixty-one inlet manifold diameter was increased from 1 3/8 inches to 1 9/16 inches. On all Harley-Davidsons, the crankpins, roller bearings, and crankcase bushings were lapped to glass smoothness.

The highlight of the 1941 announcement was the new Seventy-four overhead-valve twin, which was brought out largely to answer police requests for more power. Long-time dealer Red Wolverton remembers the era: "I'd talked the year before [1940] to Gordon Davidson [son of cofounder Walter] and he told me they were going to bring out such a machine. . . . I said, the Sixty-one suits me swell; why don't you stick to that? They can be developed to a point where they would have just as much speed as a Seventy-four. I ran one at Langhorne, in the sidecar race, and I turned a lap at 46 seconds [78-mile-per-hour average] with that sidecar outfit. The only thing is, it ran

a little hot with that compression ratio, but I think that could be overcome pretty easy. And he says, jokingly, 'Yeah, we'll bring that Seventy-four out so you fellas can sell some more chains.'"

The increased capacity was achieved by increasing the bore from 3 5/16 inches to 3 7/16 inches and the stroke from 3 1/2 inches to 3 31/32 inches. Pistons on the new Seventy-four overhead featured a milled relief on the lower skirt edge so the pistons wouldn't hit the rods near the bottom of the stroke. Piston choices offered either a 6.6:1 compression on the F model or 7:1 compression on the FL model. The company offered only one power rating for all Seventy-four overheads, 48 horsepower at 5,000 rpm. New flywheels were 8 1/2 inches in diameter, compared to the 7 3/4-inch flywheels of the Sixty-one. The Seventy-four overhead had a different crankpin design from the Sixty-one. On the Sixty-one the crankpin had a tapered section at each end with a step-up in diameter at the inboard edge of each taper. On the Seventy-four overhead the crankpin was a full taper without a step-up. Both overhead-valve models shared the same new crankcase, which had thicker walls to accommodate the additional stresses in the Seventy-four overhead. In midyear, the Seventy-four overhead's left crankcase was strengthened by lengthening the reinforcing ribs. The period of significant Knucklehead development ended with the 1941 models.

1947 Twins
For 1947 models, the instrument panel was restyled. The red-pointer speedometer was unique to 1947 models, reports Bruce Palmer, author of *How To Restore Your Harley-Davidson*. Palmer also notes this is a prototype signal lamp lens; production signal lamps were red glass with white lettering. © H-D Michigan, Inc.

Knucklehead Rideability

Although the 74-cubic-inch Knuckleheads don't ride any smoother than the side-valve Seventy-four and Eighty twins, Knucklehead dealer support is widespread. That's why Knuckleheads are better for extensive riding. Knuckleheads have a maximum cruising speed of 60 miles per hour. Some long-time dealers preferred the Sixty-ones over the Seventy-four overheads because the smaller motor was smoother running. Because of smaller flywheels, the pre-1941 Sixty-one was favored over later Sixty-ones. Among today's active Knucklehead riders, the same sentiments are expressed. Dry-sump (circulating) oiling is a big plus over earlier models. There's much dealer support, from both antique and general suppliers. Knuckleheads are excellent for logging lots of road miles.

When Versatility Was King

Whatever your riding style, you were king of the hill when you rode a new Knucklehead. It was the fastest stock road burner for Joe Rider. The Knucklehead was also tops in the comfort department. If you wanted to cow trail, you could run your Knucklehead right up at the front. In its era, having a Knucklehead was like having a full dresser, a crotch rocket, a motocrosser, and a flat-tracker, all rolled up into one package. In car terms, the image was half Packard limousine and half Ford hot-rod. The Knucklehead was a bike for the renaissance man, the jack of all trades. Knucklehead production ended just before the age of motorcycling specialization was at hand. It was a mercy killing.

Chapter 6

Panheads

The new 1948 overhead-valve Big Twins or "Panheads" refined the Knucklehead concept, bringing to the market improved oil tightness and hydraulic valve lifters that simplified owner upkeep. When the Seventy-four side-valve had replaced the Seventy-four F-head, and when the Knucklehead had replaced the Seventy-four side-valve, some Harley riders and dealers had been displeased. The same was true when the Panhead replaced the Knucklehead, which probably means the Harley world always had a strong conservative minority. There's another factor in the lukewarm feeling some veterans had about the Panhead. The Knucklehead was a hard act to follow. Dealers and riders expected the same quantum leap forward from the Panhead that they had experienced with the Knucklehead. That just wasn't in the cards.

Timing of the 1948 Panheads' introduction was perfect. Total factory production for 1948 was 29,612, according to *The Legend Begins* (probably refers to calendar year). At the time, this was the largest number of new Harley-Davidsons ever built for a single model year. The 12,924 Panheads built represented an 11 percent growth over the last Knuckleheads and accounted for about 44 percent of company production.

For the 1949 model year, Harley-Davidson initiated the Hydra-Glide series with a telescopic fork. Greatly increased comfort cost a weight penalty of about 50 pounds, with the total climbing from about 550 pounds to 598. Riders who grew up in the Harley-versus-Indian days had no problem with the size of the Panhead. In their eyes, the Panhead size was normal for a highway model, as was the size of the long-running Indian Chief.

The Sixty-one Panhead was road-tested for the June 1950 *Cycle*. The road tester was police officer Herman Filker of the Alhambra, California, department. Filker rode with his brimmed cloth cap, hip-mounted revolver, jodhpurs, and knee-high boots, just the way he would've been dressed to pull over a speeder. Filker reported: "Instant one-kickstarts were the rule, not the exception . . . the finest Harley front brake I have ever used . . . the foam rubber saddle provided a luxurious ride; the finish and plating were A-1 in every respect . . . especially suitable for high speed touring. . . ."

By 1952, the *Cycle* road tester was Bob Greene, whose uniform of the day included goggles on his bare head, and blue jeans. Greene said: "Although rather late in coming to teledraulic springing, Harley-Davidson's Hydra-glide front fork nears perfection . . . powerful, safe, comfortable and durable . . . a glutton for punishment. . . . If you're the type who likes to put on a thousand miles in one day's riding,

1957 Panhead
Welcome to the Panhead era, courtesy of this happy couple on a 1957 Panhead. No helmets. No turn signals. Just a Hydra-Glide, a girl, and a country lane. Harley-Davidson always sold motorcycling as much as it sold motorcycles. © H-D Michigan, Inc.

1948 E and F Series

Collectibility	★★★★☆
Comfortable cruising speed	60 mph
Smoothness of ride	★★★☆☆
Passenger accommodations	★★★☆☆
Reliability	★★★★☆
Parts/service availability	★★★★☆

I go for four-star collectibility status because these are the first of a long and successful line. The combination of the Panhead motor and springer fork are unique to this year (except for a few 1949 sidecar haulers). This was the last appearance of springer fork on solo Big Twins, which adds to the nostalgia.

1948 Panhead
Unique to the 1948 overhead-valve twins was the combination of springer front fork and Panhead engine (unless you count a few 1949 models sold for sidecar use). The new "wishbone" frame was bowed outward beneath the steering head. It was the last year for this style of saddlebags. © *H-D Michigan, Inc.*

1948 Panhead
The "Panhead" nickname came from the new stamped steel rocker covers that resembled inverted pans. Also new were hydraulic valve lifters and aluminum cylinder heads. The lifters were placed on the top of the pushrods, an idea that didn't work out. © *H-D Michigan, Inc.*

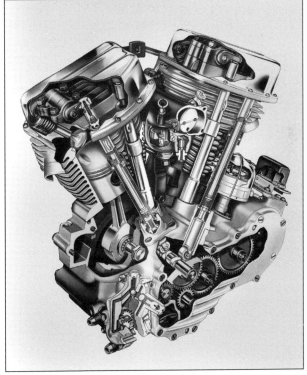

loathes frequent adjustments and yearns for solid comfort, try this one for size."

The Panhead continued to be popular with *Cycle* road testers of the 1950s. The December 1954 issue reported on the 1955 Hydra-Glide: "If you are looking for a machine capable of cruising at high speeds for long distances with a lot of power, and the ability to carry two passengers easily, as well as many pounds of extra gear, the Harley-Davidson 74 would undoubtedly be hard to beat."

For the 1958 model year, Harley-Davidson replaced the Hydra-Glide with the Duo-Glide. The swinging arm rear suspension gave the model a truly plush ride, and more than ever the biggest Harley was a Cadillac among motorcycles. The Duo-Glide weighed 710 pounds with solo saddle, front and rear crash guards, saddlebags, and no windshield. This was 72 pounds more than the 1950 rigid-frame Hydra-Glide

1948 instrument panel
Detail changes were made to the 1948–1952 speedometer. The 1953–1955 speedometer was similar but had the hash marks moved to the glass and markings of 1, 2, . . . , 11, and 12, according to Palmer's *How to Restore Your Harley-Davidson.* © H-D Michigan, Inc.

1949 E- and F-Series Hydra-Glides

Collectibility	★★★★☆
Comfortable cruising speed	60 mph
Smoothness of ride	★★★★☆
Passenger accommodations	★★★☆☆
Reliability	★★★★☆
Parts/service availability	★★★★☆

I think the first Hydra-Glides merit a higher rating than the later ones. The year 1949 was a particular Harley-Davidson strength, as Indian didn't even offer its Chief Big Twin for that season, being totally occupied with the eventually disastrous vertical twins.

"Stop the presses!" you yell. "Hatfield is rating the 1948–1949 Panheads as high as the 1937–1947 Knuckleheads, proving something unflattering about himself." Not so. These are weaker four-star ratings than for the Knuckleheads, but there's no way you know this unless I tell you. Which I have.

Rideability: Maximum cruising speed of 60 miles per hour, suitable for touring, good solo riding comfort with solo saddle, good solo riding comfort with buddy seat, poor rider comfort with buddy seat and passenger, and good passenger accommodation with buddy seat. Super soft telescopic fork makes a mountain of difference. Much dealer support, from both antique and general suppliers.

The Harley party line in 1949 called for the old springer front fork on models intended for sidecar use. If documented, such an example would be quite rare, and would merit a four–star rating; otherwise, a springer fork on a 1949 model is just a mismatched motorcycle.

Sixty-one tested by *Cycle,* even though the earlier model had a windshield in addition to the other equipment.

There was a performance penalty for the weight. As reported in the December 1957 *Cycle*: "Riding a 74 FLH Duo-Glide one finds that there is not a great deal of urge in the lower rpm range considering the size of the engine." Still, the report continued: "But once the engine is wound up and the high performance cams come into play, those 74 cubic inches go to work to haul the Harley-Davidson along at its 70 mph cruising speed with about as little strain as a bulldozer plucking a daisy. Even at 70 mph there is plenty of passing power tucked under the tank, and the engine is as silent all the way to its over-100 mph top speed as a kid in communion."

During the 1960s, the big V-twin was larger—by far—than all rivals. Moreover, British motorcycles were selling so well that their specifications had become "normal." This began to affect magazine road tests because

many of the new crop of riders grew up riding British motorcycles. The 1964 Duo-Glide with a 50 percent fuel load, buddy seat, front and rear safety guards, and saddlebags (but no windshield) weighed in at 690 pounds, reported the January 1964 *Cycle World*. The April 1965 *Cycle World* noted the touring Sportster H with half a tank of gas, buddy seat, and front safety guard, scaled 505 pounds. Typical of British 650s was the 1962 Triumph Bonneville, which with half a tank of fuel but no accessories, weighed 410 pounds according to *Cycle World* for January 1962.

Magazine road testers of the 1960s were naturally accustomed to smaller motorcycles—all bikes were smaller than the Panheads. It's a

1949 Panhead

In 1949, the Hydra-Glide fork ushered in a new era. Despite the rigid frame, the Hydra-Glides were very comfortable riding bikes. The big low-pressure tires, long wheelbase, and seat post saddle suspension gave a Cadillac ride on all paved roads. © H-D Michigan, Inc.

1949 Panhead

Other new features were the front fender, rear fender trim, larger front brake, and larger restyled saddlebags. It was the only year for black lower fork legs on the regular Hydra-Glide forks. But police models were optionally equipped with completely black forks for several years. © H-D Michigan, Inc.

1950–1957 E- and F-Series Hydra-Glides

Collectibility	★★★☆☆
Comfortable cruising speed	60 mph
Smoothness of ride	★★★★☆
Passenger accommodations	★★★☆☆
Reliability	★★★★☆
Parts/service availability	★★★★☆

Collectibility: These are solid-value machines. For saddlebags, I prefer the leather variety that were available throughout the era to the Royalite plastic bags also offered beginning in 1954. To one accustomed to the later fully equipped Duo-Glides and Electra-Glides, the Hydra-Glides look small even with a buddy seat and saddlebags. I like the compactness. One expert says the 1955–1957 Hydra-Glides are more sought after than the 1950–1954 models for the same reason that 1957 Chevrolets are so popular—the "baby boomer" phenomenon.

1950 Panhead
The chrome-plated "Mellow-tone" muffler was new for 1950. Improved carburetors and rubber-mounted fuel lines were also featured. Military riding gear was falling out of favor. © H-D Michigan, Inc.

1951 Panhead—dreams
The dream of weeks on the open road, of riding to Yellowstone, California, and other magical places, was embodied in that Harley-Davidson in the garage, even if the long ride never happened. © *H-D Michigan, Inc.*

fact of life that a sudden change in motorcycle types can be unnerving. So road testers griped about the Panhead's weight. But the unnerving process could work both ways. One of the scarier rides in my life was when I rode the local Harley shop's 50-cc Suzuki home, while my 1,200-cc Duo-Glide was in for maintenance.

Flash forward from 1964 to 1984. Proud of my restored 1947 Indian Chief, I rode alongside my friend on his (pardon the expression) Honda Gold Wing. Ah, the Honda Gold Wing, the most nothing motorcycle in the universe—oops, wrong book. After we traded off, and the Gold Wing had completely lived down to my expectations, we traded remarks. He wanted to know how I liked his Gold Wing. I dodged the issue the same way I dodge the issue when an ugly baby is shown to me by proud parents. "That's a baby, er, I mean, motorcycle," I said. I was amused at my buddy's remark: "Your Indian Chief is so small!"

Big and small are simply relative terms, so 74-cubic inch (1,200-cc) V-twins were big in the 1960s but are medium-sized in the 1990s. But in the eyes of 1960s magazine staffers, the Panhead was too big solely because nothing else was as big. Milwaukee had to be wrong, reasoned the editors.

The final version of the Panhead was the 1965 Electra-Glide. This was the beginning of a new era. The electric starter had a cultural impact. The time-honored kickstart process was a macho exercise that conveyed grace as well as strength. As an envious Duo-Glide owner back in 1965, I noticed some owners of new Electra-Glides occasionally opted for the

1958 FL and FLH Duo-Glides	
Collectibility	★★★★☆
Comfortable cruising speed	60 mph
Smoothness of ride	★★★★☆
Passenger accommodations	★★★☆☆
Reliability	★★★★☆
Parts/service availability	★★★★☆

Surprise, surprise, first-year Duo-Glide status merits a collectibility promotion. These are tied for the honor (?) of the weakest of the big-twin four-star collectibility ratings.

Yes, I know that Duo-Glides have a softer ride than Hydra-Glides. But on modern highways there's not enough difference to reflect in the ratings. In fact, and I know this sounds crazy, there's something good about all the little jiggles that come through the saddle on a Harley rigid-frame Big Twin. So, in my opinion, a more noticeable difference between the Duo-Glides and the Hydra-Glides is that the Duo-Glides are heavier and slower.

1951 Panhead
The 1951 models had new tank trim. Oil seepage was a problem due to the different expansion rates of the steel rocker covers and the aluminum cylinder heads. To reduce the problem, steel "D" rings were added between the heads and the covers. © H-D Michigan, Inc.

19525

1952 Panhead
A few late 1951 Hydra-Glides were fitted with a foot shift and hand clutch, but these features officially debuted on the 1952 models. The long chrome-plated device on the left front down tube is the clutch booster assembly, which took on the nickname "mouse trap" (see text for operating details). © H-D Michigan, Inc.

kickstart process. To them, kick-starting was a part of the manly art of motorcycling. As well as electric starting, the model brought with it an improved primary drive setup (see development section).

The new 5-gallon "Turn-pike" gas tanks were another source of envy for this Duo-Glide rider. To me, the big tanks conveyed power. Moreover, in my 1965 opinion, the tanks looked better on the full-dress Harley than did the smaller tanks. I still believe that the smaller tank looks too small for a Big Twin outfitted with windshield, buddy seat, and saddlebags. To me, the buddy seat, especially after it became white or half-white in 1960, dwarfs the tanks on the late Duo-Glides. Incidentally, Electra-Glide buyers could opt for the old 3 3/4-gallon tanks; one of our Montgomery (Alabama) Motorcycle Club members did so.

I'll close with a look at the Panhead's production history, which is also a gauge of its popularity. After the 1948 surge in sales, having satisfied the bottled-up and surging demand of the postwar market and confronting an explosive growth of low-priced British imports, Harley-Davidson's total production began to decline gradually. *The Legend Begins* documents total production for 1949 (calendar year, probably) as 23,861 units, a 20 percent drop from the previous year. However, the 12,685 1949-model Panheads represented 53 percent of company totals, and Panhead production was off less than 2 percent from model year 1948.

From 1950 through 1964, Panhead production wavered up and down around an average of 5,974. Despite a 10 percent price hike, the 1965 Electra-Glide sold better, and 6,930 units left the factory.

The Panhead's greatest sales rivals were motorcycles of an entirely different type, the Triumph and BSA 650-cc (40-cubic inch) vertical

1953 Panhead
The Deluxe Solo Group accessories package included the chrome-plated oil filter. All 1953 model Panheads had 74-cubic inch engines; for police and others preferring the characteristics of the former 61-cubic inch version, there was a new FLE model with the special "Traffic Combination" of carburetion and cam profiles. The timing cover ribs were longer. © H-D Michigan, Inc.

1954 Panhead
These "Royalite" plastic saddlebags were first offered on the 1952 Model K and became available on the Hydra-Glide in 1954. Meanwhile, leather saddlebags were also offered up through 1956. The "OHV" fender trim was used on 1952–1954 models. On top of the fender is the "Golden Anniversary" emblem, used in 1954 only. © H-D Michigan, Inc.

twins. At speeds above 60 miles per hour, these British motorcycles vibrated as badly as Panheads. Compared to the 650s, the Panheads had a vibration of lower frequency but greater amplitude. The Panheads shook, while the 650s trembled. While we're at it, the smaller Japanese road bikes electrocuted, or as somebody said, their high-rpm vibrations would shake the fillings out of your teeth. Unique among motorcycling's offerings were the BMW flat twins. Although the BMWs were smooth, they were about as pricey as the Panheads. The Beemers' somber black finish and super quiet exhaust were just too civilized to appeal to many motorcyclists. As World War II was still strong in everyone's memory, lingering hostility toward German products also reduced the impact of BMWs.

So the Panhead remained the dominant touring bike of its era, as a tour through old magazines will confirm. Big road rallies of the 1960s, like Southern California's Indio and Death Valley events were Panhead affairs. To many Americans, bigger is always better. In those pre-Gold Wing days, the Panheads were the biggest, and therefore the best.

1948–1965 Panhead Development

The outstanding feature of the new Panheads was the pair of stamped-steel rocker covers. To distinguish this series from the earlier overhead-valve Big Twins, the nicknames "Knucklehead" and "Panhead" came into use for the 1936–1947 and 1948–1965 series, respectively. The Panhead nickname became popular because the rocker covers resembled an inverted cooking pan.

Other major changes of the Panheads were aluminum cylinder heads and hydraulic valve lifters. Aluminum cylinder heads had been common among Harley and Indian side-valve models, as well as among the foreign makes. However, the use of hydraulic valve lifters on the Panhead was a first for the motorcycle industry. There was a separate hydraulic valve lifter for each valve. Each lifter consisted of a small pair

1955 Panhead
The 1955 Hydra-Glide got this new primary chain cover. The generator end cap and the clutch booster springs were cadmium-plated instead of painted black. © H-D Michigan, Inc.

of male and female pistons, one of slightly larger diameter than the other, so that the cylinders fit one within the other and with the closed surfaces (or tops) on opposite ends of the piston-pair set. Within the closed volume formed by the mated pistons was a supply of engine oil pumped there under pressure. The oil pressure expanded the piston-pair set until one end contacted the pushrod, and oil pressure ensured constant contact of the piston-pair set with the pushrod. Thus, the engine ran with zero valve clearance and owners never had to adjust valve clearance on the Panheads.

There were other engine refinements. External oil lines were replaced by drilled passages in the crankcases, cylinders, and heads. Oil was pumped to the rocker arm bearings, as in the Knuckleheads. But the oil returned to the crankcase by gravity instead of by vacuum, as in the Knucklehead series.

1955 Panhead
The 1955 Hydra-Glide was fitted with a new tank badge. The 1955-only "V" front-fender medallion was similar to the 1954 anniversary medallion. Note the new style of solo saddle. © H-D Michigan, Inc.

1955 Panhead
From *Enthusiast,* September 1954, "An O-ring and clamp arrangement has been devised to attach the manifold to the cylinder head intake shoulders on the 74 OHV. A tight seal results." © H-D Michigan, Inc.

1956 Panhead
This 1956 Hydra-Glide shows off the new "King of the Highway" accessory group, the first standard offering with cross-over exhaust and dual mufflers. © H-D Michigan, Inc.

1957 Panhead
The trumpet-shaped "Jubilee" horn first appeared on the 1954 Panheads. The timing cover with four decorative ribs was introduced on the 1955 Hydra-Glide, while the FLH decal was introduced on the 1956 high-performance model. It was the last year for the rigid frame Hydra-Glide series. © H-D Michigan, Inc.

Despite the new rocker covers, veteran dealers Tom Sifton (dealer, 1929–1953) and Red Wolverton (dealer, 1929–1958) remembered Panhead oil seepage as a disappointment. The basic problem was the interplay between the aluminum cylinder heads and the steel rocker covers. Because of the different expansion rates of aluminum and steel, it was impossible to retain oil tightness under all conditions. Still, the Panheads ran cleaner than the Knuckleheads.

The 1948-model Panheads suffered from three other problems. Some dealers and owners complained about the long warm-up time required on some motorcycles before the hydraulic lifters fully expanded. During this warm-up period the valve-gear noise was excessive due to too much clearance. Contributing to the problem was the location of the hydraulic lifters, which were at the top of the pushrods. A second problem was a ringing noise produced by vibrations within the rocker covers. A third problem occurred for the small minority of owners who "babied" their new overheads during the break-in period. The problem with "babying" the Panheads was that the oil pump didn't work well under

1958 Panhead
The Duo-Glide arrived as a 1958 model. To simplify the rear brake layout, as well as to give the stopper more bite, operation was changed from mechanical to hydraulic. White sidewall tires were a new feature, too. © H-D Michigan, Inc.

sustained low-rpm running. This problem didn't receive priority attention because of its rarity, and it wouldn't be solved until the 1954 season.

Along with the new Panhead motor, the overhead models got a new frame, which was eventually termed the "wishbone" frame. The nickname arose from the twin front down tubes, which for a short distance angled outward from the bottom of the steering head before turning down again. The front down tubes thus resembled the shape of a chicken wishbone.

For 1949, the most important Panhead change was the fitting of a telescopic Hydra-Glide front fork, so that the overhead-valve Big Twins were called "Hydra-Glides." Dealers and riders gave the Hydra-Glides rave reviews. The increase in rider comfort was dramatic. There were, however, some instances of fork fluid leakage. The Hydra-Glide fork was fitted to a new steering head containing roller bearings instead of ball bearings. At the fork base was a new brake with 34 percent more braking surface.

In the 1949 Panhead motors an oil spigot was fitted to route oil from the inlet rocker arm bearing to the inlet valve spring and then to the top of the inlet valve stem. The 1949 Panhead cylinders and exhaust pipe exteriors were coated with silver silicone resin, and the exhaust mufflers were coated with black silicone resin, to reduce the corrosive effects of high temperature and moisture. As these hot parts cooled off, water condensed on the surfaces, which tended to corrode the metal, especially when the motorcycle was left in the sunlight. All those little water droplets acted as miniature magnifying glasses for focusing sun rays on the metal. Remember how you used to burn leaves with a magnifying glass?

1948–1949 Models E, EL, ES, F, FL, and FS Specifications

Engine ....45-degree overhead-valve V-twin with hydraulic valve lifters
Bore and stroke
Models E, EL, and ES......3 5/16x3 1/2 in
Models F, FL, and FS.......3 7/16x3 31/32 in
Displacement
Models E, EL, and ES......60.33 ci (989 cc)
Models F, FL, and FS......73.66 ci (1,207 cc)
Compression ratio
Models E and ES.............6.5:1
Model EL........................7:1
Models F and FS.............6.6:1
Model FL.........................7:1
Power
Models E and ES.............37 bhp @ 4,800 rpm
Model EL........................40 bhp @ 4,800 rpm
Models F, FL, and FS.......48 bhp @ 5,000 rpm
Transmission ....Four-speed, constant-mesh type, mounted remotely to frame, positive gear locking
Shift ....Left hand, indicator gate on tank
Primary drive ....Double-row chain, oil-mist lubricated
Clutch ....Dry, multiple disks, left-foot actuated
Wheelbase......................59 1/2 in
Wheels and tires ....Drop-center rims, quickly detachable, interchangeable, 5x16 in
Suspension
Front, 1948.....................Leading-link, drop-forged fork
Front, 1949.....................Telescopic Hydra-Glide fork (leading-link fork recommended for 1949 sidecar models)
Rear ....Rigid
Weight
1948 ....515 lb (fully serviced, with standard solo group)
1949 ....637 lb (fully serviced, with windshield, solo saddle, and saddlebags)
Saddle height.................26 in
Fuel consumption...........35–50 mpg
Top speed (all without windshield and saddlebags)
Model E.........................85–90 mph
Models EL and F ....90–95 mph
Model FL........................95–100 mph

1959 Panhead
The 1959 Duo-Glides were graced with "arrow flight" name plates and "jet sweep" panels. It was in the age of automotive tail fins, when it was considered chic to emphasize aviation themes. This style of toolbox debuted on the 1958 Duo-Glide. © H-D Michigan, Inc.

1959 Panhead
According to the 1959 models press release, "Duo-Glides have a bright green indicator light on instrument panel that tells you at a glance whether the transmission is in neutral." © H-D Michigan, Inc.

The 1950 Panheads got larger inlet ports. The carburetor venturi diameter for the Seventy-four was increased to 1 5/16 inches, while the venturi diameter for the Sixty-one remained as 1 1/8 inches. The carburetors were further modified to provide a richer mixture during acceleration. Harley-Davidson promised improved power and acceleration, but didn't quantify the improvements.

Changes were made in the 1950 Hydra-Glide fork to reduce oil leakage. Six baffle plates, a deflector in the upper fork tubes, and a rubber breather valve in each fork leg were the new components. A stronger front brake backing plate was fitted. Also, an adjustable-rake version of the fork was built for use on sidecar-haulers.

For 1951, the Panheads were fitted with steel "D-rings" to improve the oil sealing around the rocker covers. These D-rings provided a stiff surface to more evenly distribute the load of the rocker cover screws. The piston rings were chrome plated. During the break-in period the chrome-plated rings established smoother cylinder walls with consequently reduced long-term wear. The inlet and exhaust cams were redesigned with opening and closing "ramps" to smooth the movement of the valves off of and on to the valve seats. On the pushrod end of the

1960 Panhead
When they leave the beach, there's a fun ride ahead all the way home. "Twin Flare" styling was applied to the 1960 Duo-Glide. The 1960 Duo-Glide got a headlight nacelle a year after the XLH Sportster. © *H-D Michigan, Inc.*

1961 Panhead
On the 1961 Duo-Glide, the old double-fire (or wasted-spark) ignition system was replaced by a dual-coil, dual-points system hidden beneath the chrome cover just in front of the oil tank. The FLH decal was a new design. © *H-D Michigan, Inc.*

The Price of Progress

Harley-Davidson, like most motorcycle manufacturers, added features and weight to its models as the years went by. Accessories were also emphasized over the years, which added to the bulk. The first of the Knuckleheads, the two-wheeled hot-rods of their time, weighed 515 pounds with no accessories. The last of the Hydra-Glides weighed 660 pounds when equipped with front and rear guards, solo saddle, and saddlebags—figure at least another 20 pounds for a windshield and buddy seat, and you have the typical 1957 Hydra-Glide weighing over 680 pounds. A motorcycle's dimensions had a way of growing, too, as seen by the two accompanying photos. Considered individually, each new feature and added accessory was a good idea. Considered altogether, the cumulative impact was a new breed of Big Twins that mimicked Cadillacs instead of Ford V-8 hot-rods. Harley-Davidson didn't care; they had the Sportster ready for the old Knucklehead role.

Riding position on 1948 Panhead
A 5-foot, 9-inch rider poses on a 1948 Panhead with his legs well bent, though they're drawn up to the sides of the bike. In a riding situation, he would move his legs out, farther to the side, to easily balance the motorcycle when stopped. Even with the typical thinly padded buddy seats of the mid-1950s, the average-sized rider would have plenty of leg room.

Riding position on 1957 Panhead with buddy seat
A 5-foot, 9-inch rider straddles a 1957 Hydra-Glide with his legs in the only possible stance, drawn in to the sides of the bike. With the late 1950s or later thickly padded buddy seat, he can't stretch his legs out to a wider perch, so balancing the stationary bike is a chore.

1962 Panhead
Here's the new tank styling for 1962. There were no significant technical changes except for a new midseason oil pump with changes in the internal routing. © H-D Michigan, Inc.

rocker arms, the pressed-in sockets were eliminated in favor of sockets machined directly into the forgings. Reduced oil leakage and improved reliability were thus claimed. Late 1951 Panheads were available with a hand clutch and foot shift.

The headline feature of the 1952 Panheads advertising was the availability of a hand clutch and foot shift. These optional features had actually appeared quietly on the scene as late 1951-model offerings.

To provide the human hand with the leverage to disengage the big-twin clutch, Harley-Davidson came up with the so-called "mousetrap" booster mechanism—the nickname came into common use over the years. The mousetrap consisted of an over-center arrangement with springs. When the hand lever was first pulled in there was little resistance. Then, with momentum of the hand squeeze established, the lever passed quickly through a very small region of stiff resistance. Immediately there-after, helper springs in the mechanism came into play, so that again only slight hand pressure was required. All of the clutch action occurred with the helper springs along for the ride. So to fully disengage and reengage the clutch plates required only the quick pass through the stiff point, fol-lowed by slight hand pressure over the bulk of the hand lever movement. In slow traffic, feathering the clutch in and out of engagement could be done entirely within the region of slight hand pressure.

On late 1952 Panheads, a rotating action was incorporated into the valve lift. This feature provided uniform heat stress around the valve heads, thus minimizing warpage and loss of effective valve seat contact.

All 1953-model Panheads were Seventy-fours. After introduction of the Seventy-four, the Sixty-one had sold in relatively low numbers, primarily as a docile police model. In place of the defunct Sixty-one, Harley-Davidson offered a 74-cubic inch Model FLE fitted with the "Traffic Combination," consisting of special cam and a 1 1/8-inch car-buretor venturi instead of the standard 1 5/16-inch venturi. On 1953

1962 Panhead
This instrument panel was used on 1962–1965 Panheads. Harley fans now call this the "tombstone" speedometer. © H-D Michigan, Inc.

1959–1964 FL and FLH Duo-Glides	
Collectibility	★★★☆☆
Comfortable cruising speed	60 mph
Smoothness of ride	★★★★☆
Passenger accommodations	★★★☆☆
Reliability	★★★★☆
Parts/service availability	★★★★☆

Although these lack 1930s or 1940s nostalgia, you get the plush rear suspension. The Duo-Glides look more interesting with each passing year.

1963 Panhead
The 1963 chain guard was larger. A 40-percent larger rear brake was fitted, and a redesigned rear-wheel hydraulic brake cylinder reduced brake pedal pressure. © H-D Michigan, Inc.

Panheads, the hydraulic valve lifters were relocated to the bottom of the pushrods, thus effectively eliminating excessive warm-up time before the lifters came into full effect. The excess oil from the rocker covers no longer drained directly into the rear of the crankcase (the scraper area). Instead, the oil drained onto the cylinder walls, at a point in each cylinder just below the piston skirt when in top-dead-center position.

For the 1954 season, Harley-Davidson at last solved the problems a few riders had experienced under prolonged low-speed running, primarily due to excessive caution during break-in. The company learned that under these unusual conditions the oil pump delivery was inadequate. Improved low-speed oiling was achieved by modifying the oil-pump bypass system, with a piston-type valve replacing the previous ball valve.

Late 1954 Panheads had a new frame that featured the return of twin straight front down tubes. Very late 1954 Panheads were fitted with new, cast-aluminum D-rings to assist in oil sealing of the rocker covers. The new D-rings were much thicker than the preceding steel D-

rings and were secured with 6 mounting screws instead of 12, a change which eventually proved detrimental to oil tightness.

The 1955 Panhead engines featured three changes. The inlet manifold was secured to the cylinders with hose clamps and O-rings, instead of hex nuts and flat seals. A tighter seal was claimed, plus the advantage of being able to remove the carburetor and manifold without a special wrench. On the sprocket main shaft, Timken tapered roller bearings replaced the earlier standard uniform-diameter roller bearings. And the cylinder base gaskets were changed from rubber-impregnated fiber to rubber-impregnated asbestos, with the aim of improving oil tightness.

During the course of the 1955 season, Harley-Davidson introduced the top-of-the-line FLH series. The FLH had polished and flowed inlet ports, and with new high-lift "Victory" cams, the factory claimed a 10 percent power increase over the FL models. Longtime dealer Red Wolverton didn't think highly of the FLH models. In Wolverton's opinion, the extra power was short-lived and not worth the extra cost. Late-season models had the rocker cover D-rings changed back to a 12-screw design.

The 1956 models officially reintroduced the 12-screw D-rings. The sprocket shaft had a shoulder added to back up the Timken bear-

1964 Panhead
The 1964 Duo-Glide was the last of the kick-starting big-twins. These fiberglass saddlebags were first offered for 1963 Duo-Glides. Royalite bags were also offered on 1963 and 1964 Duo-Glides, reports Bruce Palmer, in *How To Restore Your Harley-Davidson*. © H-D Michigan, Inc.

1965 Panhead
The new "Turnpike" tanks held 5
gallons instead of 3 3/4. The old 3
1/2-gallon tanks remained optional,
most of these going to police
motorcycles. *Petersen's The
Complete Book Of Motorcycling*
described the Electra-Glide: "The
grandaddy of motorcycles . . .
preferred by devoted tourists . . .
solid comfort for lengthy trips." ©
H-D Michigan, Inc.

ing. Crankcase oil passages were redrilled to route the oil to the
hydraulic lifters and the valves through the oil pump check valve. This
prevented oil from draining from the tank through the lifters into the
crankcase. Power was claimed to be 12 percent more than for the 1955
FL, but there was no explanation for where the extra 2 percent of punch
came compared to the late 1955 FLHs.

No significant technical advances were announced for the 1957
Panheads. Undoubtedly, the engineering department was totally
absorbed with the forthcoming Duo-Glide series.

The 1958 season saw the introduction of the Duo-Glide series,
named in honor of the new swinging arm rear suspension. As with
the K, KH, and Sportster series, the rear shock absorbers were
enclosed in a forward-sloping tube mounted far forward. The new
spring frame produced an acceptable appearance that still had similar overall lines to the rigid frame models. Also, with the suspension
units far forward, larger saddlebags could be fitted than with the

spring units nearer the rear axle. Weight had now climbed to 710 pounds, when equipped with saddlebags, front and rear safety guards, and twin exhausts (*Cycle* December 1957). By comparison, the 1948 Panhead weighed 515 pounds with front safety guard; and the 1950 Panhead with windshield, front and rear safety guards, and saddlebags weighed 637 pounds (*Cycle* June 1950). The resulting reduction in acceleration brought with it the end of any pretense toward sporting capabilities. From now on, the biggest Harley was a tourer, pure and simple.

All Duo-Glides got new cylinder heads with larger cooling fins extending to about 1 inch. A rubber discharge fitting replaced the metal fitting for the front chain oiler, with the intent of eliminating damage resulting from a slack chain. The rear brake was changed to hydraulic operation. A new higher output generator was fitted to the 1958 Panheads. On the FLH, the inner and outer valve springs were stronger and longer (free length). The FLH also got new exhaust valves made from stellite, a more heat-resistant material.

The 1959 Duo-Glide was fitted with a cast-iron rear brake in lieu of the former stamped steel brake. On the foot-shift models a neutral indicator light was provided.

On the 1960 Duo-Glide there were no important technical changes except for a new kickstarter ratio providing a faster engine spin. A styling change was the headlight nacelle, which followed by a year its incorporation on the Sportster H.

On the 1961 Duo-Glide the historic wasted-spark ignition system was replaced by a new dual-fire, dual-points unit, in order to eliminate backfire when the ignition was fully retarded. This improved starting and idling. Also, a new 1961 generator had bearings that didn't require frequent lubrication. The 1962 Panheads continued without significant technical changes, except for a new midseason oil pump with changes in the internal routing.

For 1963, the Duo-Glide was fitted with a 40 percent larger rear brake and a redesigned rear-wheel hydraulic brake cylinder that reduced brake pedal pressure. A larger rear chain guard extended from its top down to within a couple of inches of the swinging arm. A rear chain oiler was provided. External engine oil lines returned. Harley-Davidson offered no reasons for the return to the Knucklehead practice of external lines, but in his book, *Harley-Davidson Panheads* (Motorbooks International), author Greg Field offers two theories. First, external lines would deliver oil to the cylinder heads at a cooler temperature. Second, an oil line with two fittings is easier to seal than an oil passageway that must be sealed at the gasket surface above and below the cylinder.

The year 1964 saw the debut of the last of the Duo-Glides. There were no important technical changes to the 1964 Duo-Glides because of the impending launch of the new Electra-Glide series.

The 1965 Electra-Glide marked the start of a new Harley-Davidson era. The biggest change, of course, was the electric starter. While Electra-Glide riders welcomed the new starter button, they bid the kickstarter an extended and affectionate farewell, often kicking the bike to life just for the fun of it.

The Lost Art of Kickstarting

Does anybody know why straddling a kick-start motorcycle fell out of favor as part of the starting drill? Kickstart motorcycles—those with the starter on the right side—start so much easier when you straddle the bike and put all your weight on the kickstarter—really. Or do you believe that people were so stupid during the 40-plus years that kickstarters were the only starters, that riders failed to learn the modern "correct" way of starting.

Yeah, that's it. We modern types do 98 percent of our starting with our right thumb, which, apparently, has some direct communications link with the front (smart) part of our brain. Thus, we modern types have a big advantage over riders of the kickstart era, for in pushing the button 98 percent of the time we therefore gain great insights in how we do the other 2 percent of our starting with a pedal. Sure.

The modern way of kickstarting a motorcycle consists, first, of standing on your left knee, your left knee being on the saddle. This way, all your body weight except for your right leg remains on the saddle. Then you kick the motorcycle 9 or 10 times, with no power other than your right calf muscle, never swinging the starter through more than a 45-degree arc, and you have the nerve to wonder why your leg cramps and your motorcycle is hard to start. The modern dumb-ass technique works on Big Twins and battery-ignition Sportsters, but it takes longer to get rolling. If you try modernism on a magneto-ignition CH Sportster, and the temperature is less than 50, you might want to time the starting process. A calendar will be fine for that task. Truly we are a nation in decline.

One other thing about kickstarting—and nowhere in any of the instruction books of 1903–1965 does this appear. If you flood the motorcycle: turn off the ignition; ensure the choke is wide-open (no-choke position); roll the throttle on all the way; kick the engine over about eight times; return the throttle to about one-eighth roll-on; turn on the ignition;

The feel of it all
The feel of it all. Much of the old motorcycle experience is in the sense of touch. The classic bicycle-pedal kickstarter of 1915–1962 gets a rider started on a different-feeling ride. Along the way, the footboards, a foot-clutch, a hand-shift, a spring-loaded saddle, and a throttle without a return-spring, all take the motorcyclist back in time.

Improper kickstarting
Right top: The johnny-come-lately method of exercising one's right leg. Nobody started a Harley this way in the old days. The rider needlessly gives up weight on the kickstarter and reduces the effective length of the kicking stroke.

Proper kickstarting
Right bottom: Here's the right way to start an old Harley. The rider straddles the bike, uses all his weight, and gets a full stroke on the kickstarter. The kicker is J. D. DeVries.

kick, and the motorcycle should start. If the bike doesn't start, repeat the process but give the motor about a dozen key-off/throttle-open kicks. If the bike still doesn't start: remove the plugs and wipe them off; repeat the key-off/throttle-open procedure with the plugs out; install the dry plugs; turn the ignition on; set the throttle to one-eighth; kick, and the bike should start. If the bike still doesn't start, get a truck.

1965 Panhead
A cast aluminum primary chain cover absorbed the torque loads of the electric starter and made for a more oil-tight seal. The engine and transmission were mounted together, so primary chain adjustment was accomplished by a moveable slipper shoe in the chain case. This design was a big improvement over the old system of moving the transmission and readjusting the rear chain. © H-D Michigan, Inc.

New 5-gallon "Turnpike" tanks were a styling improvement, as they fit in better with the buddy seat and large saddlebags. However, buyers could still obtain the earlier 3 3/4-gallon tank set. Another major Electra-Glide advancement was the new and massive cast-aluminum primary drivecase. The primary chain was now adjusted by a movable "shoe," over which the bottom of the chain ran, instead of by the bothersome task of moving the transmission. Also, with the new setup it was no longer inevitably necessary to tighten the rear chain each time the front chain was tightened.

Still another 1965 improvement was the incorporation of a 12-volt electrical system. With twice the voltage, only half the amperage was required, so that smaller wiring could be used. This had the by-product of increasing the output of the new generator because more wiring was wound within the same volume.

To make room for the new large 32-amp-hour battery, the traditional horseshoe-shaped oil tank was replaced by a rectangular tank. The oil tank was offset to the left. On the right side of the oil tank was the new battery, offset to the right. Both of these could be serviced without lifting the saddle, thus saving your hands from the inevitable grease coating they got with the earlier Big Twins.

Panhead Rideability

I might as well talk about the 1948–1957 rigid rear end versus the 1958 and later Duo-Glides and the 1965 Electra-Glide. On modern highways, and with a sprung saddle, there's little difference between the comfort of Harley rigid-frame Big Twins and the comfort of Duo-Glides and Electra-Glides. Really. That's why Harley-Davidson got away with the rigid frame through 1957, making the Hydra-Glide the last rigid-frame motorcycle sold in large numbers. So, for smoothness of ride the ratings are three stars for the 1948 Panhead with the springer front end, and four stars for 1949 and later Panheads.

Cadillacs and Jaguars

In 1948, the Harley-Davidson factory was running full-bore, yet was unable to meet demand for the new Panheads. Dealers were assigned new motorcycle quotas, based on prewar sales.

If you walked into the local Harley shop, you got one of two reactions, depending on whether you were one of the in-crowd. You were "in" if you belonged to the motorcycle club the shop sponsored, or if you rode a Harley you bought from the shop. As an insider you would get a friendly hello or two, be called by your name or nickname, and perhaps be offered a cup of coffee out back in the repair shop. There were no new motorcycles in the showroom, so you didn't linger there long. In the repair shop, with a little discretion, you could stand around sipping your coffee and talking to the mechanics. It was an even bet the shop owner would also be turning wrenches, because he didn't have to be out front giving sales pitches. One of the things you might talk about would be your position on the waiting list for a new Harley. Aha! you say. This was just like today! Not really. Today, a ton of money is made in the showroom selling Harley T-shirts, whatnots, videos, and you name it. In 1947 and 1948, a dealer made most of his money selling and fixing motorcycles. In short, if you were part of the in-crowd you dissolved into the scene, an equal participant with the owner and mechanics in the society of the shop. You might not want to live there, but the Harley shop was a fun place to visit.

If you didn't ride a motorcycle, or if you rode another brand, you weren't an in-crowd member at the Harley shop. When you walked in, you would get the same friendly hello or two. Things were different after that. The shop owner would stand behind the counter and offer a few words of small talk. Then, you might walk over to a used bike or, on rare occasions, to a new, already-sold bike sitting there for a day or two before the owner claimed it. The boss would stay behind the counter, either doing some book work or pretending to do so, while he kept an eye on you. If you looked responsible, he might tell you to make yourself at home while he went in the back to the shop, and to please holler for him if you have a question. He didn't have to follow you and give you a running sales pitch on the joys of motorcycling and the advantages of doing it on a Harley-Davidson. The shop owner already had more motorcyclists than he could handle. To sell a new Harley, all he had to do was take your

Collectibility	★★★★☆
Comfortable cruising speed	60 mph
Smoothness of ride	★★★★☆
Passenger accommodations	★★★☆☆
Reliability	★★★★☆
Parts/service availability	★★★★☆

The first Electra-Glides and last Panheads in one package, making a four-star collectibility rating an easy call.

down payment and put you on the waiting list. You weren't part of the shop society so you were left alone as you stood there amid the merchandise. You felt like you were in a hardware store.

If you were an in-crowd rider you gritted your teeth when confronted with postwar prices. But you didn't hold a grudge against the dealer who was also your friend. He had managed to keep the doors open during the war, by selling a handful of police motorcycles and keeping them in running order, and by the occasional repair job on a commuter's Harley-Davidson. Chances are, his had been a one-man shop. Now it was his turn to be prosperous.

If you weren't part of the in-crowd in 1948, you had options other than the big, clean Harley-Davidson shop. You walked around the corner to the dirty little cramped shop with a Triumph or BSA sign out front. The outside appearance didn't inspire confidence. But inside you found new motorcycles were on hand. You got a running sales pitch for both motorcycling and his British brands because the dealer in British bikes had to fight for every sale. No waiting list for his stuff, which was cheaper—and different. If you liked his stuff and him, you went British. When you did, you decided the Harley shop was an arrogant bunch. They weren't, but you decided that anyway.

Briefly, Harley-Davidson's ancient rival Indian made a run for success, but by the end of 1948 Indian was on the ropes. Thereafter, riding a Harley-Davidson put you in one of the two feuding camps: Harley or British. By 1950, the British invasion was sweeping across the continent. The Brit-bike dealerships improved, though few of them ever matched their local Harley shops in size and profitability. If you rode a Harley, you referred to "lousy Limey pipsqueaks." If you rode British, you ridiculed Harley "iron," especially the full dressers.

Multiply by a hundred times any image differences you sense between riding today's Harleys and riding today's Japanese motorcycles. Today, most Harley riders don't question your patriotism if you ride a foreign bike; back then, they did. Today, most riders of foreign bikes don't question your sanity if you ride a Harley; back then, they did. Most enthusiasts couldn't separate the motorcycles from the emotionalism.

To those able to view Panheads objectively, to look at the motorcycle instead of the politics, they saw a rugged model that had few equals for comfortable long-distance touring. If they could look even beyond the motorcycle to the factory and dealer network, objective observers could see that no broken Panhead would stay broken long. There were dealers in every city and even in many towns; there were parts in every bin; and there were mechanics with decades of Harley-Davidson experience. British motorcycle dealerships were a different matter. Many were underfinanced and, dealing with a wide variety of models, they couldn't afford to stock the parts bins. Their mechanics had little or no experience with their motorcycles. British motorcycle dealerships were also scarce outside of the larger cities. A broken British bike usually involved a parts shipment from some distant place. Support for British bikes got much better in the 1950s, but never matched support for Harley-Davidsons.

On the other hand, objectively, there were two Panhead drawbacks: price and size. You had to really want a Harley-Davidson to pay the extra 30 or 40 percent over the price for a British bike. As for size, many of the new generation of learners were intimidated by the extra weight and length of the Panheads. A Panhead was a tough sell as a first-time motorcycle.

Panheads were part tradition, part patriotism, part social statement, part luxury, part fast, part reliable, part pricey, and part heavy. One thing they weren't—for very long—they weren't successful all-around competition motorcycles. Lighter British bikes ushered in the age of specialization, because they were more suitable for off-road riding (though less suitable for touring). So big Harley-Davidsons could no longer do triple-duty as the best touring bikes, the best off-road bikes, and the best anythings in-between. That versatility had been unique to the Knuckleheads in the pre-import days.

In their prime, to capture the Knuckleheads' image you stirred in equal parts of Packard limousines and Ford hot-rods. Then, in 1948, came the Panheads with a new image. The Panheads' image was simpler. Panheads were just big, flashy, expensive, and comfortable. If you owned one, it was a sure sign you had arrived. Panheads, in other words, were Cadillacs. Motorcycling's Caddy kept that image until the last Panhead rolled down the assembly line in 1965.

On the other side of the game, BSA Gold Stars and Triumph Bonnevilles were two-wheeled analogies to the Jaguar XK-120. In the car world, Cadillac drivers felt superior to Jaguar drivers but that was okay because Jaguar drivers felt superior to Cadillac drivers. In the motorcycle world, it was the same way. Harley riders knew they were more intelligent and good-looking than Brit-bike riders, and Brit-bike riders knew they were smarter and more dashing than Harley riders. It could be no other way because the other camp's motorcycles were so different, and in being so different, they challenged everything you believed about your bikes and every statement you made by riding your brand.

1962 Duo-Glide Ownership

Back in 1966, I put about 10,000 miles on a 1962 Duo-Glide Police Special, equipped with hand shift and foot clutch. The Duo-Glide had mild tuning, which I liked a lot because of the incredibly slow idle. Starting was so easy and dependable. I don't recall the Duo-Glide ever taking more than one or two ignition-on kicks—you did have to give it two or three (I've forgotten) ignition-off priming kicks when cold. Kicking it over was a cinch, thanks to the low-compression police pistons.

The Harley had better acceleration than most cars, and there was plenty of power on hand for any situation. With the police gearing, the bike wasn't as smooth as it might have been running a little taller gearing. The maximum comfortable cruising speed was 60 miles per hour; anything above quickly wore out your hands from the vibration. The top speed was about 90 miles per hour, I guess, as the speedometer bounced around between 95 and 100, and I figure it probably read a little on the fast side. When running flat out the bike handled as light as a Schwinn. I had to park my feet on the passenger footrests; no way they would've stayed on the footboards up front. The Harley was rough at 90 miles per hour, but no rougher than a new Triumph 650 at 80 miles per hour.

I took two long trips, one from Alabama to Daytona and the other from Alabama to the Springfield (Illinois) mile-track race. On the Daytona trip the battery quit, apparently from the generator overcharging. On the Springfield trip the primary drive chain became so loose it flopped around—I've never been very good about preventative maintenance. Eventually, the primary chain stretched so much it bounced up against the oil feed pipe and pinched it off. With no oil feed, the primary chain quickly became hot, loud, and rough. I managed to find a Harley shop before ruining the chain and vowed to pay more attention to its adjustment in the future.

Gas mileage ranged from 35 to 40 miles per gallon. Oil consumption was about 500 miles per quart, if the oil tank was full at the start. If not topped off after the first 500 miles, the next quart would only last about half as long. Some years later, I had identical oil-consumption experience with a 1947 Indian Chief.

Sore points: I never did learn to like the backwards clutch—heel-down for disengagement, toe-down for engagement, and to the very end of the 10,000 miles I was capable of absentmindedly trying to grind the shift into low with the toe pedal down.

Other sore points were the oil tank and battery under the saddle. Checking either one meant removing the seat-post security pin and lifting the saddle up and forward to rest on the tanks. Since the seat-post tube was necessarily greasy, a battery or oil check was a messy-hands operation that I tended to neglect.

I was mystified at why Harley-Davidson riders had to put up with the sloppy passenger footrests. These were affixed to stamped brackets that were entirely too weak for the task, with the inevitable result of bending downward anywhere from about five degrees (on my bike) to 20 or more degrees on some bikes that hauled a heavy passenger. The brake pedal was curious, too, as it was mounted right at the midpoint of the footboards. The forward-mounted brake and the heel-up-to-go clutch, I decided, were intended to provide support for your boot heels which might otherwise slip back and off the busily vibrating footboards.

Finally, the primary-chain setup wasn't to my liking. Rider inattention, my specialty, runs the risk of chain failure. Roadside primary-chain adjustment isn't practical because you need a jack to get the rear wheel up; also, the rear chain must be readjusted every time you adjust the primary chain. Then there's the sheet-metal cover that permits oil to drip out. As the saying went, if the ground was clean under your Harley, you were out of oil.

Sounds like I didn't like my Panhead. Not so. I had a helluva good time with the Duo-Glide, selling it only because I wanted to try trail riding and couldn't afford more than one motorcycle. There was something indescribably pleasant about cruising on the old battleship. Partly it was the throbbing V-twin sound and feel; partly it was the plush suspension; partly, it was the assurance that I had at last moved up to a "real" motorcycle. Selling the Duo-Glide was the easiest chore I've ever had. A guy at the newspaper advertising department saw my ad request and wanted the bike, so the ad never was printed! No price haggling at all. I looked forward to a new motorcycling experience, but I hated to see the Duo-Glide go.

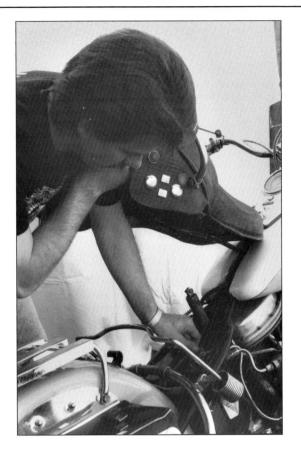

**Adding oil to Big Twin
with buddy seat**
Messy! Rider Mark Dye has greasy
hands from pulling the saddle-
mount pin from the greased seat
post. The well-padded buddy seat
won't flip forward over center, so
underseat road grime makes its way
to Mark's shoulders, and, if he's not
careful, he will spread the grease to
his clothes. It was (and is) easy to
put off checking the oil and battery.

Bent passenger footrest
Right: The bent passenger footrest
is a steel stamping, and it's not up
to the job. A hefty passenger
makes short work of the footrests,
especially the mount/dismount
footrest on the left side.

Anti-vibration device
Old Harleys have the brake pedal
mounted midway along the
footboard. Above 60 miles per
hour, you park your feet ahead of
the brake and clutch pedals, and
the pedals help keep your feet on
the trembling footboards.

Chapter 7

American-Made Two-Strokes

Harley-Davidson entered the lightweight field after World War II, but typically, this was no hurry-up move. In 1942, the company had purchased a New Orleans-built Servi-Cycle for evaluation. The Servi-Cycle was a belt-drive, one-speed, two-stroke single. The management concluded a similar Harley-built bare-bones machine wouldn't be accepted by Harley-Davidson dealers. Cost considerations undoubtedly figured into the equation. Milwaukee had long believed its manufacturing costs were stretching the limit of acceptability for V-twin riders, and the cost factor would be even more critical for an entry-level model.

Victory in World War II brought an unexpected opportunity. German engineering designs were confiscated, and among the blueprint packages was the design of the DKW 125-cc two-stroke single. The little DKW was considered the state-of-the-art lightweight, so Harley-Davidson and the English company BSA rushed at the opportunity.

Engineering costs for Harley-Davidson were very low because the engine and transmission were faithfully copied. BSA spent more engineering effort because it built the Bantam lightweight as a mirror image so the foot shifter and kickstarter were on the right side. Both Harley and BSA added their own front fork and styling touches, but a Russian version, the Mockba M1A, was an exact copy the DKW. In 1954, Yamaha marketed its imitation DKW as the YA-1, with Yamaha front and rear suspension and styling—and no, I've no idea how they got the engine blueprints.

The Model S 125-cc two-stroke went into production in early 1948, too late for the new-models edition of *The Enthusiast* and the 1948 sales literature. The 125 was targeted at beginners and to a lesser extent commuters, so mild performance was acceptable. The rated output was only 3 horsepower, but an all-up weight of only 170 pounds helped matters. Verbally, the lightweight was termed the "One Twenty-five."

The battery ignition and lighting systems of the 1948–1959 models were luxurious compared to the magneto ignition and lighting of contemporary motorscooters. Bright lights at low speeds set the little Harleys apart from the scooters, whose lights could only muster an orange glow at slow speeds. But in my high-school years, it seemed the little Harleys often suffered electrical failures. One long-time Harley-Davidson mechanic told me the generator design was faulty. He believed the generator driveshaft was too long, thus giving a whip action to the points breaker mechanism on the end of the shaft. Mean-

1952 125

Here's "The Make-Out King" and his admirers. All you needed to get girls was your trusty Harley-Davidson One-twenty-five. Well, a little Wild Root Cream Oil on your hair didn't hurt. The bikes are 1952 models, but the scene typifies the era. © H-D Michigan, Inc.

1948-1950 Model S	
Collectibility	★★☆☆☆
Comfortable cruising speed	30 mph
Smoothness of ride	★★★☆☆
Passenger accommodations	
Solo saddle and pillion	★☆☆☆☆
Retrofitted buddy seat	★★★☆☆
Reliability	★★★☆☆
Parts/service availability	★★☆☆☆

while, the stone-age Cushman and Allstate motorscooters, orange lights and all, just kept going and going and going.

Strangely, two Harley-Davidson dealers with plenty of experience had opposite opinions of the little Harleys, and no, I can't figure this out. Tom Sifton, a California dealer for 25 years, didn't think a lot of them. Sifton much preferred Cushman motorscooters, which he sold for awhile before Harley-Davidson brought out the 125 in 1948. In the hands of youngsters, the Cushmans were less likely to be damaged than were the little Harleys. That's because the Cushmans had an automatic clutch that prevented over-revving, "popping" the clutch, and stalling. All of these things could happen with the little Harleys and all of these things produced shock loads on the 125 engine and transmission. Sifton said his 125 riders had plenty of problems.

1948/49 125

The Model S was commonly referred to as the "one-twenty-five" verbally, or as the "125" in writing. The One-twenty-five engine was a direct clone of the German DKW one-twenty-five designed in the late 1930s. Victory in World War II entitled the winners to the designs and patents of German businesses. The One-twenty-five name denotes 125-cc (7.5-ci) displacement. © *H-D Michigan, Inc.*

On the other hand, Charles "Red" Wolverton, a Pennsylvania dealer for 29 years, was very enthusiastic about the 125. Wolverton said his riders had very few failures with them. One of his teenage customers rode a 125 to the West Coast and back, with no problems along the way.

To counter complaints about low performance, the 125 was replaced in the 1953 lineup by the 165 cc Model ST, commonly termed the "One Sixty-five." Maximum output went up from the 125's 3–3 1/2 horsepower (as it was variously reported) to a range of 5 1/2–6 horsepower.

Although still equipped with a three-speed transmission and a rigid rear end, the 165 had a high-quality image because of top-quality paint and plating, plus a wide variety of colors, including deep metallics. Said the January 1953 *Cycle*: "Overall, the Harley 165 is rugged, very good-looking, economical and handles exceptionally well." Thereafter, only detail changes were made to the 165 until its replacement in the 1960 lineup.

A low-cost 125-cc Hummer was offered from mid-1955

1948/49 125

Just the ticket for your paper route, back when dailies were small enough to be thrown. The name Harley-Davidson on the tank meant you had a "real" motorcycle. But the Harley mystique could backfire, because parents often had a dim view of real motorcycles, while offering fewer objections to slower-looking motorscooters. © *H-D Michigan, Inc.*

1950 125
A new bucket saddle and new
saddle springs improved the
appearance of the 1950 One-
twenty-five. © H-D Michigan, Inc.

through 1959. Following the 165 came the Super 10 in 1960 and the
Pacer and Scat variants in 1962, as detailed in the section on development.
These models used magneto ignition and lighting as cost-cutting features.

The Topper motorscooter barely got into production as a 1959 model,
so the 1960 models were the first built in significant numbers. Power from
the 165-cc (10.1-cubic inch) engine was transmitted through a V-belt to a
variable-diameter pulley and then to the final drive chain. The range of
ratios was 18:1 (low) to 6:1. The engine featured a reed-valve intake instead
of the piston-controlled intake used on other Harley-Davidson two-strokes.
Starting was by a pull cord. The front suspension was by leading-link fork,
and the rear suspension was by swinging arm. Twenty-inch disk wheels
were fitted. According to those who rode them, the Topper was quite peppy
and reliable. Surprisingly, the suggested retail price was $430, which was 7
percent lower than the companion Super 10 motorcycle.

The Topper's best year was 1960, its first full year, when 3,801 were
produced, and then production fell steadily until the final model year of
1965, when only 500 were built. The main obstacle to Topper sales was the
timing, for by 1961 Japanese lightweight motorcycles were arriving in great
numbers, especially Hondas. The little Japanese motorcycles offered amazing value in terms of performance versus cost. Japanese-motorcycle shops
were successful in selling the idea that little motorcycles are safer than
motorscooters—I know, I was a Honda salesman. So, scooters were "out"
and little motorcycles were "in." Two Topper features didn't help a bit. The
pull-cord starter seemed out of place and less effective than a kickstarter.
Worse still, refueling required the rider to mix the oil with the gas. Although
hand-mixing was still required on a few Japanese two-strokes, the practice
was very unpopular. The Topper was last offered in the 1965 season.

When the 125 hit the market in 1948, the model was unquestionably
state-of-the-art. When the last Pacers and Scats were made in 1965, they
were unquestionably behind the times. The technological turning point
was probably 1953, when Harley-Davidson opted for boosting the dis-

1950 125

Topping the girder front fork was an attractive headlight nacelle, predating by several months Triumph's introduction of this feature, which they made famous. Underneath the headlight nacelle, four rubber bands handled the fork suspension chore. © H-D Michigan, Inc.

placement to 165 cc while retaining the three-speed transmission. The transmission probably cost more to build than the engine, and in any event, adding another gear would've been more costly than enlarging the cylinder.

American-built two-strokes were an important part of the total production picture from 1948–1965. Typically, the introductory year of a new lightweight model was also its year of highest production, and in those introductory years the lightweight entries accounted for 20–30 percent of total Harley-Davidson production. Thereafter, production of a single lightweight model typically fell to a range between 10 and 20 percent of company totals. There was a continual influx of new lightweights: in 1948, the 125; in 1953, the 165; in 1955, the Hummer; in 1959, the Topper motorscooter; in 1960, the Super 10; and in 1962, the Pacer. The Hummer in 1959 and the Topper motorscooter in 1960 (first full year), were com-

1951 125

The 1951 One-twenty-five was graced by a telescopic front fork, dubbed the "Tele-Glide" and lubricated by grease. A new larger (7-inch) Cycle-Ray headlamp perched atop the upper fork panel. © H-D Michigan, Inc.

1951 125
These are production One-twenty-fives with the correct front fender; many advertising photos of the era showed a prototype model with a nonproduction front fender like the later Sportsters. The new muffler was quieter yet permitted more power delivery. © *H-D Michigan, Inc.*

panion models to already-fielded entries, so that combined lightweight production for those years was about a third of overall production.

The 1950s saw two forms of increased competition for the Harley-Davidson lightweights. Production levels of American-built Cushman motorscooters and Mustang lightweight motorcycles were increased, while mass marketer Sears-Roebuck sold Cushman-built motorscooters and the Italian-built Vespa, all under the "Allstate" label. The 1960s saw the rapid growth of Japanese imports. Considering the strength of these rivals, Harley-Davidson American-built lightweight production was remarkable.

However, after 1960 the profit picture for the home-grown two-strokes was less and less attractive. The factory got its money, always, but by the middle 1960s, dealers had an increasingly tough time selling the lightweights. More and more Harley dealers were taking on a Japanese line. (More often than not, Suzuki motorcycles were chosen because Honda and Yamaha had established most of its dealerships in the early 1960s, when Harley dealers weren't yet impressed.) With the imports offering more features at less cost, many little Harleys were probably sold for little or no markup.

1948–1965 American-Made Two-Strokes, Development

The 1948–1950 girder front fork was unusual for its suspension system of rubber bands under tension. The 1948 and 1949 electrical system included a two-brush, direct-current generator attached to the right end of the engine mainshaft. A 10-amp-hour battery was fitted.

On the 1948–1950 models, the upper end of the connecting rod had a brass bushing. Roller bearings were fitted to the bottom end. The mainshaft was carried in ball bearings. From the engine, sprocket power was transmitted through an endless nonadjustable single-row chain on the left side to the wet clutch. The hand-operated clutch worked with a left-side foot-shift lever to operate the three-speed, constant-mesh transmission that was in unit with the engine. The shift pattern was

Model S Specifications

Engine ....Single-cylinder, two-
    stroke cycle, domed piston without
    deflector, loop scavenged
Bore and stroke...............2 1/6x2 9/32 in
    (55.0x57.94 mm)
Displacement ....7.6 ci (124.9 cc)
Lubrication ....Oil mist
Compression ratio..........6.6:1
Power..................................3 hp (rpm not specified)
Transmission ....Three-speed,
    constant-mesh type, unit construction
    with the engine
Shift ....Left foot
Shift pattern ....Down for low
Primary drive ....Nonadjustable endless
    chain
Clutch ....Multiple cork disks,
    wet, hand actuated
Gear ratios, overall
3rd 8.45:1
2nd 15.4:1
1st 29.23:1
Wheelbase......................50 in
Wheels and tires
1953–1955......................3.25x19 in
1956–1959......................3.50x18 in
Suspension
Front ....Girder fork,
    suspended by rubber bands
Rear ....Rigid
Weight..............................170 lb (fully serviced)
Saddle height.................27 in
Foot-peg height..............9 in
Fuel capacity ....1 3/4 gal
Oil capacity ....Mixed with fuel, 6 oz
    per gallon
Fuel consumption
@ 20 mph ....133 mpg
@ 30 mph ....120 mpg
@ 40 mph ....93 mpg
Top speed in gears
3rd @ 5,120 rpm ....46 mph
2nd @ 5,880 rpm.............29 mph
1st @ 6,640 rpm..............17 mph

1953 165

To answer performance complaints, the capacity was upped to 165 cc for 1953. The enlargement gave the little Harley a new name, verbally the "one-sixty-five," and in writing the "165." Wheels and tires were 19x3.25 instead of 18x3.50. The ignition coil was moved from the tank bottom to the front down tube. © H-D Michigan, Inc.

down for low, then up for neutral, second, and high. The mixture of recommended unleaded "white" gasoline and oil was done manually, using the measuring cup that was integral with the fuel cap, the mix being set at 6 ounces per gallon. The juice was provided to the engine by a Linkert carburetor.

For 1950, a new four-brush generator offered improved reliability. The new unit had four brushes, 1-inch poles instead of 13/16-inch poles, and fiber insulators between the brushes and springs in order to prevent spring overheating and consequent setting. Heavier-gauge wiring was also used, and the electrical system was changed to a negative ground. The company said only 10-mile-per-hour running was required to maintain system strength with lights off, and only 15 miles per hour with lights on. Generator strength was sufficient to permit push-starting in second gear with a dead battery. A drop-forged steering head was the response to a few broken 1948 and 1949 frames. The kickstand (Harley called this a "Jiffy stand") was fitted with a return spring, so the stand no longer had to be manually stowed like a bicycle stand.

The 1951 and later connecting rods had needle bearings on the top end. The 1952 Tele-Glide fork was changed from grease lubrication to oil lubrication. Removable oil caps with integral measuring cups were placed atop each fork leg. The kickstand was redesigned for better return-spring action. New oil seals were placed around the shifter shaft.

For 1953, the little Harley was enlarged to 165 cc (10.1 cubic inches) and was given the new official designation of Model ST. The increased capacity was achieved by enlarging the bore from 2.0625 to 2.375 inches, while maintaining the stroke at 2.281 inches. The engine output was increased from 3 horsepower maximum to a cited maximum in the range of 5.5–6 horsepower—and no, I don't know why they didn't pick a single number. The spark plug was moved from the rear to the middle of the cylinder head. The crankpin was strengthened

1951–1952 S Series

Collectibility	★★☆☆☆
Comfortable cruising speed	30 mph
Smoothness of ride	★★★☆☆
Passenger accommodations	
Solo saddle and pillion	★☆☆☆☆
Buddy seat (retrofit on 1951, current on 1952)	★★★☆☆
Reliability	★★★☆☆
Parts/service availability	★★☆☆☆

Like the first Knuckleheads, these offered styling excellence that comes only once in a generation. There was more than the 1948 and later tank, the outline of which we still see on some new Harley-Davidsons. The 1951–1952 models also had the fender contours used on the 1952–1954 K and KH middleweight twins. Up front, the Tele-Glide fork and fork-top panel were entirely graceful. You could buy a gutted one, paint it and plate it, and get your money's worth just to have it around to look at.

by making the diameter uniform across its full length. In some instances, the main bearings had corroded because of prolonged lack of riding and because owners disregarded instructions and used leaded gasoline. Accordingly, two Alemite fittings were provided to grease the engine main bearings every few thousand miles.

Inevitable carburetor drippings and blow-back caused a mess on the earlier 125. This was combated by a cast-aluminum carburetor cover on the 165. A pocket in the crankcase below the carburetor caught the drippings and drained them out near the rear chain. A larger air cleaner was fitted, with corrosion-proof metal mesh.

Working with the larger motor were a new clutch with canvas-coated plates and a new set of wider transmission gears, so that the engine ran slower at any given road speed. The transmission filler neck was relocated for greater accessibility.

Cycle magazine found the maximum speeds of the 165 to be: low, 25 miles per hour; second, 42 miles per hour; high, 58 miles per hour. These speeds were well up on the old 125s and substantiated the 37–50 percent power increase claimed by Harley-Davidson. This power improvement followed naturally from the 32 percent displacement increase.

Some states restricted minors to 5 horsepower or less, and for these states, Harley-Davidson offered a lower-powered 165, the Model STU. The STU had a carburetor with a more restricted orifice plate. (The standard 165 also had a restrictor plate, but with a larger orifice.)

For 1954, a new high-silicone aluminum-alloy piston reduced drag. The new piston was slotted 1 1/2 inches wide and 1/4 inch deep

Model ST Specifications

Engine	Single-cylinder, two-stroke cycle, domed piston without deflector, loop scavenged
Bore and stroke	2 3/8x2 9/32 in (60.33x57.94 mm)
Displacement	10.1 ci (165.5 cc)
Lubrication	Oil mist
Compression ratio	6.6:1
Power	5.5–6 hp (rpm not specified)
Transmission	Three-speed, constant-mesh type, unit construction with the engine
Shift	Left foot
Shift pattern	Down for low
Primary drive	Nonadjustable endless chain
Clutch	Multiple cork disks, dry, hand actuated
Gear ratios, overall	
3rd	7.23:1
2nd	12.2:1
1st	20.8:1
Wheelbase	50 in
Wheels and tires	3.25x19 in
Suspension	
Front	Girder fork, suspended by rubber bands
Rear	Rigid
Weight	170 lb (fully serviced)
Saddle height	27 in
Foot-peg height	9 in
Fuel capacity	1 3/4 gal
Oil capacity	Mixed with fuel, 6 oz per gallon
Fuel consumption	
@ 20 mph	117 mpg
@ 30 mph	106 mpg
@ 40 mph	82 mpg
Top speed in gears	
3rd @ 5,550 rpm	58 mph
2nd @ 6.570 rpm	42 mph
1st @ 6,850 rpm	25 mph

1954 165

Externally, only the Golden Anniversary medallion on the front fender distinguished the 1954 One-sixty-five from the 1953 model. Mechanical improvements included a piston with less drag, a larger cylinder exhaust boss to reduce oil leakage, and a more rugged foot shift lever. © H-D Michigan, Inc.

1955 165

For 1955, the exhaust pipe had a sharper curve to permit raising it and the muffler by an inch. Few girls were interested in the little Harley, but such photos helped draw attention to the ads. © H-D Michigan, Inc.

near the bottom of the rear side. To eliminate damage to the foot-shift mechanism caused by a few rough riders, the foot-shift lever was enlarged around the pivot point. Also, the lever was no longer serrated but was attached to the shaft by a pinch bolt. To reduce oil leakage from exhaust residue, the cylinder exhaust boss was lengthened, cut with an exterior groove, and fitted with a split-ring. The exhaust pipe was then clamped over the split-ring, and the ring expanded under heat to maintain a tight seal while running.

The 1955 165 incorporated minor improvements. These included a larger kickstarter segment gear, ball bearings for the clutch hub instead of a graphite thrust washer, and several speedometer changes.

The bigger story for 1955 was the new bare-bones Hummer model announced in midseason. The Hummer reincarnated the 125-cc engine but offered the minimum of fittings to reduce the price. Cost-cutting Hummer specifications included a magneto-generator instead of a battery, black-painted instead of chrome-plated wheels, no front brake, no upper fork panel, black instead of chrome-plated handlebars, no speedometer, a squeeze-bulb horn instead of an electric horn, a kill button instead of an ignition key, cadmium plating instead of chrome plating on the exhaust pipe, and no rubber covers for the footpegs and kickstarter.

The 1955 Hummer motor was listed at 3 1/2 horsepower, although its specifications were identical to those of the old 1948–1952 125, for which a 3-horsepower maximum had been cited, and which in turn was identically configured to the BSA Bantam. Since BSA claimed 4 horsepower for the Bantam, it's unclear why the 125 and the Hummer would have had, respectively, 25 and 12 percent less output. Although the

1955 Hummer
Apparently a vast nerd market was envisioned for the new low-bucks Hummer. The Hummer was a reincarnated One-twenty-five without the amenities of battery ignition, battery lighting, and front brake. © H-D Michigan, Inc.

Hummer satisfied states with the 5-horsepower limit, the "hopped down" Model STU 165 cc was continued for those desiring more deluxe specifications.

For 1956, the 165 specifications listed only a larger taillight as a functional improvement, and no changes were listed for the 1956 Hummer. The 1957 165 got needle bearings for its front wheel, and the 1957 Hummer got a front brake. Both 1957 lightweights had a sturdier muffler mounting.

The 1958 165 and Hummer were equipped with a stoplight that was legal in all states, bragged *The Enthusiast* in one of its more curious blurbs. On the Hummer, the magneto-generator was changed from using one breaker-point set to two sets. Half of the Hummer circuitry operated the headlight and taillight, and the other half operated the ignition and stoplight. On both light-weights, the brake lining material was harder, in order to prolong brake life. Both lightweights also were fitted with a new torsion-wound brake return spring fitted at the pedal.

The 1959 165 was equipped with a 5 3/4-inch headlight in lieu of the former 7-inch unit. The 165 had a new speedometer with a trip meter. The 1959 Hummer continued without technical changes.

In May 1959 the Topper motorscooter joined the Harley-Davidson lineup. The Topper used an all-new 165-cc (10-cubic inch) two-stroke engine that featured a reed-valve inlet system instead of piston porting. An automatic centrifugal clutch transmitted power through a rubber belt across front and rear variable-diameter pulleys, and then to a rear drive chain. The final drive ratios varied from 18:1 to 6:1, making the Topper gearing slightly taller than the 165's. The Topper was offered through the 1965 season without any significant changes during its production life.

For the 1960 season Harley-Davidson consolidated its former two-model lightweight-motorcycle range into a single compromise model. The

1956 165
A larger taillight and 3.50x18 tires distinguished the 1956 One-sixty-five and Hummer. © *H-D Michigan, Inc.*

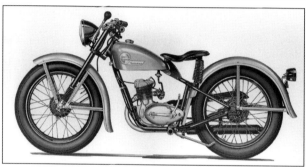

1957 Hummer
Notice the cable running to the front wheel; this was the first year for a front brake on the Hummer. © *H-D Michigan, Inc.*

1958 165
Believe it or not, this was the first year for a standard stoplight switch on the One-sixty-five and the Hummer, making the as-delivered models legal in all states. © *H-D Michigan, Inc.*

1959 Hummer
Following tradition, the 1959 Hummer got new tank styling. The same tank "swash" was used on all other models. © *H-D Michigan, Inc.*

1953–1965 ST and BT Series, 1955-1959 Hummer, 1959–1965 Topper

Collectibility	★★☆☆☆
Comfortable cruising speed	40 mph (BT, ST), 30 mph (Hummer)
Smoothness of ride	★★★☆☆
Passenger accommodations	
Solo saddle and pillion (BT, ST)	★☆☆☆☆
Buddy seat	★★★☆☆
Reliability	★★★☆☆
Parts/service availability	★★☆☆☆

The long downhill road started with the 1953 165, which offered improved performance by the simple expedient of enlarging the engine size, as opposed to adding a fourth gear ratio. Effective, true, but this power strategy and the continuing rigid rear end advertised Harley-Davidson's inability to manufacture a lightweight model that was cost-competitive with foreign makes. The mid-1955 through 1959 Hummer was another flashing neon light advertising Harley-Davidson's high manufacturing costs. The 165's appearance, in my opinion, suffered because of the carburetor cover and taller cylinder. The low-bucks Hummer looked like a low-bucks bike, the rubber bulb horn being particularly cheesy.

new Super 10 replaced both the 165 and the Hummer. The new Super 10 was so named for its nominal displacement of 10 cubic inches (165 cc, nominally). The Super 10 selling price was held down by elimination of the battery, a la Hummer. The Hummer-style single-cap fuel tank also was less costly than the previous tank with both cap and built-in ignition switch. The new model also had deeper finning on the cylinder and cylinder head. For the Topper motorscooter, no technical changes were announced.

The 1961 Super 10 was equipped with 3.50x16-inch tires in lieu of the previous 3.50x18-inch tires. No technical changes were announced for the 1961 Topper motorscooter.

For 1962, the name "Super 10" name was replaced by "Pacer." The Pacer came in two variants, the 175-cc BT and the 165-cc BTU. The 175-cc (11-cubic inch) Pacer had a 2.41-inch stroke, and the 165-cc (10-cubic inch) version had a 2.28-inch stroke; both retained the previous 2.38-inch bore. The compression ratios of the larger and smaller versions were 7.63:1 and 6.6:1, respectively. The cited outputs were 10 horsepower and 4.7 horsepower, making the smaller of the two legal in areas where horsepower was restricted for young riders.

There were no announced engineering updates to the Topper motorscooter. Joining the 1962 lightweight lineup were two new models,

Riding a 1952 125

Wow! This is it! I finally get to ride a "light Harley"—that's what my gang of 10-year-olds had called them. I finally get revenge against my parents for not letting me have one of these beauties. You see, I did my internship on Cushman motorscooters because scooters, with those little wheels, looked different from motorcycles, and to my parents that made Cushmans look safer than little Harleys. Mom and Dad figured anything that said Harley-Davidson on the side had to be dangerous, and if it was a Harley-Davidson 125, didn't that mean it would go 125 miles per hour? So, 40 years later, I get revenge.

First off, I take a long look at this glamorous little job. No doubt about it, Harley-Davidson put a perfect styling treatment on the 125. The front and rear fenders are shaped just right, with the little flair along the trailing tip, and are in fact the same fenders used on the mighty (it seemed so, then) 45-cubic inch (750-cc) K-model. How about that telescopic fork! It's just as lovely as I remembered it, especially with the fork-top panel. The handlebars are perfect, with the graceful bend that leaves an unobstructed view of the speedometer. A telescopic fork and a speedometer are two signs of a "real" motorcycle, and other "real motorcycle" stuff includes a foot shift, a hand clutch, and a battery. Most of all, everything blends together so perfectly, with the flat-bottomed gas tank, bucket saddle, and saddle mounting somehow looking beyond improvement. That tank—so good it had to be called into duty later for the Sportster CH! Looking is so much fun that I walk around the 125, and slowly, stopping every few inches and trying to commit the images to memory.

Starting is a cinch. The two-stroke engine burbles steadily like a subdued popcorn popper. I flick the skinny kickstand back. I pull in the clutch lever and snick the left-side foot-shift lever down into low. I roll back the throttle until I get a 30-mile-per-hour sound and then ease the clutch lever out. I'm away.

Quick—up with the shift lever! That was a close call; I almost over-revved by the time I'd rolled 20 feet.

In second, the motor pulls steadily, but the acceleration is anything but brisk. Louder and louder the exhaust yells, still no strong wind attacks my face. I know it's not time to shift to high gear yet, so to relieve the boredom I check the speedometer—20 miles per hour, 22 miles per hour, 24 miles per hour.

I pull the shift lever upward into high gear. I'm rolling almost 30 miles per hour now, and now I finally hit 30 miles per hour. A steady drone trails out behind me. I keep the throttle wide open and slowly the speed moves upward to 35 miles per hour. From 35 miles per hour the acceleration—if it can be called that—is even slower.

I get bored waiting for the speed, hopefully, to reach 40 miles per hour. Long ago as a Cushman rider, I memorized the sound of this "real" motorcycle when it's downshifted. I call the memory in from deep storage. I downshift into second, to see if the memory is correct. My memory is spot on, as the 125 momentarily screams at the increase in engine speed. Carefully, lest I do real harm, I come almost to a walk before downshifting into low, and again the familiar memory of decibels and the actual sound bounce against each other.

I decide to do a torque test. With the throttle at idle, I let the clutch slowly engage. The 125 pulls confidently away, so I roll on some throttle, but by the time I'm at a fast walk the little engine seems to be running at almost half-maximum. The lack of muscle is the reason for the bizarre gear ratio. This 125 wouldn't unwrap a burrito. If only Mom and Dad had known, they could've had me riding on something slower than a stump-pulling Cushman, with the little Harley's better handling thrown in as a bonus. Plus all those looks and the name "Harley-Davidson" on the tanks!

Checking fuel
The Harley lightweights had a tank cap with a built-in measuring cup. The rider filled the cup with oil, then filled the tank, preferably with "white" (unleaded) gas, which, unfortunately, wasn't offered by many gas stations then. To finish the process, the cap was secured, and the bike was shaken several times. This ensured the oil and fuel were well mixed.

1952 125
How a real motorcycle looked to a kid lucky enough to have one. So what if a Cushman Eagle would outrun your little Harley? A Cushman was a scooter but your Harley was a motorcycle! © H-D Michigan, Inc.

Accessory handlebars
This was probably the all-time most over-leveraged handlebar set. These extra-cost bars were called "spaghetti bars" by some during the 1950s.

1959 Hummer
The Hummer had a magneto-generator instead of a battery. The new right crankcase was bulkier in order to house the magneto-generator, and a new left crankcase was required to match up with the new right case. © H-D Michigan, Inc.

1960 Super 10
The Super 10 combined the money-saving ignition system of the Hummer with the deluxe features of the old One-sixty-five. The cylinder and head were more deeply finned than the old One-sixty-five. © H-D Michigan, Inc.

1961 Super 10
For 1961, 3.50x16 tires replaced the previous 3.50x18 tires. © H-D Michigan, Inc.

1962 Ranger
The company brought out the Ranger trail bike for the 1962 season. Its 84-tooth rear sprocket meant it was strictly a low-speed job. As with the dual-purpose Scat, 18-inch wheels were used. The Ranger was offered for the 1962 season only. © H-D Michigan, Inc.

the 175-cc Scat and the 165-cc Ranger. The Scat was an off-road version of the Pacer that had a front fender mounted motocross style to the upper fork legs and with substantial clearance over the tire. Other Scat features included a normal street-legal lighting set, a high exhaust system, and a bobbed rear fender. The Ranger was a stripped-down off-road model designed for hunting and fishing. The 165-cc Ranger motor had a listed output of 10 horsepower, instead of 4.7 horsepower of the BTU Pacer. The Ranger had no front fender, no lights, and had a smaller muffler than the Scat. With no envisioned street use, the Ranger used a rear sprocket that was about 12 inches in diameter. This facilitated very slow going and provided plenty of urge for hilly sections. The 1962 lightweights were the last American-made Harley-Davidsons without rear suspension.

The 1963 Pacer and Scat were fitted with a swinging arm rear suspension. The stamped-steel rear legs acted against a horizontally mounted spring unit beneath the rear of powerplant. The low-output Pacer BTU had a 175-cc motor instead of the previous 165 cc unit, but output was still held to a maximum of 5 horsepower. The stripped-down Ranger was discontinued; in its place was an optional large trail-riding sprocket for the Scat. For 1964 and 1965, no engineering changes were announced for the Pacer and Scat.

American-Made
Two-strokes, Rideability

What you see is what you get. The 1948–1952 125 and the 1955–1959 Hummer deliver the as-advertised mild around-town performance. A 30-mile-per-hour cruising speed is about tops. Excellent solo comfort is provided by the softly sprung solo saddle. Passenger accommodation with the period pillion pad—the little bit of stuffing over the luggage rack above the rear fender—is poor. Solo acceleration is acceptable.

1962 Topper

The 165-cc (10 cubic inch) Topper motorscooter was offered from May 1959 through the 1965 season. Power from the all-new 165-cc (10-cubic inch) reed-valve two-stroke was transmitted through a centrifugal clutch and variable diameter pulley/belt system similar to today's Japanese motorscooters. Performance was brisk, but homely styling, high sales price, and the rising flood of small Japanese motorcycles, combined to keep Topper sales small. © H-D Michigan, Inc.

On the other hand, the 125-cc models have very poor get up and go when riding double. The little jobs strain their every fiber to climb ever so slowly up the revolutions scale, and then power falls way off when shifting up to second or third. Riding double in the era's traffic was acceptable because cars were a lot slower away from the stop lights, and traffic generally moved more slowly than today. In today's congested traffic, surrounded by fast cars, and with higher speeds between stops, the little Harleys are unsafe.

But I think you have to cut the little 125s some slack because they're adequately designed for their role—with one rider aboard. Also, reliability and dealer support are good.

In 1952, more comfort came with the telescopic Tele-Glide fork, but on the paved streets for which the model is intended there isn't a substantial improvement over the rubber-band front end. For the 1952 season a two-passenger bench-style buddy seat was available. Depending on your philosophy, you could install this on an earlier 125 in the same way a rider of the era could've done, and still have a correct motorcycle. Judges might consider this incorrect, however. The buddy seat with mattress-style springs gave reasonable comfort, although two-up performance was still weak, then, and is still scary, now.

1962 Scat

This was the only year for the rigid frame Scat, a dual-purpose mount. Like the road model BT Pacer, it used a 175-cc engine derived from the 165-cc 1960–1961 Super 10. The 1962 Scat came with street gearing because trail riders could opt for the strictly off-road Ranger. © H-D Michigan, Inc.

1962 Pacer
Harley-Davidson was always on the prowl for bored commuters who could be convinced that they were saving money by motorcycling. "Honest, Honey," Joe Commuter would say to his wife, "I'm only buying this motorcycle to save money, which is the responsible, mature thing to do." Although savings could mount up over the long haul, most of the appeal was the fun of riding. Usually the fun disappeared with the first autumn frost, and Dad's fling was over. © H-D Michigan, Inc.

The 165-cc and 175-cc models brought substantial power improvement. The larger models are still slow with two riders, but you shouldn't be terrorized.

Gee, Dad, It's a Wurlitzer, er, I Mean a Harley-Davidson!

Wow! A real motorcycle! It has two brakes, instead of one like the motorscooters, and the big wheels on the Harley-Davidson mean it holds the road better. It has a speedometer, which keeps you from accidentally exceeding the speed limit, Dad, and an electric horn, not some squeeze-it or push-it thing. No, Dad, it's not very fast. The "125" on the tank stands for the engine size, not the speed. It's the real thing,

1963 Pacer
Although the new rear suspension helped, the continued three-speed transmission and a high selling price kept Pacer ($485) and Scat ($495) sales low. © H-H Michigan, Inc.

1963 Pacer
Wow! Rear springs on the Pacer and Scat! The neat looking setup predated the Evolution Soft Tail by 21 years. Moto Guzzi pioneered this layout in the late 1930s. © H-D Michigan, Inc.

1964 Scat
The dual-purpose Scat had this spring frame layout from 1963 through 1965. In the company's two-page new-models flyer, there was no text about the Scat except for the brief photo caption "Scat—Top value for '64." © H-D Michigan, Inc.

Reverse Tapered-Cone Muffler is better looking; gives motorcycle a hotter, racier appearance.

Multiple-Disc Clutch is ruggedly built to give years of smooth, trouble-free service on or off the road.

Handlebar Grips are more comfortable. Ball-end clutch and brake levers provide safe control of cycle.

Scat What's Scat made of? A hi-mount front fender. Upswept rear fender. Racing saddle. And 175 c.c.'s of lean 'n lively engine — just to name a few. Who's Scat made for? Hunters, fishermen — anyone under the sun who enjoys real riding adventure, especially in the rough. In mud. Through water. Or across rugged countryside. Nothing stops Scat. With its telescopic spring front fork and swing-arm rear suspension plus Glide-Ride springs, you go anywhere, comfortably, on a Scat — even over the roughest roads and trails. No worries when the sun goes down either. Scat's fully equipped with legal lighting: headlight with Hi-Lo beam, tail and stop light plus hi-fidelity horn. And a reverse tapered-cone muffler adds a sporting flair to Scat's already "hot" look. Add it all up? Scat's for you, if you're looking for an entirely new kind of motorcycling experience.

RLEY-DAVIDSON SCAT and PACER models ... 175 c.c. versatile lightweights

Swing-Arm Rear Suspension smoothes out the rough spots in any road for greater comfort and stability.

175 c.c. Engine has deep-finned cylinder and head to transfer heat more quickly and efficiently.

Pacer Go ahead. Try the Pacer on for size. Climb a hill. Take it around a curve. Now open it up on the straightaway. Notice how the miles go by smoothly, effortlessly. And notice how Pacer's able to find all the fun and excitement that's in a road, mile after mile. A hearty 175 c.c. engine and front and rear suspension system that just won't quit over the roughest of roads is just part of the answer to Pacer's agile ways. Take it to work, school or play. Take it shopping. Or out for fun. A gallon of gas carries you about 80 miles. Like the Scat, Pacer is legally equipped for nighttime riding. Has headlight with Hi-Lo beam, tail and stop light. Hi-fidelity electric horn, too. And an easy-to-operate hand clutch and foot shift makes learning to ride a cinch. Climb aboard this unique kind of excitement known as Pacer.

● TWO PEPPY MODELS FOR EVERY RIDING PURPOSE ...

Dad, not some fly-by-night toy. Just look at the high quality of the paint and the chrome; you know it has the same high quality inside. It has battery ignition and lights, just like our car, so the lights are bright even when you're riding slow or stopped. I could never run it out of oil, like Bobby Wright did with his Cushman, Dad, because the oil is mixed in with the gas, just like on your outboard motor. It only costs a hundred bucks more than some Cushman motorscooters, Dad, and it's a genuine Harley-Davidson! You had a Harley-Davidson years ago, remember, and you didn't get hurt. I could pay for it myself—all I need is the down payment. I could make enough money with my paper route to buy all my own clothes, plus you wouldn't have to give me an allowance, and I'd learn all about having a job and responsibilities and stuff. Can't I have one, Dad? Can't I?

1965 Pacer & Scat

For 1965, there were no significant engineering changes for the Pacer and Scat. The following year, a restyled version of the Pacer was dubbed the "Bobcat." That marked the end of an 18-year run of Milwaukee-made two-stroke motorcycles. © H-D Michigan, Inc.

Models K and KH

The 1952 Model K, commonly called the "K-model," was Harley-Davidson's answer to the British invasion. British motorcycle imports grew rapidly from 1946 and by 1949 had become a frightening situation for Harley. During 1949, Indian came under the effective control of a British company, and Indian began to import several lines of British motorcycles for display alongside the American-built Indians. Clearly, Indian was on the ropes, and to a great extent had been put there by "Limey" bikes. Boasting both lower prices and advanced technical specifications, the British bikes posed a serious threat to Harley-Davidson's survival.

Upon its debut, the Harley-Davidson K was the greatest single leap forward the company had ever taken. Consider a comparison of the key specifications of the preceding W models with the K models. The WL had a "springer" fork, rigid rear end, foot clutch, hand shift, three-speed transmission, and had the transmission separately mounted in the frame. The K had a telescopic fork, swinging arm rear suspension, hand clutch, foot shift, four-speed transmission, and had unit construction of the engine and transmission. In one step, the company had moved from specifications rooted in the 1930s to specifications that were ahead of most 1952 rivals.

The swinging arm rear suspension was a trendsetter. Most British motorcycles and Indian, which had become a minor player, used a plunger rear suspension. Part of the popularity of plunger rear suspensions stemmed from the looks, because the sloping rear frame structure looked about the same as the rear part of a rigid frame. Plunger units looked more impressive than they were, because half of the springs were below the axle to provide rebound damping, so only a couple of inches of movement were in the picture in normal road use. Elsewhere, the biggest-selling British bike, Triumph, had an even-less-adequate rear suspension dubbed a "spring hub." The device was a large wheel hub with internal coil springs that provided about an inch of movement under normal road use. In contrast, the Harley-Davidson K swinging arm provided over 4 inches of movement under normal road use. Of major rivals, only Associated Motorcycles' Matchless and AJS marques also used a swinging arm rear suspension. The K setup surpassed the Matchless/AJS layout because the sloping rear suspension units were mounted well ahead of the axle, giving the rear section of the bike a light look reminiscent of a rigid frame, while leaving room for the traditional large Harley-Davidson saddlebags.

The K unit construction also was ahead of its time. Harley-Davidson's biggest rivals, Triumph and BSA, would turn to unit construction

1953 K
What is so rare as a day in June? Maybe a Model K (they weren't big sellers). But (and these are big exceptions) the Model K was the basis of the highly successful KR-series racers, and the K paved the way for the later ever-popular Sportster. © H-D Michigan, Inc.

1952–1953 Model K

Collectibility	★★★★☆
Comfortable cruising speed	50 mph
Smoothness of ride	★★★★★
Passenger accommodations	★★★★☆
Reliability	★★★☆☆
Parts/service availability	★★☆☆☆

I would rate the 1953 model three stars except that there was no observable differences from the 1952 inaugural Model K. In other words, the 1952 and 1953 models make up one set. The first Ks were important as the eventual, though not yet planned, basis of the later overhead-valve Sportsters. The sires of the K line also bask in the glory of the KR and KRTT racers that had their way in American racing for nearly twenty years.

1952 K

The 1952 Model K was the most radically new model Harley-Davidson ever built. A telescopic fork replaced the W-series leading link (springer) fork. The four-speed foot shift transmission replaced the W-series three-speed hand shift box. Out back, a swinging arm rear suspension replaced the W-series rigid frame. © H-D Michigan, Inc.

1952 K

The August 1952 *Cycle* reported, "The Sultan's magic carpet never rode like Harley-Davidson's K model. . . . the K stands second to none at ironing out the bumps." But the road test bike was unable to keep buzzing in the gears, prompting *Cycle* to report, "The bike's acceleration . . . was good but not sensational." © H-D Michigan, Inc.

1953 K

The buddy seat and saddlebags became available late in the 1952 season. © H-D Michigan, Inc.

more than a decade later. Unit construction of the K added rigidity to the engine-transmission package, ensured accurate alignment, and reduced manufacturing costs. It was not the first unit-construction Harley-Davidson. The 1919–1923 Sport model had unit construction, as did the contemporary 125, but this was the first American-designed unit-construction motorcycle engine since the 1931 Super-X. As an aside, the Indian V-twins were sometimes labeled unit construction, but the Indian design was more properly termed "semi-unit" because the engine and transmission were separate units, which were bolted together instead of housed in shared castings.

Although unit construction was a good idea, the K design was seriously flawed by lack of accessibility to the transmission. Accessibility was the keynote of the separate engine and transmission approach favored elsewhere in the industry, and Harley-Davidson had failed to retain this feature in the unit construction. Any transmission work on the K, even the replacement of the footshift return spring, required removal of the entire powerplant from the frame. This, in turn, required disconnecting the controls for the throttle, ignition timing, and clutch—a major hassle. But the hassle wasn't over; the crankcases then had to be split. Splitting the crankcases meant removing the cylinders. Not since the last 1942 Indian Four had gearbox work been such a nightmare, and even the Four didn't require cylinder removal. Moreover, the old Indian Four had an "Acme Indestructo" clutch and transmission that almost never required the ordeal. In the hands of some owners, the K would prove to need both transmission and clutch work.

Sales of the new Model K weren't helped by the price, which was $997 f.o.b. at Los Angeles, less than $100 under the Panhead price. Some of the cost was due to the rear suspension, which was both vastly superior to—but more expensive than—the Triumph and BSA springing. But customers often looked at the price tags of the 650s, which hurt less by about 15 percent, and figured they were making an apples-to-apples comparison.

On the other hand, the Model K wasn't a world-leader in every department. Take the engine—please! That seemed to be the American reaction. From the sales standpoint, the biggest drawback to the K was its side-valve engine. The post-World War II influx of British overhead-valve motorcycles brought with it new images as well as new motorcycles. By 1952, most potential K buyers hadn't grown up in the prewar side-valve era, and to them a side-valve engine was obsolete. The side-valve approach was to add engine size to compensate for lack of sophistication. Although increasing engine size was a simple and effective solution, the fact that a K needed 45 cubic inches (750 cc) to compete with 30.50-cubic-inch (500 cc) British bikes just reinforced notions of obsolescence.

Even with the 45-cubic inch displacement, which made the K engine 50 percent larger than the British 30.50-cubic inch engines, the K didn't have a surplus of power and speed for street fights with these common British bikes, and was really inadequate when pitted against the popular 40-cubic inch (650-cc) Triumph Thunderbird and BSA Golden Flash. These 650s had entered the market in the 1950 sales season, at a time when Model K development was well along. Consequently, the Model K had been designed to shoot at easier targets. *Cycle* editor Bob

1954 KH

For 1954, the middleweight was stroked to achieve 54.2-cubic inch (888-cc) displacement and parity with 40-cubic inch (650-cc) British vertical twins. Rechristened the KH, the model also got new big-twin-style flywheels with a tapered crankpin. The fork got new rubber accordion boots, and the timing case was polished.

Greene noted in the August 1952 road test that maximum speed couldn't be reached in low and second gears because of carburetor spit-back—a common complaint. The Model K required 16.86 seconds to negotiate a standing-start quarter-mile acceleration run, a pace that put the K well behind the 650s. The top speed of 98.9 miles per hour was only about 1 mile per hour under that of the 650s. A midseason KK variant offered faster running via polished inlet ports and sportier cams.

Swayed by the K's stunning good looks and major technical features, Harley-Davidson dealers were initially enthusiastic about the model. Their enthusiasm was short lived. Much transmission and clutch repair was accomplished under factory warranty, and the dealers weren't compensated for their labor costs. One of the clutch problems was buildup of oil in the primary case, which in turn crept into the clutch housing and ruined the action of this "dry" clutch.

Reading, Pennsylvania's, Red Wolverton related that overall he lost money on every K, and San Francisco's Dud Perkins told Wolverton the

1955 KH

More glitter was added by polishing the outside of the cylinder heads. A heavier rear wheel hub and spokes were fitted. The fork trail was increased, the speedometer was rubber mounted, and the cylinder heads were mirror polished.

1955 KH transmission door
The much needed transmission door arrived on the 1955 KH models. No longer did transmission repair require removing the powerplant and cylinders and splitting the cases. © H-D Michigan, Inc.

1955 KHK
These special high lift "racing" cams made the KHK breath deeper, while special lightweight roller tappets let the KHK spin faster. © H-D Michigan, Inc.

1955 KHK
Built off-line were limited production high-performance KHK models with polished inlet and exhaust ports and deeply relieved cylinder heads to make room for the higher lift cams. © H-D Michigan, Inc.

same story. Wolverton was put off by the short and high stance of the Model K. He never parked a Model K next to a Big Twin in his showroom, because a K looked bigger than a Panhead. Ever the gentleman, Wolverton never cursed. But in remembering the K, Wolverton's face turned red, his voice got louder, and he permitted himself expressions like "gosh-darned" and "doggone" that otherwise never passed through his lips. He wished he'd never ordered a K!

Wolverton had warned the factory about the transmission inaccessibility the first time he saw the Ks in Milwaukee. Long-time San Jose, California, dealer Tom Sifton had conducted a mini-test program on the K using his star racing rider, Joe Leonard. Sifton had predicted transmission problems.

But, eventually, the factory turned the transmission from a weakness into a strength. The great Carol Resweber, four times consecutively the top racer in the nation, related racing at a late 1950s Laconia, New

1952–1953 Model K Specifications

Engine ....Side-valve V-twin with an individual camshaft for each valve

Bore and stroke...............2.75x 3.1825 in

Displacement

Actual ....45.3 ci (742 cc)

Nominal...........................45 ci (750 cc)

Lubrication ....Dry sump

Compression ratio..........6.5:1

Power ....30 hp @ 5,800 rpm

Transmission ....Four-speed, constant-mesh type, unit construction with the engine

Shift ....Right foot

Shift pattern ....Down for low

Primary drive ....3/8-inch triple chain in oil bath

Clutch ....Multiple disks, dry, hand actuated

Gear ratios, overall

4th 4.77:1

3rd 6.21:1

2nd 8.74:1

1st 12.37:1

Wheelbase......................55 1/2 in

Wheels and tires ....3.25x19 in, front and rear

Suspension

Front ....Telescopic fork

Rear ....Swinging arm and shock absorbers

Weight.............................450 lb (fully serviced)

Saddle height..................28 1/2 in

Foot-peg height..............8.9 in

Fuel capacity ....4 1/2 gal

Oil capacity ....3 qt

Fuel consumption...........45.7 mpg* (city riding)

Top speed

4th @ 6,320 rpm..............100.5 mph*

3rd @ 6,650 rpm ....81.2 mph*

2nd @ 6,910 rpm.............60 mph*

1st @ 7,340 rpm ....45 mph*

Acceleration, 1/4-mile.....16.86 sec at 53.3 mph*

* Figures from *Cycle*, August 1952. Speed and acceleration tests were run without a muffler and with altered carburetor jetting.

1954–1956 Models KH and KHK

Collectibility	★★★☆☆
Comfortable cruising speed	50 mph
Smoothness of ride	★★★★★
Passenger accommodations	★★★★☆
Reliability	★★★☆☆
Parts/service availability	★★☆☆☆

These were better motorcycles with power that at last made the middleweight Harleys competitive in the street wars with 650-cc British vertical twins. But they were not history-making machines. The polished parts look a little gaudy to me, but you might prefer the shine. Weakest of the lot is the 1954 model, which didn't have the transmission door.

Hampshire, 100 Mile National Championship Road Race. As a rider with factory backing, Resweber had to start the race, although he would've preferred to skip the race because he had a severe hangover. Resweber decided to make it a short day by breaking his KRTT. Despite full-throttle clutch-less gearshifts, and stomping on the shift lever, the KRTT ran the entire 100 miles.

Back to the issue of power, as in "not enough." For the 1954 season, the factory responded to the British 650s by replacing the 45-cubic inch K with the 55-cubic inch (nominal) KH. With more than a 20-percent displacement increase, the results were predictable. Said the March 1954 *Cycle*: "Look Out It's Loaded . . . the 45-inch predecessor to the KH just did not have go-power in relation to its displacement. This is where the story changes in testing the KH . . . the new 55-cubic inch KH has horsepower that most riders would hardly ever use. . . . The factory's claim of 38 horsepower at 5,000 rpm seems indeed modest to me now. . . . Harley-Davidson's golden anniversary surprise, the 55-cubic inch KH, is a different kind of motorcycle. It is a side-valve wonder that will make many others scamper to keep up."

The KH ran through the standing-start quarter-mile acceleration test in 14.75 seconds, compared to the Model K's time of 16.86 seconds (*Cycle*, August 1952). Triumph's top gun for 1954, the 40-cubic inch (650-cc) Tiger 110, turned the quarter in 15.28 seconds (*Cycle*, April 1954), proving the 650s would no longer scare the middleweight Harleys. The KH accelerated faster than the K, despite the KH's taller gearing in every ratio. In fourth (high) gear, the KH engine spun 4 percent slower than the K engine. The KH topped out at 100.55 miles per hour, practically identical to the top speed of the Triumph Tiger 110.

Three KH variants were offered for the 1955 and 1956 model years. The KHK was a super sports version with polished internals and special

Riding a 1952 K-model

Like the 125, the K-model is long on looks. The K has the same beautiful fenders. The fork has the in-look of the era, with the top part bigger than the bottom. The handlebars, too, were a sign of the times. Most West Coast customs had these sit-up-and-beg bars, and even star dirt-track racers got into the high-bar act.

I throw my right leg over the K and pull the bike erect and off the kickstand. I settle into the plush sprung saddle and feel it go down under my weight (got to start that diet!). I also feel the rear suspension settle. This is a kick. I rise out of the saddle, turn my head to watch, and sit down again. The rear shocks compress about 1/2 inch. I do this several times, finding it so amusing because of high school memories. I remember Jackie Dean Anderson sitting on his K and all those saddle and rear suspension springs doing their thing. This was heady stuff in the days when other new Harleys and many new British bikes still had rigid rear ends. I notice that the rear suspension tops out every time I lift out of the saddle, resulting in a quiet clunk.

I rise out of the saddle again and unfold the bicycle-style kickstarter pedal. Foot in place, right leg bent at the knee, I jump about a foot off the ground so that my right leg nearly straightens, then I let the full force of my weight come down through my nearly straight right leg and onto the kickstarter. The K squats under the load, roars to life, and rises on its springs, ready for a ride. If Jackie Dean Anderson could only see me now.

With the fully warmed engine settled into a steady fla-flump, fla-flump, fla-flump, I pull in the clutch lever, ease the right-side shift lever down into low, roll on the throttle, and ease out the hand clutch. As soon as we're fully away, I grab some more throttle. It takes some doing, as there's about a yard of slack in the throttle cable. The back end settles and the fork rises while we move briskly through low. The clutch action and shifting are delightful, and I quickly get the bike in high gear (fourth) and settled into a 60-mile-per-hour cruise.

I ease off the throttle above 60, and at 65 the riding position becomes tiresome because I'm sitting absolutely upright. An unexpected plus is mechanical quietness, with most of the motor noise trapped under the flat-bottomed tank. The "double-decker" cylinder heads probably help too.

I never do performance tests because, a) I'm not brave, and b) the performance story is well documented. To paraphrase British road testers of the era, I find the power entirely adequate (not

Rider's view of K
The handlebars feel strange. It's not just the high rise that's so unusual; it's also the angle of the handlegrips. If you relax your grip, your hands almost slide down and off the handlegrips. The high and wide bars combine with the 3.25-inch tires to produce very light steering. The gas tank, to me, is the best-looking one to ever grace a mid-sized Harley.

Kicking K Model
The K, by far, was the softest sprung motorcycle on the market. A vigorous prod on the kickstarter compresses the rear springs about an inch, while the front fork springs expand to lift the steering head noticeably. That was heady wine in 1952.

very fast) and the vibration well within keeping of the grand tradition of V-twin motorcycling that has so enriched our experiences (shakes like hell). But this is one beautiful bike, and it irons out the bumps so well. I was right to want one so much.

1954–1956 KH Specifications

Engine ....Side-valve V-twin with an individual camshaft for each valve

Bore and stroke...............2 3/4x4 9/16 in

Displacement

Actual ....54.2 ci (888 cc)

Nominal ....55 ci (900 cc)

Lubrication ....Dry sump

Compression ratio...........6.8:1

Power ....38 hp @ 5,200 rpm

Transmission ....Four-speed, constant-mesh type, unit construction with the engine

Shift ....Right foot

Shift pattern ....Down for low

Primary drive ....3/8-inch triple chain in oil bath

Clutch ....Multiple disks, dry, hand actuated

Gear ratios, overall

4th 4.58:1

3rd 6.37:1

2nd 8.35:1

1st 11.55:1

Wheelbase......................55 1/4 in

Wheels and tires ....3.50x18 in, front and rear

Suspension

Front ....Telescopic fork

Rear ....Swinging arm

Weight............................450 lb (fully serviced)

Saddle height..................28 1/2 in

Foot-peg height..............8.9 in

Fuel capacity ....4 1/2 gal

Oil capacity ....3 qt

Fuel consumption...........41.2 mpg (city riding)*

Top speed

4th @ 6,190 rpm..............100.55 mph*

3rd @ 7,050 rpm ....82.37 mph*

2nd @ 7,300 rpm.............65 mph*

1st @ 7,450 rpm..............48 mph*

Acceleration, 1/4-mile.....14.75 sec*

* Figures from Cycle, March 1954.

cams. The KHRM was an enduro model, and the KHRTT was for TT racing. (*The Legend Begins* lists one KHR flat-tracker produced for 1955, but this would have been a prototype.) A total of 3,994 KHs of all varieties were built 1954–1956, says *The Legend Begins*, with the KH series accounting for about 10 percent of total production. It was an improvement over the 1,723 Model Ks, which averaged 6 percent of total production, but both the K and KH series were disappointing sellers in a market flooded by less-expensive British 650s. Model year 1956 was the last for the KH series, which was replaced in model year 1957 by the Sportster.

The importance of the basic K layout went well beyond sales figures, though the middleweights did have to pull their weight. The K design work paid off handsomely with the KR-series racers, and the derivative KH series gave the Harley speed enthusiasts enough ammunition to do battle on equal terms with the 650s. The KH bikes were ridden mostly by younger and faster riders who moved among the middle-aged Panhead pilots, within the social sphere of the Harley shops and their related clubs. Though the effect can't be quantified, Harley-Davidson dealers must have benefited from KH bragging rights that shined a halo over the Panhead scene, even as the KR series racers also reflected Harley glory.

K and KH Development

The K received no announced technical improvements for 1953, except for a faster-acting throttle. The first Harley-Davidson Royalite plastic saddlebags were offered as accessories.

Reacting to complaints about the price, Harley offered a 1953 lower-cost optional finish package, the Standard Solo Group, in addition to the Deluxe Group. The low-bucks Model K had cadmium plating instead of chrome plating on the wheel rims, fork sliders, tank cap, horn, and horn cover. Black paint substituted for chrome plating on the handlebars and headlight shell. The taillamp cover, fork panels, and fork-tube covers were finished in the standard color specified instead of chrome; for example, these would be blue on a blue motorcycle. Other cost-cutting features included brush finish of the steering-damper adjusting knob and brake side panels (front and rear). These alternatives lowered the suggested retail price $44.75, not much, but enough to keep the price under the magic $1,000, even with freight charges and sales tax.

The first significant upgrades occurred with the successor model, the 55-cubic inch (900-cc) KH of 1954. The major change was the displacement increase, which made the side-valve model competitive with British 650-cc overheads. Peak output was up 26 percent, from 30 to 38 horsepower, while torque was up by 40 percent.

The displacement boost was achieved by increasing the stroke from 3 13/16 inches to 4.562 inches; the bore remained at 2.745 inches. New cast-iron flywheels had a tapered crankpin, the same approach used on the Big Twins. New pistons had eight holes drilled beneath the oil-control rings instead of horizontal slots. Inlet valves were increased to a diameter of 7/16 inch. New valve springs of the KR type reduced likelihood of valve float by dimensional changes that ensured the coils couldn't close at maximum valve lift.

Buildup of oil in the primary case was eliminated by a one-way siphon valve, thus reducing the likelihood of clutch slippage. To handle the increased engine output, a new seven-plate clutch replaced the former five-plate unit. Lubrication of the second and third countershaft gears was improved by an oil passage through the center of the transmission countershaft and with vertical passages to the gears. The main drive clutch gear was fitted with needle bearings instead of a bronze bush. The transmission gears were "redesigned," but the factory didn't make clear what the changes were. But despite these improvements, the hoped-for transmission accessibility still wasn't there.

Other detail changes were incorporated on the KH series. Foremost of these was new fork geometry with increased rake and trail. Pressed-steel brake shoes replaced the former aluminum units, and the brake lining material was new.

For 1955, the KH got a transmission door that at last permitted transmission removal with the engine in place. Lubrication of the needle roller bearing on the right side of the transmission was improved, by carrying the oil from a pocket on top of the transmission case through a duct. A heavier rear wheel hub and spokes were fitted, and the fork trail was increased 1 inch. The frame was stronger because it was made from chrome-moly steel instead of C 1026 steel. The speedometer was rubber mounted, and the cylinder heads were mirror polished.

A new top-of-the-KH-line model was the 1955 KHK, with polished inlet and exhaust ports and cylinder heads that were deeply relieved to accommodate the higher valve lift imparted by "racing type" cams. Special lightweight roller tappets lifted the valves. The factory warned that stocks of KHKs wouldn't be built up, necessitating that dealers allow for lead time when ordering KHKs. The high-performance KHK variant was given a distinctive decal for the oil tank and toolbox. All in the KH series got stronger transmissions.

The 1956 KH series got a lower frame, which was achieved by changes to the steering-head casting and the forgings that supported the rear spring arms. The shock absorbers were redesigned for 9/16-inch-shorter length, larger diameter, and a larger oil volume. The KH-series oil pump was redesigned to reduce the likelihood of oil draining into the crankcase. The mainshaft and countershaft second and third gears were redesigned for increased tooth section and strength.

The K/KH generation ended with the 1956 models. Ultimately, their development was the foundation of a spectacularly successful racing program. As road models, they set the stage for the much-more-successful Sportster series.

Models K and KH Rideability

These aren't very rideable motorcycles. In fact, they're not as rideable as any of the big overhead-valve twins up through the KH years.

What am I, some kind of nut? After falling all over myself with praise of the K and KH magic-carpet riding quality, I rate the rideability lower than the old rigid-frame Big Twins. The problems isn't in the physical ride, it's in the consequence of riding. To put it bluntly, Ks and KHs are rare motorcycles. During the era, the factory built three two-stroke Harleys for every K and KH. The world isn't exactly overflowing with the littlest Harleys, is it? Because of the low build rate, the Ks and KHs are seen even less. At most AMCA events you won't see a single K

1956 KH

A 1956 KH, just what your average well-to-do sports enthusiasts admired. The 1956 frame was lowered in anticipation of the forthcoming 1957 Sportster, which would need more engine room. The forward section of the chain guard was eliminated to clear the lower oil tank. © H-D Michigan, Inc.

or KH. K-unique and KH-unique parts are conspicuously absent from most parts dealers' catalogs. A lot of Sportster stuff will work for chassis restoration and repair, and a lot of W-series engine internals will work in a K or KH. But the dealers have left the homework for you, so these are difficult motorcycles to restore and maintain.

Beauty and the Beast

The 1952 and 1953 Ks were your basic schizophrenic motorcycles. In stock trim, each was the gentle Dr. Jekyll, mild mannered and civilized. But in racing trim, as KRs and KRTTs, the type was the sinister Mr. Hyde, ready to explode in anger. In the street wars, the stock Ks were no more than average performers—mild mannered, as I said. The average 30.50-cubic inch (500-cc) British vertical twin could give a Model K a real challenge, and the average 40-cubic inch (650-cc) vertical twin would invariably come out on top. Unfortunately for the K, it debuted at the same time that the 650s replaced the 500s as the most popular size of Brit-bike.

In the 1954 season, the performance gap was closed with the long-stroke KH series. The KH series was an improvement in every respect except that it messes up the imagery. Okay, I'll try. The KH was Dr. Hyde.

Riding either a K or KH on the streets and highways marked you as a stronger Harley-Davidson loyalist than the average Panhead rider. The Ks and KHs were good enough, but there were competitive British models of similar size and performance that cost a lot less. This was a different situation from riding a Panhead because there were no other motorcycles like the Panhead. So if you rode one of the Harley middleweights, you were making a statement about yourself. You said to the motorcycle world that no matter how good a foreign bike might be, it wasn't good enough for you.

Riding a new K made you feel like a patron of the arts. The K's sweeping lines and bold engine design made the motorcycle so easy to look at, and from any angle. Like the first Knuckleheads and Hydra-Glides, and the first skirted-fender Indians, here was a bike that gave so much pleasure just parked in the garage. By the time the KH came along, the lines were just as good, yet familiarity had taken a little off of the edge. But there was more to the KH than good looks. Riding a KH wasn't exactly like looking for a fight, but you knew no bully was going to pester you with his Triumph or BSA. Street racing was now a fair fight. Your beauty was a beast.

Chapter 9

Sportsters

March 1957 *Cycle*: "The power is there in any gear, throughout the speed range, without hesitation, which provides riding thrills that have to be experienced to be appreciated."

March 1959 *Cycle*: ". . . terrific acceleration through the gears . . . extremely smart in appearance."

Motor Cycling (date unknown, reprinted in January 1960 *Cycle*): "Shattering acceleration was perhaps the most impressive of the single-carburetor Sportster's many capabilities."

October 1962 *Cycle World*: "It is big, powerful, and goes in a manner that will make hair grow on your chest (if you've already got the hair, it will part it down the middle)."

What the K and KH models had lacked, the Sportster brought to the scene. Power! Granted, the 55-cubic inch KH could hold its own with British 40-cubic inch vertical twins. But in the Sportster, Harley-Davidson riders found a model that, every time it was asked, showed its taillight to any other new motorcycle on the road.

In the mid-1950s, Harley-Davidson was under pressure because of hot sales competition from Triumph and BSA, whose 40-cubic inch (650-cc) vertical twins were winning too many of the street battles against the 55-cubic inch (883-cc) KH to suit Milwaukee. Behind the scenes, engineering was working hard on the solution. But the Sportster, as we know it, wasn't supposed to be the solution. Instead, Harley-Davidson planned an all-aluminum Model KL engine with either a high camshaft or overhead cam. The picture of the KL in the author's *American Racing Motorcycles* looks like a high cam, pushrod job to me, but I'm told old-timers called it an overhead-cam model. One thing is for sure, it had parallel valves. Although prototype testing was favorable and some production tooling had already been ordered, the company canceled the KL because too much time was required for its development. At that point, engineering began development of the Sportster, which, in principle, was an overhead-valve conversion of the existing KH engine.

In its initial touring trim, the 1957 Sportster XL seemed to be a model looking for a mission. Although noting the "terrific acceleration" of the 1957 Sportster, the *Cycle* magazine road test said the model was ". . . designed primarily with an eye for the touring motorcyclist." A 7.5:1 compression ratio and mild-mannered cams made the new model docile, but the overhead valves brought a new standard to touring-model performance. Only the British-built Vincent outperformed the Sportster, but the Vincent died during 1955, and in any case was always

1957 Model XL

Collectibility	★★★★☆
Comfortable cruising speed	60 mph
Smoothness of ride	★★★★★
Passenger accommodations	★★★★☆
Reliability	★★★★☆
Parts/service availability	★★★★☆

There's no time like the first time. The 1957 Sportster announced clearly that Harley-Davidson had the fastest and quickest motorcycle.

1957 Sportster
What's wrong with this picture? Answer: With the solo saddle, he won't likely talk her into riding away on this summer day. The 1957 Sportster came on the scene as a mildly tuned combination touring and sport model. © H-D Michigan, Inc.

1957 Sportster

The Sportster was an overhead-valve conversion of the KH series, but the engineering involved more than simply grafting on new jugs and heads. Nominally, both the Sportster and the earlier KH were 55-cubic inch (900-cc) motorcycles, but the Sportster had a bigger bore and a shorter stroke. The Sportster exhaust system was less restrictive than the KH layout. © H-D Michigan, Inc.

1958 Sportster

In 1958, five out of every six Sportsters was a touring version, either the low-compression XL or the high-compression XLH. The rest were the new CH (Competition Hot). © H-D Michigan, Inc.

sold in numbers too small to bring its impact face to face with most riders of other marques. Among new motorcycles, the Sportster was king!

The genre was produced in 1957 in touring trim only as the model XL (low compression). Three variants were added for the 1958 season. These were the XLC (low-compression) magneto-equipped competition Sportster without lights, XLH (high-compression) road model, and the "Competition Hot" XLCH, which was a high-compression, magneto-ignition competition version without lights. The "CH," as it came to be called, got lights for the 1959 season. Sixteen percent of the 1958 Sportsters were CH models. The ratio of CH models to H models continuously increased over the years, and by 1965, 75 percent of all Sportsters were the CH version. The low-compression XL was produced for only three model years, 1957–1959.

Sportster production varied from 12 to 21 percent of the Harley total during the 1957–1965 era. Accordingly, Sportsters accounted for a lower percentage of Harley-Davidson production than the American-built two-strokes. However, Sportsters sold for almost three times the

1958 Sportster
Some say the Sportster engine, with its long stroke and hemispherical combustion chambers, was a throwback to the old J. A. Prestwich motors used by the Brits in the 1920s and 1930s. What of it? Low- and mid-range power still is the choice for many, and the first Sportsters had plenty. © *H-D Michigan, Inc.*

1958 Sportster
The 1959 transmission countershaft was beefed up by increasing the diameter 1/8 inch and increasing the number of splines from six to eight. A new oil seal was aimed at eliminating oil seepage into the dry clutch, which had been a problem under engineering attack since the first K models. © *H-D Michigan, Inc.*

prices of the lightweights, so the Sportsters represented 25 or more percent of total revenues each year.

As well as being a profitable line, the Sportsters brought status to the Harley-Davidson lineup. Panhead riders could feel that their honor as Harley-Davidson riders was defended by the Sportsters. A Duo-Glide might be slow compared to a Triumph or BSA, but that didn't matter if another Harley-Davidson was around to teach the Brit-bike riders some manners. Whether Panhead sales benefited from the Sportster connection can't be verified, but the hundreds of

1958–1965 XL Series

Collectibility	★★★☆☆
Comfortable cruising speed	60 mph
Smoothness of ride	★★★★★
Passenger accommodations	★★★★☆
Reliability	★★★★☆
Parts/service availability	★★★★☆

Of the roadsters, I like the 1958 best of this range, as it doesn't have the imitation Triumph headlight nacelle and the larger front fender. The move to a nacelle happened about the time Triumph was dumping that idea, so Harley nacelles never made sense to me. I don't distinguish between the H and CH series, but you might feel the first street-legal CH of 1959 deserves a bump upward. The CH series is a little murky because the first ones were the 1958 strictly competition bikes, so is 1958 or 1959 the first year for the series? The low-slung tank of the 1961 and later Sportster H road models is attractive, but lacks the charisma of the earlier tank.

clubs sponsored by Harley shops clearly enjoyed the knowledge that Sportsters were on the prowl.

The Sportster held the "quickest" (fastest standing-start quarter mile) title until the arrival of the 1966 Suzuki X-6 Hustler, which bettered the XLH by 0.2 seconds in the *Cycle World* quarter mile, with an identical 84-mile-per-hour terminal speed; next, the 1968 Kawasaki Mach III turned the *Cycle World* quarter mile a whopping 2.2 seconds faster than the CH, and bettered the CH's terminal velocity by a score of 100.22 miles per hour to 92 miles per hour. The "fastest" title was

1958 Sportster CH
The first CH models were designed purely for competition, and so they were delivered with neither lights nor provisions for lights. The CH was the fastest accelerating of all stock motorcycles. At the time, they were so quick they were scary. © H-D Michigan, Inc.

1959 Sportster
"Arrow-Flite" styling on the Sportster XLH included the same new tank badge and white "Jet sweep" panel as used on the Duo-Glides. The new headlight nacelle followed the fashion lead of Triumph motorcycles. © H-D Michigan, Inc.

valid until the 1969 Honda CB 750 four-cylinder won that *Cycle World* comparison by 123.24 miles per hour to 122 miles per hour. No matter. The CH never lost its chest-hair-parting image.

I'll get in trouble for this, but I thought then, and still think now, that the main stateside appeal of British vertical twins was low pricing. In 1967, British 650s cost between $1,200 and $1,500, but Sportsters were around $2,000, making them about 50 percent more expensive. To me, no Triumph, BSA, or whatever, compared favorably with a Sportster in looks, sound, or raw power. I say this as a guy who used to sell BSAs— or at least I tried to sell them.

1957–1965 Sportster Development

With the same nominal 55-cubic inch (900-cc) displacement

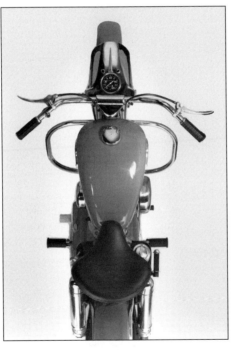

1959 Sportster
The March 1959 *Cycle* says the following of this 1959 Sportster, ". . . terrific acceleration through the gears . . . extremely smart in appearance."
© H-D Michigan, Inc.

as the KH, one would naturally think that creating the Sportster was simply a matter of moving the valves upstairs. Actually, other engineering thought went into the design, for the Sportster had a shorter stroke than the KH, measuring 3.8125 inches compared to the KH's 4.562 inches. The Sportster bore was 3 inches compared to the KH's 2.745 inches. According to the factory press releases, there were no significant changes to the frame and running gear bequeathed by the displaced KH side-valve middleweight. Apparently, the lowering of the 1956 KH frame had paved the way for the taller 1957 Sportster engine. The

1957 XL, 1958 XLC, 1958–1965 XLH, and 1958–1962 XLCH Specifications
Engine ....Overhead-valve V-twin with an individual camshaft for each valve
Bore and stroke...............3x3.81 in (76.2x96.8 mm)
Displacement
Actual ....54.9 ci (883 cc)
Nominal............................55 ci (900 cc)
Compression ratio
Models XL and XLC 7.5:1
Model XLH 9:1
Model XLCH....................9:1
Power
Model XLH ....55 hp @ 6,300 rpm (*Cycle World*, April 1965)
Model XLCH....................55 hp @ unspecified rpm (*Cycle World*, October 1962)
Transmission ....Four-speed, constant-mesh type, unit construction with the engine
Shift ....Right foot
Shift pattern ....Down for low
Primary drive ....3/8-inch triple chain in oil bath
Clutch ....Multiple disks, dry, hand actuated
Gear ratios, XLH, overall (*Cycle*, March 1959)
4th 4.21:1
3rd 5.82:1
2nd 7.69:1
1st 10.63:1

1959 Sportster CH
The 1959 CH was at last street legal. Eleven percent more power was claimed from new high-lift cams. *Motor Cycling* (reprinted in January 1960 *Cycle*) commented: "Breathtakingly fast. . . . Shattering acceleration." © *H-D Michigan, Inc.*

Sportster got a new exhaust system that smoothed the flow. The front pipe continued along the side of the motor and then to the muffler in one sweeping curve, and the rear pipe blended in with this one-curve concept. Previously, the K and KH had a Y-connection of the front and rear pipes at the rear of the transmission, with the tailpipe exiting in the middle as the stem of the Y.

Changes to the 1958 Sportsters involved details. Cams and small cam gears were made in one piece to increase strength and to dispense with the former key and keyway used for each cam-camshaft pair. The transmission countershaft was beefed up by increasing the diameter 1/8 inch and increasing the number of splines from six to eight. A new oil seal was aimed at eliminating oil seepage into the dry clutch; this had been a problem under engi-

1959 Sportster CH
The primary drive cover was the same as used on the KR-series racers. © *H-D Michigan, Inc.*

1960 Sportster
Harley-Davidson rested on their Sportster laurels, and for the 1960 season made only minor modifications to the suspension damping plus the traditional tank trim change, now called "Twin-Flare" styling. © H-D Michigan, Inc.

neering attack since the first K-models. Midseason additions were the XLC and XLCH, which were low- and high-compression competition variants sold without lights and generator. No, I have no idea why there would be a need for a low-compression competition model. Maybe the XLC was a trail bike? At any rate, the XLCH was eligible for TT racing and hillclimbing. Both of these go-fast models had twin, low-mounted straight pipes to handle the exhaust.

Headlining the 1959 Sportsters was the new street-legal XLCH with lighting powered by a magdyno; there was no need for a battery. The CH had a muffled, high-mounted exhaust. The CH was fitted with new high-lift inlet cams that produced 11 percent more power. Elsewhere, the touring XL Sportster received no technical changes.

1957 XL, 1958 XLC, 1958–1965 XLH, and 1958–1962 XLCH Specifications

Wheelbase.......................55 1/4 in
Wheels and tires ....3.50x18 in, front and rear
Suspension
Front ....Telescopic fork
Rear ....Swinging arm
Weight............................450 lb (fully serviced)
Saddle height..................28 1/2 in
Foot-peg height..............8.9 in
Fuel capacity ....4.4 gal
Oil capacity ....3 qt
Fuel consumption............55–60 mpg (*Cycle*, March 1957)
Top speed, XL (*Cycle*, March 1957)
4th @ 5,740 rpm.............101.40 mph
3rd @ 6,690 rpm ....85.53 mph
Top speed, XLH (*Cycle*, March 1959)
4th @ 5,970 rpm.............105.4 mph
3rd @ 6,690 rpm ....85.5 mph
2nd @ 6,520 rpm............63.1 mph
1st @ 6,500 rpm.............45.5 mph
Top speed, XLCH (*Cycle World*, October 1962)
4th @ 6,600 rpm.............122 mph
3rd @ 6,800 rpm ....90 mph
2nd @ 6,800 rpm............68 mph
1st @ 6,800 rpm.............49 mph
Acceleration, 1/4 mile
XLH ....15.5 sec at 84 mph
(*Cycle World*, April 1965)
XLCH ....14.3 sec at 92 mph
(*Cycle World*, October 1962)

1960 Sportster CH
More "Twin-Flare" styling here. From *Motor Cycling* (British, date unknown, reprinted in January 1960 *Cycle*): "Shattering acceleration was perhaps the most impressive of the single-carburetor Sportster's many capabilities." © *H-D Michigan, Inc.*

1962 Sportster CH Specifications

Frame type	Tubular, two-loop
Suspension	
Front	Telescopic fork
Rear	Swinging arm
Tire size	
Front	3.25/3.50x19 in
Rear	4.00x18 in
Brake lining area	36.0 sq in
Engine type	Overhead-valve V-twin
Bore and stroke	3.00x3.81 in
Displacement	53.9 ci (883 cc)
Compression ratio	9.0:1
Power	55 hp
Carburetion	L&L, 1 5/16 in
Ignition	Magneto
Fuel capacity	2.25 gal
Oil capacity	6.0 pt
Oil system	Dry sump
Starting system	Kick, folding crank
Clutch type	Multiple disks
Primary drive	Duplex chain
Final drive	Single-row chain
Gear ratios, overall	
4th	4.22:1
3rd	5.82:1
2nd	7.72:1
1st	10.6:1
Wheelbase	57.0 in
Saddle height	30.5 in
Saddle width	11.0 in
Foot-peg height	11.5 in
Ground clearance	4.1 in
Curb weight	480 lb

1961 Sportster CH
Ads in the era never tired of the flying theme, which was extended in the 1961 season to include outer space. Harley-Davidson called the tank trim "Astro-Flite" styling. Nineteen sixty-one saw no significant engineering changes to the Sportsters. © H-D Michigan, Inc.

The 1960 Sportsters featured recalibrated damping rates on the front fork and rear suspension. No Sportster technical changes were announced for the 1961 season. For the 1962 model year, an aluminum upper fork bracket was introduced. The 1963 Sportsters had a taller third-gear ratio (1.323:1 instead of 1.381:1), resulting in third and fourth gears being "closer." The 1963 CH magneto was fitted with a higher output coil and a tachometer takeoff drive, and the CH headlight was rubber mounted. The 1964 models had full-width aluminum hubs, aluminum tappets, and a polyacrylic clutch oil seal. A 12-volt electrical system debuted on the 1965 Sportsters, hinting at the electric starting that would come two years later.

1961 Sportster
Although the rest of the motorcycles got "Astro-Flite" styling with white tank trim, the Sportster H had a new tank without white trim. The press release said the new Sportster tanks were graced with "Jet-Stream" styling. © H-D Michigan, Inc.

LUMINUM UPPER FORK
ET—The Upper Fork Bracket
arley-Davidson SPORTSTERS
nade of lightweight aluminum.
nother weight-reduction feature
hese popular speed twins easier
—faster on the move.

VIDSON SPORTSTER H

1962 Sportster H
Following Harley-Davidson tradition, the XLH Sportster got new tank trim for 1962. © H-D Michigan, Inc.

1961 Sportster
No Sportster technical changes were announced for the 1961 model year. © H-D Michigan, Inc.

1962 Sportster CH
The new tank trim wasn't given a name, as in previous years, on any of the 1962 Harley Davidsons. © H-D Michigan, Inc.

1963 Sportster CH
The 1963 CH got a rubber mounted headlight, a tachometer, and an improved magneto. A CH rider didn't need a tachometer to beat a 650-cc Brit bike to the next stop light, but tachometers had become a styling necessity on high-performance motorcycles. © H-D Michigan, Inc.

Sportster Rideability

No worries—be happy. A 40-year-old Sportster rides pretty much the same as a brand new 883-cc model. Comfort and power are excellent for street and touring use. Parts are plentiful, and dealer support is strong.

Fountain of Youth

When you rode a Sportster CH, your chest was bigger and your waist was smaller. Everybody was looking at you. At a stoplight, even if you turned your head quickly and found that car driver next to you was staring straight ahead, you knew he'd been looking at you—and wishing. Wishing he was in your T-shirt, tight jeans, and loafers, and holding on to your handlebars, looking for action. Instead, he was in his sport coat, button-down-collared shirt, and polyester pants, holding on the steering wheel of his Chevrolet Delray, and on his way to the Jay Cees meeting. You were 30 going on 20; he was 30 going on 50. He was your basic domesticated male, made with a cookie cutter to be just like every other guy in his suburb. You were you.

1963 Sportster

Hold on tight! In 1963, the Sportster was the baddest stock motorcycle you could buy. A properly running stocker would eat a stock Triumph's lunch. That's what mattered. © H-D Michigan, Inc.

1963 Sportster

Twin "shorty" exhaust pipes debuted on the XLH and XLCH models. The 1963 Sportsters had a taller third-gear ratio (1.323:1 instead of 1.381:1) resulting in third and fourth gears being "closer." © H-D Michigan, Inc.

1964 Sportster CH

As usual, new tank panels graced both the H and CH Sportsters in 1964. © H-D Michigan, Inc.

1964 Sportster
The 1964 XLH and XLCH had full width aluminum hubs, aluminum tappets, and a polyacrylic clutch oil seal. © H-D Michigan, Inc.

1965 Sportster H
A 12-volt electrical system debuted on the 1965 XLH, hinting at the electric starting that would come a year later. © H-D Michigan, Inc.

1965 Sportster H

Mystery bike. This is the 1965 Sportster road tested by *Cycle World*, but the motorcycle doesn't have the white tank-top trim shown in the catalogs. The road tester said the bike ". . . had flecks of dirt, or something, in its paint." So was this Sportster repainted by the dealer or did it leave the factory this way? © Cycle World

1965 Sportster CH

The tachometer was moved to the side of the speedometer. The Sportster CH was still the performance king in 1965. "A brute for strength in any situation," reported Petersen's *The Complete Book Of Motorcycling.* © H-D Michigan, Inc.

Chapter 10

Italian-Built Models

In the 1950s, Harley-Davidson was wrongly accused of showing no interest in the market for medium-sized motorcycles popularized by British manufacturers. Actually, from 1956 through 1959, the company made three attempts to launch a smaller and less costly model aimed at the bulk of the market. All three attempts were undone by projected high costs.

In January 1956, a huge price, weight, and performance gap existed in the lineup between the ST 165 cc two-stroke and the KH 900 cc V-twin. Based on dealer and rider feedback, the sales department and management concluded there was a need for an "in-between" model to bridge the gap. Over the next six months, the engineering department prepared layout drawings for a 30.50-cubic inch (500-cc) overhead-valve single-cylinder model with front and rear suspension. It was to be equipped with a four-speed, foot-shift transmission, and intended for riding on and off the roads; the model had a projected weight of 350–400 pounds. From the layout drawings, the production staff estimated the tooling and materials costs, and in turn the necessary sales price was clearly established. In July 1956 the management concluded the necessary selling price would be too high, so the 30.50 single was dropped from further consideration.

In October 1956, the engineering department began consideration of a 350-cc two-stroke twin-cylinder in-between model. In May 1957, a progress report was presented to management, which then approved further engineering effort. It was to be a completely new motorcycle in every respect. In late 1958, time schedules, tooling and pricing estimates were solidified. The time schedule called for 1962 introduction. The management concluded the extended schedule was too risky and the projected selling price was too high, so the all-new twin was removed from further consideration.

In April 1959, the management approved preliminary engineering design of a compromise in-between model. This was to consist of a 400-cc two-stroke twin-cylinder engine housed in a Sportster frame. By using the Sportster frame, the estimated tooling cost fell from $400,000 to $100,000. Also, the compromise model could be launched in 1961, a reduction in lead time from four years to two. Engineering work continued until June 1959, at which time the management concluded the necessary selling price would still be uncompetitive.

In June 1959, the management decided to investigate the feasibility of importing the Italian-made Aermacchi 250-cc single-cylinder motorcycle. The management also decided to consider the possibility and feasibility of entering into a joint production arrangement with

1965 Sprints
And the last shall be first, said the prophet, so this 1965 scene is our tone-setter for the 1961–1965 Italian-built models. Clever advertising, this is, because the foreign-built (gasp!) Sprints are immersed in an All-American scene. © H-D Michigan, Inc.

1961 Sprint
For the 1961 season Harley-Davidson introduced the Sprint, built by Harley's newly-purchased Italian subsidiary, Aermacchi. The fully serviced weight of only 270 pounds combined with the high torque 250-cc (15-cubic inch) engine to produce peppy performance. © H-D Michigan, Inc.

Aermacchi. The Graham Parker consulting firm was hired to study these possibilities, after good references were obtained from A. O. Smith (consultant) and the Chain Belt company. Chain Belt had used Graham Parker in the process of purchasing an Italian subsidiary, Regina. For Harley-Davidson, Graham Parker studied possibilities in Japan and the nations of the European Common Market. The Harley-Davidson management concluded business conditions weren't good in Japan. Among

other factors, except for the Aermacchi machines, the European models that might possibly be imported were deemed inadequate. Harley-Davidson decided to pursue the possibility of buying a majority interest in Aermacchi, as the management felt they needed executive control in order to retain dealer confidence.

In 1961, Harley-Davidson brought out the Italian-made Aermacchi 250-cc (15-cubic inch) single-cylinder overhead-valve motorcycle and renamed it the Harley-Davidson Sprint. The company was at last ready with an in-between model.

The Sprint had an up-to-date look because of its unusual nearly horizontal cylinder disposition. The 250-cc (15-cubic inch) engine itself, however, was a conservative design. The "under-square" bore and stroke measured 2.60 and 2.84 inches, respectively, and valve actuation was by conventional pushrods. The single-cylinder configuration was in the mainstream but at a time when Japanese 250-cc twins were hitting our shores in larger and larger numbers.

Engine ....Overhead-valve single-cylinder with pushrod valve actuation
Bore and stroke...............2.60x2.84 in
Displacement ....246 cc (15 ci)
Lubrication ....Automotive-style wet sump
Compression ratio
Sprint 8.5:1
Sprint H 9.2:1
Power
Sprint ....18 hp @ 7,500 rpm
Sprint H ....21 hp @ 7,500 rpm
Transmission ....Four-speed, constant-mesh type, unit construction with the engine
Shift   Right foot
Shift pattern ....Up for low
Primary drive ....Helical gears
Clutch ....Multiple disks, wet, hand actuated
Gear ratios, overall
4th 5.94:1
3rd 7.54:1
2nd 10.4:1
1st 17.3:1
Wheelbase......................52 in
Wheels and tires
Sprint, front ....3.00x17 in
Sprint, rear ....3.00x17 in
Sprint H, front ....3.00x18 in
Sprint H, rear..................3.50x18 in
Suspension
Front ....Telescopic fork
Rear   ....Swinging arm
Weight
Sprint ....270 lb
Sprint H ....280 lb
Saddle height
Sprint ....29 in
Sprint H ....29.7 in
Foot-peg height
Sprint ....11.5 in
Sprint H ....12.6 in
Fuel capacity ....4 gal
Oil capacity ....4 qt
Fuel consumption...........35–50 mpg
Speeds
Sprint 75 mph (top speed without windshield or saddlebags)
Sprint H ....76 mph (after 1/2-mile acceleration)
Sprint H ....90 mph @ 7,600 rpm (top speed; requires tail wind or downhill)

1961–1965 Sprints

Collectibility	★★☆☆☆
Comfortable cruising speed	60 mph
Smoothness of ride	★★★★☆
Passenger accommodations	★★★☆☆
Reliability	★★★☆☆
Parts/service availability	★★☆☆☆

Sprints felt great, but the company couldn't convey the feel of this motorcycle in advertising print. Worse yet, Sprints were overpriced and underfeatured for successful marketing, a game in which statistics were the whole show. The competition Sprints were another matter entirely; check them out in the next chapter. Along with the American-made two-strokes, the Italian models offer the least costly way to get into old Harleys. But are the Italian-born machines really Harleys? That's the problem. The tanks were labeled "Harley-Davidson," and Harley-Davidson dealers sold them. Harley-Davidson made some bucks every time an Italian model was sold, here or anywhere else, because Harley-Davidson was majority holder of Aermacchi stock. Milwaukee ran the Italian outfit, in other words. So Aermacchi-built motorcycles are closer to being Harleys than foreign-built bikes were to being Indians. So I guess the Aermacchi bikes were Harleys. I guess.

Journalists of the era said the Sprint engine ran backwards, meaning it spun in the opposite direction of the rear wheel. I fail to see how this made the engine run backwards in as much as the motorcycle didn't back up when the clutch was dropped. Anyway, the motor ran that way for two reasons. First, this permitted the helical-gear primary drive to use only one driving gear and one driven gear. Conventional engine spinning would've required an intermediate idler gear between the engine gear and the transmission gear. The second reason for the unconventional engine rotation was that this slung crankcase oil up into the cylinder bore instead of away from the bore.

Incidentally, the constant phraseology of writers—then and now—to the effect that flywheels sling crankcase oil has become rather tiresome. The truth of the matter is that the flywheels probably do about 1/10 of 1 percent of the slinging. Most of the oil is slung by the crankpin and the connecting rods. In fact, I have a hunch that if an experiment were set up with an electric motor spinning a flywheel half immersed in a trough of thin oil (as it is when it's hot), that it would take quite some time to make a significant amount of oil leave the trough. One hopes to educate—don't one.

The rest of the Sprint showed some of the postwar European influence that had, until the upstart Japanese movement, put Continental

1961 Sprint
In 1961, most Americans held Italian motor vehicles in higher esteem than Japanese motor vehicles. The Aermacchi company, builder of the Sprints, was ripe for takeover, but no such opportunity existed in Japan. These factors led to Harley-Davidson's purchase of the controlling interest of Aermacchi. © H-D Michigan, Inc.

lightweight motorcycle engineering ahead of all others. The gear-driven primary drive wasn't found on any of the British 250s. The frame featured a single large-diameter tube as its main component, a configuration that offered great strength and minimum weight. In fact, the Sprint tipped the scales at a relatively light 270 pounds, fully serviced. Another reason for the light weight was the compact layout. The Sprint fork and rear suspension units were about 10 percent shorter than such units on British rivals. You know that it's easier to break a new long pencil than an old short one; in the same way, the compact configuration of the Sprint allowed additional weight-cutting without sacrificing strength.

How did the Sprint measure up? Not so well. The problem was that the Italian machine was designed to compete against other European 250s and against a rather humdrum array of British 250s. Harley-Davidson didn't fully appreciate the strength of the Japanese brands, which were just beginning to come to the United States in large numbers.

Here is a chilling comparison of the Sprint versus the Honda Super Hawk on road test data from *Cycle World,* February 1962 (Sprint) and May 1962 (Super Hawk).

Item	H-D Sprint	Honda Super Hawk
Number cylinders	One	Two
Valve actuation	Pushrod	Overhead cam
Horsepower	18	28
Starting	Kick	Electric
Top speed	75 mph	104.6 mph
1/4-mile accel.	19.4 sec, 63 mph	16.8 sec, 83 mph
Price	$695	$665

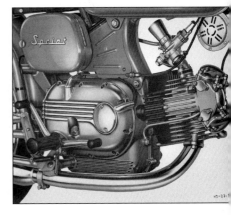

1961 Sprint
The horizontal engine layout was unusual, as was the automobile-style wet-sump lubrication system. But the pushrod valve actuation and single-cylinder configuration were conservative design features. © H-D Michigan, Inc.

The higher-performance Sprint H fared little better in the comparison. Worse still, the 250-cc Sprint H performed no better than the 160-cc Honda CB-160. According to *Cycle World* road test data for the Sprint H (April 1963) and the Honda CB-160 (May 1965), the 21-horsepower Sprint could turn the quarter in 19.2 seconds with a terminal speed of 66 miles per hour. The little 160-cc CB-160 used its 16.5

1962 Sprint

In the Harley-Davidson tradition, each new model year brought some styling change to the tanks. Here we see the slightly different white tank trim of the 1962 Sprint. Folding foot pegs were a new feature. The company said the chrome quality was improved for 1962. © H-D Michigan, Inc.

1962 Sprint

The large tank, narrow bars, and compact riding position suggested the Sprint's Italian origin and its readiness for spirited riding along twisty roads. On the 1962 Sprints traditional large handle-grips and a larger tank cap were fitted. © H-D Michigan, Inc.

horsepower to go the same distance 18.6 seconds with a terminal speed of 69 miles per hour. The top speed of the Sprint H was 76 miles per hour. No top speed was listed for the CB-160; Honda claimed 72 miles per hour; I can personally swear to an indicated 72 miles per hour top speed, and an indicated 67-mile-per-hour cruising speed for hundreds of miles on the CB-160. Kick in the groin time: the Sprint H was listed at $720 and the CB-160 at $530. Oh yeah, the little Honda had electric starting and two cylinders.

Hold the phone. After a year of CB-160 fun, your author traded up (?) to a single-cylinder BSA 250 Starfire. The BSA 250 had about the same performance as the Sprint. The Beezer would run an indicated 85-mile-per-hour top speed, probably an actual 80 miles per hour, but that wasn't the issue with me. Nor was the very smooth BSA cruising speed of 60 miles per hour. No, I just liked the BSA's handling, looks, and sound. The point is: I would very likely have bought a Sprint for the same reasons, but that would have been frowned on by the BSA shop where I worked part time! In the ensuing two years of my motorcycling apprenticeship, I'd covered the spectrum with, in this order, a BSA 650, a Harley-Davidson Duo-Glide, a Suzuki 120 trail bike, and a Honda CB-160. I learned during this time that much of what I like or don't like in a motorcycle has to do with how the motorcycle feels. Comparing motorcycles can be like comparing a nylon-string classic guitar with a state-of-the art electric guitar. Comparisons can become pointless.

Or how about this? The standard piano keyboard has 88 keys. Suppose somebody added an 89th key at the high (right) end of the keyboard, but removed, say, 12 keys from the left end of the keyboard. A musical engineer could then brag about a "higher" performance piano because a higher pitch could be achieved. But such a wood cutter would've given up plenty of versatility to get a marginal gain at the top end. That, in my opinion, is what often happened with recent motorcycle designs. No, I'm not saying that the Japanese bikes stunk after all. Just that, for me, evaluating motorcycles became a more subjective process. I stopped limiting myself to the raw numbers.

But meanwhile, back in the fiercely competitive American motorcycle market of the 1960s, most buyers stuck to the raw numbers.

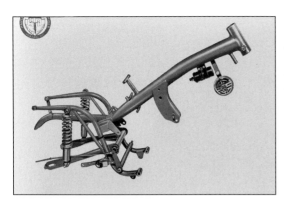

1962 Sprint
One of the keys to the Sprint's lightweight was the unusual frame. The large diameter single-backbone produced great torsional strength with a minimum of metal. © H-D Michigan, Inc.

1962 Sprint H
For enthusiasts inclined to a little off-road riding, Harley-Davidson introduced the 1962 Sprint H in midseason. The Sprint H had a larger carburetor and higher compression ratio, resulting in a maximum output of 21 horsepower compared to the regular Sprint's 18 horsepower. © H-D Michigan, Inc.

1963 Sprint H
According to the April 1963 *Cycle World*, "Riding this lightweight, whether on dirt or pavement, was great fun." *Cycle World* also liked the large handlebar grips. © H-D Michigan, Inc.

Sprint sales averaged 2,143 per year for 1963–1965 (1961 and 1962 figures unavailable), reports *The Legend Begins*. In the years beyond the scope of this book and available in *The Legend Begins*, 1966–1969, Sprint sales were much better. In the late 1960s, the yearly average was 5,756. Still, in comparison to the tide of Japanese lightweights, the Sprint and Sprint H never became popular. I liked them anyway.

In 1965, Harley-Davidson began importing an Aermacchi 50-cc step-through, that is, a lightweight styled somewhat like a girl's bicycle.

1963 Sprint
The new 1963 tank styling is shown here. Heavier gauge rear frame tubing, a larger battery, and a new 60-watt generator were features of the 1963 Sprint. © *H-D Michigan, Inc.*

1964 Sprint
A big Sprint plus was the helical gear primary drive, which was rugged and smooth. On the 1964 Sprints, the primary gears were made wider. © *H-D Michigan, Inc.*

Dubbed the Harley-Davidson M-50, the little single featured oil-mist lubrication that required the rider to hand-mix the engine oil with the gasoline. A three-speed twistgrip-operated transmission and hand-operated clutch enabled the tiddler to get away and climb up to a cruising speed of 20–25 miles an hour and a top speed of about 35 miles an hour. The M-50 was woefully lacking in comparison to Japanese 50-cc bikes. Still, Harley-Davidson managed to sell 9,000 of the 1965 models, says *The Legend Begins*, which was almost one-third of total sales. The M-50 and 65-cc derivatives were carried in the lineup through 1969, with steadily decreasing sales.

Sprint Development

The Sprint was first imported as a 1961 model. The 1962 model year saw a number of functional changes. Harley-Davidson claimed

1964 Sprint H
The 1964 Sprints got detailed mechanical improvements and new tank panels. © *H-D Michigan, Inc.*

1964 Sprint
He seems to have said,"Why don't we get a pizza for lunch and get the complete Italian experience?" The 1964 saddle was wider and softer. © *H-D Michigan, Inc.*

improved finish of internal parts, changes in the valve keys and collars for longer life, waterproofing of the circuit breaker, sturdier wheel rims with full-seating spoke nipples, a new kickstarter segment gear to disengage at the bottom of the stroke, stronger chain, wider primary drive gears, improved automatic spark advance to provide full retard for better starting, and carburetor float bowl moved to the right side to eliminate overflow.

The new dual-purpose Sprint H was introduced in the middle of the 1962 season. The H was equipped with a high-level exhaust, a high-clearance front fender, and a shorter rear fender. Enhancing the off-road capabilities was a large canister air cleaner. The compression ratio was upped from 8.5:1 to 9.2:1, and the carburetor size from 0.95 inch to 1.18 inches, so that peak output rose (17 percent) from 18 to 21 horsepower.

I walk up on the left side, the normal thing to do, but notice something abnormal. The Sprint is leaning to the right, resting on its right-side kickstand. I've never seen a motorcycle parked this way.

I've read the magazines, about how hard it is to kickstart a Sprint. But I have an advantage over riders of the era. I've been able to listen to the old hands, and they've told me what sometimes causes a starting problem. The occasional problem is the lack of a suitable ignition control. The Sprint automatic ignition advance doesn't delay the spark long enough. All other pre-1966 Harley-Davidsons have a manual ignition control, with which it's possible to retard (delay) the spark so much that the engine will idle like a tractor. Although the tractor idle is fun, that's not the reason for manual control. The super-retarded spark, happening at top dead center, or maybe even slightly later, robs other Harley engines of the ability to kick back. But here's the Sprint, ready to snap back if I hesitate. So I won't be timid.

I grab the bars and pull the Sprint vertical. The "key" is one of those curious push-pull things like those used on old BMWs. I push it into the receptacle on top of the headlight, push until I feel the first detent mate with the ball-and-spring holding mechanism. This is the "off" position.

I look down, searching for the so-called carburetor tickler. They aren't ticklers to me, because pushing the thing up and down doesn't pump any fuel. I press down on the tickler, which holds the float down, and I hold the tickler down until I see a little gasoline seeping through the carburetor-cover gasket. Gasoline has now overflowed into the inlet port, providing a rich mixture for starting. I release the tickler. With a tickler you don't need a choke, even in cold weather.

I unfold the kickstarter. Its left-side perch drew criticism in period magazines, and I'd also prefer a right-side starter so I can get my full weight on the pedal. But, hey, it's only a 250. I push the key down until the next detent signals the key is in the "on" position. I roll the throttle back until about the one-eighth-on position and kick smartly downward. Instant thump-thump-thumps. Nothing to it.

I sit on the saddle, which is quite hard, in the Italian tradition. Theoretically, I'm letting the engine warm up, but the Sprint's steady beat signals it's ready whenever I am. I'm not ready to ride. First comes the flick-about test. I lean the Sprint to the left, then to the right, and repeat this with a quicker action. The all-up weight of only about 300 pounds and the lowness of the Sprint make this child's play.

I've had the briefing. The shifter is on the right side, and it's up for low and down for the rest, just the opposite of industry standards. I pull in the left-hand clutch and pull up on the foot-shift lever, then rev the motor until it has that 30-miles-an-hour sound and ease out the clutch. We're away, and smartly.

We move swiftly into second, as I imagine the muted single-cylinder sounds like a polite BSA Gold Star flat-tracker. I play out second gear until 30 miles an hour, about 5,000 rpm and three-fourths of maximum engine speed. I back off on the throttle, de-clutch, and almost pull up on the lever, but remember to press down again to engage third.

I cruise at 30 miles an hour in third gear, for about a minute, the Sprint signaling it's happy at this pace. I shift into fourth and hold the 30-miles-an-hour gait. Pleasant sounds. And the low-speed thumping feels so good. I slow to a pace between 20 and 25, about as slow as the engine wants to spin. The gear-driven primary lends a solid feel, and there's no chain snatch. I down-shift to third, roll on the throttle, and the speed climbs leisurely to 30, then more briskly to 50, where I shift to fourth (high).

Through the gears, and now in fourth, the Sprint vibrates more than I'd expected. It's not rough, as singles go, but I'd imagined the horizontal cylinder would make the Sprint smoother than my BSA 250-cc Star Fire of long ago. If my 20-year-old memory is correct, the Sprint isn't smoother.

The medium-rise handlebars produce the classic American sit-up-and-beg riding position. This is fine for a motorcycle without a windshield, provided most of the riding is below 70 miles an hour, and that's the case with the Sprint. The typically large Harley-Davidson grips feel a little strange at first on such a small motorcycle, but I decide I like the grips. The rubber-mounted handlebars produce a strange sensation, wiggling ever so slightly at the fork mounting.

While the handlebars are okay, I question the wisdom of the foot-peg location. There's not much distance between the saddle and the pegs, so my legs are bent back sharply at the knees. This is okay for short jaunts or road racing behind a fairing. In fact, the high pegs signal the Sprint's Italian roots, where the home versions are equipped with flat, low handlebars. In Italy, they say, grandmothers on 50-cc tiddlers on their way to the supermarkets settle into the racing crouch and troll for challengers. I think if I were crouched over low bars or clip-ons and with my torso straight, my hips would be rotated on the saddle enough to reduce the bending at the knees. Anyway, with these bars and footpegs I wouldn't want to go more than 100 miles down the road.

Handling is excellent, as I expected for a motorcycle not all that different from its road-racing cousins that won many international grands prix as well as some Daytona races in the 1960s. I flick the Sprint right and left through sharp curves with abandon, its light weight and low-down geometry inviting me to go ever faster along this twisty road.

The brakes are good, not that I do a panic stopping test, but they work well. Down-shifting isn't as easy as on other foot-shift bikes because of the upward action, but up-shifting is easier once you remember the pattern. I finish the ride and put the Sprint in neutral. I listen to the steady thump-thump idle. There's something indescribably pleasant about the sounds and the feel of a one-lunger, and like the V-twin bug, you either have the single-cylinder bug or you don't. I have it.

Sprint and M-50 Rideability

Sprint: You can comfortably cruise a Sprint at 60 miles per hour. Handling is delightful. One- and two-passenger riding is accommodated by the bench-style saddles (more than one design over the years), though the saddles are too stiff. I don't rate them highly rideable for the same reason I penalized the Ks and KHs. There just isn't enough dealer support. So restoring and maintaining one means you will have to personally honcho the tasks.

M-50: Okay for around-the-corner runs and one homo sapiens on board. But don't carry another homo sapiens, or, for that matter, even a canis familiaris or felis catus as a passenger. If you had an M-50 30 years ago and want to relive that part of your youth, go ahead. Otherwise, these don't make much sense because of the lack of power.

DOO Dah Dah DOO Dah Dah DOO Dah

Sprints were designed by Rod Serling. They had to be. Didn't Serling and his Twilight Zone have the copyright to the old "parallel universe" plot? You know, the idea that there's another earth running side-by-side with this one, accessible for mere moments and only through a rare and accidental portal opened up by a lightning strike or a nuclear accident. Interlopers into parallel-earth always find things are strikingly similar to main-earth, yet different in important ways. For example, in parallel-earth you actually see people riding around on Sprints. No, not at the short track races or the Daytona oval, but down Main Street and County Road Number 1. In main-earth, Sprints were very seldom ridden. They were mostly used to fill up the empty showroom floor spaces between real Harleys. When purchased, the terms of the agreement required the new owner to take the Aermacchi to another city, or, preferably, to another state. If the invisible man had been a 1960s motorcyclist, he would've bought a Sprint.

1965 Sprint
New adjustable footrests were provided on the 1965 Sprint and Sprint H. © H-D Michigan, Inc.

1965 Sprint H
The new low-level exhaust system signaled a retreat from the previous dual-purpose theme of the Sprint H. © H-D Michigan, Inc.

Both the 1961 and 1962 Sprint road models were designed for the traditional European riding position. The semi-racing crouch was inspired by motorcycle road racing, which was the third most popular spectator sport in Europe (after soccer and car racing). But, and I was surprised to learn this by trying it, a crouched riding position can be quite comfortable. The European tradition was to lean forward with the spine straight. The spinal muscles are very strong, and they take up the strain so that the weight on the wrists isn't excessive. With the spine kept straight, one's hips are rotated slightly, and the upper body weight is supported by both the hips and the thighs. The American tradition was to sit up straight, so Americans didn't know how to posture themselves on the earlier Sprints. Instead of keeping the back straight, Americans would bend at the waist. On long rides this produced both a sore back and sore arms.

1965 M-50
The Aermacchi-built M-50 was a simple low-cost machine. Lubrication was by oil mist spray from the hand-mixed fuel/oil mixture. Amazingly, one of every three 1965 Harley-Davidsons was an M-50, according to *The Legend Begins*. © H-D Michigan, Inc.

1965 M-50

Collectibility	★☆☆☆☆
Comfortable cruising speed	20 mph
Smoothness of ride	★★☆☆☆
Passenger accommodations	★☆☆☆☆
Reliability	★★☆☆☆
Parts/service availability	★☆☆☆☆

The M-50 is your basic pre-Columbian motorcycle. On the plus side, it has inflatable tires rather than solid rubber.

The 1963 model year saw Harley-Davidson give up on the European riding position designed into the previous Sprints. "Hi-Level" bars were fitted. With a "sit up and beg" riding position, one's hips take up all the body weight, so a new saddle was also provided. Other functional improvements included a stronger lower end bearing, lightweight racing tappets, improved oil filter, provision for a tachometer drive, and a redesigned shifter spring. The standard Sprint also got a 60-watt-output generator, a larger battery, and heavier-gauge rear frame tubing.

For model year 1964, the following updates were made: new clutch lining material, stellite-faced tappets, and a new oil pump with higher pressure and output. A conventional ignition key was installed on the left side near the saddle.

For the 1965 model year the Sprint and Sprint H got wider saddles. The Sprint H was fitted with a low-profile exhaust system and a new crankcase breather tube that discharged below frame level.

Racers and Hillclimbers

Today, Harley-Davidson has a rich racing heritage, but prior to 1914 the company had nothing to do with the sport. The 1914 lineup of stock F-head motorcycles saw the first indication of Harley-Davidson interest in speed. Optional faster "A" motors with a larger (3/4-inch) inlet manifold were offered. The A motors had looser clearances and probably also had larger valves; this isn't absolutely clear from factory documentation. In 1914, the first Harley-Davidson factory racing team rode motorcycles that were simply stripped-down stock models with motors further evolved from the stock A motors. The success of the A motors (and perhaps other experiments) led to the 1915 stock motors with larger valves and inlet manifold.

In 1915 the "Chicago" F-head motors debuted at the Chicago speedway for the 300-Mile National Championship. Although a Chicago-built Excelsior won the race, a Harley-Davidson established a new 100-mile record. The Chicago motors featured special cylinders to work with the narrow 1914-style crankcases. (I was mistaken in my earlier book, *Inside Harley-Davidson*; the spark plugs were not placed in the combustion chamber proper.) At about this time, for dealers and non-factory riders, the company began building "500"-series fast motors, so named because the motor numbers were all in the 500–599 range. These replaced the A motors as the fastest engines produced in quantity. The 500-series motors used looser clearances throughout.

In 1916, three racing models were advertised: the 16-R twin-cylinder speed roadster, the 16-S single-cylinder stripped stock model, and the 16-T twin-cylinder stripped stock model. Most key features, such as fork, handlebars, clutch, and brake, were optional. All racing models were cataloged with shorter-than-standard "short-coupled" frames, made possible by a rear-hub clutch that did away with the countershaft. But the wheelbase for each was listed along with the modifier "or optional."

Too late for inclusion in the 1916 model announcements were the exciting new eight-valve twins and four-valve singles, featuring all overhead valves. To get the best possible results, Harley-Davidson hired England's Harry Ricardo, who was the leading free-lance theorist and practitioner in the young science of cylinder-head-flow physics. In designing the eight-valves and four-valves, Ricardo enjoyed the benefit of recent engine design advancements brought on by the rapid aviation buildup for World War I. Therefore, the Harley racers featured hemispherical combustion chambers, domed pistons, and valves with a 90-degree included angle. This was in contrast to the 1911 Indian four-

1915 Chicago-Motor F-Head Racer

Collectibility	★★★★★
Other factors	N/A

The first really fast Harley racers. Rare. The distinguishing feature is the narrow 1914-style crankcase coupled with the 1915 and later cylinders.

1916 Model 16R Twin

Collectibility	★★★★★
Other factors	N/A

These were the first cataloged racing twins. Find one if you can.

1916 Model 16S Single

Collectibility	
Usually	★★★★☆
With documented championship history	★★★★★
Other factors	N/A

The singles had less charisma than the companion racing twin; they were mainly used for half-mile dirt-track races of lesser stature than one-mile dirt-track and road-race courses.

valve racing singles and eight-valve racing twins designs, which used parallel valves and flat-topped pistons.

The 1916 eight-valve and four-valve motors were laid out with the standard F-head bore and stroke of 3 5/16x3 1/2 inches Also in line with F-head practice were the one-piece combined cylinders and cylinder heads. Exiting each head were two short exhaust pipes. The F-head valve mechanism was modified so that the valve action was generated by a four-lobe cam instead of a two-lobe cam. This enabled valve timing to be set strictly by reshaping the cams, instead of by the less-clear and more-difficult F-head racing practice of reshaping the valve lifters (or cam followers). About six first-generation eight-valve twins were built, and they were immediately successful, one of them providing the winning ride at the 1916 Dodge City 300, the nation's most prestigious race.

The year 1919 saw the next eight-valve update. The valve gear was changed to the so-called "two-cam" principle. Rather than meaning the introduction of a second cam lobe—there had always been at least two lobes—the term meant a switch from one camshaft to two camshafts, with each of the two shafts supporting two cam lobes. The reason for changing to a two-cam configuration was to incorporate shorter and therefore lighter

F-head racer
This is a Two-Cam racer from the 1924–1927 era. Factory rider Joe Petrali rode a similar motorcycle at the 1925 Altoona, Pennsylvania, board track race. He set the all-time 100-mile board-track record, averaging over 100 miles per hour.

valve lifters (cam followers), which would permit higher engine speeds. These racers (and later road-model derivatives) became known as "Two Cams." Although the two-cam principle debuted on the eight-valve twins, the new valve action was incorporated on F-head racers, and in fact, most Two Cam racers were F-head configured.

Externally, the first Two Cams were distinguished by the timing case cover, which eventually was termed a "banjo" cover. Only one intermediate idler gear was used to separate the rear cam gear from the magneto drive gear, so the idler gear had to be large in order to bridge the gap. The shaft of this idler gear drove the oil pump, which was mounted to the gear-case cover. Because the idler gear was large, it spun slowly, and therefore the racing oil pump was unusually large. Drilled connecting rods were fitted. As with the road models, the flywheels were "spoked;" that is, they were cast with large openings between the crankpin web and the other flywheel supporting webs. Over the years these Two Cam motors were referred to as "banjo motors." Only four are known to have survived, two with F-head cylinders and two with eight-valve cylinders. Incidentally, from this era only three F-head racers with the standard (not Two Cam) valve gear are known to have survived.

Circa 1920 board track action
From 1919 through the late 1920s, board tracks of one mile or longer were used for motorcycle and automobile racing. Harley-Davidson fielded teams of salaried riders, backed up by a full racing department. Riders rode as a team, using a thorough signaling system to communicate. Harleys won most of the long races from 1915 through 1930, at Indian's great expense. © H-D Michigan, Inc.

1922 Model 22-S Single Racer
The Model 22-S was basically half of a V-twin. Singles of this shape and size were used for half-mile dirt-track racing from the 1910s through the mid-1920s. This photo was used in the 1922 competition catalog. © H-D Michigan, Inc.

In 1920, for dealers and favored riders interested in racing, Harley-Davidson introduced "E" motors to replace the 500-series motors used since about 1915. The E motors were fitted with drilled connecting rods and aluminum pistons. Factory instructions stressed the need to vary the compression ratio according to the race length; the longer the race, the lower the compression ratio. The compression ratio was varied by inserting various thicknesses of plates under the cylinders. Other racing tips included sprocket options and the use of low-grade fuel to reduce overheating during long races. Tear-down and inspection were recommended at 100-mile intervals. As with the 500-series motors, fittings were looser throughout.

In 1920, a "dealer's racing frame" was introduced. The frame was open at the bottom. This permitted the installation of either the latest E motors or the earlier 500-series motors by using different motor-supporting side plates.

As of 1921, the A motors were still optional. Superseded as racers about 1915, the A motors were used for police work, where the looser clearances of the A motors added both speed and reliability in this environment. The 1921 eight-valve and four-valve motors were new. Each cylinder still was combined with its head in one casting. Instead of two conventional round exhaust ports, each head had two moderately elongated, somewhat-triangular open exhaust ports.

In 1923 the racing Two Cam timing case was redesigned. A new magneto drive gear train featured two intermediate idler gears between the rear cam gear and the magneto drive gear, and since these idler gears were smaller than those on the old banjo-cover Two Cam, the idler gears spun faster. The faster-spinning idler gears resulted in a normal-sized oil pump, which was driven by the idler gear closest to the rear cam gear. Like many Harley-Davidson features, the timing-gear cover of the 1923 and later Two Cams eventually got its own nickname. They were eventually known as "peanut" covers. On the top of the new right crankcase were four small cast-in cylindrical protrusions that housed the valve lifter blocks (tappets). The lifter blocks transmitted the motion of the valve lifters (cam followers) to the pushrods. As with the banjo motors, some were eight-valves but most were F-heads.

1916–1927 Eight-Valve Twins

Collectibility	
Authentic	★★★★★
With remanufactured cylinders, frame, etc.	★★★★☆
Other factors	N/A

These are ultimate in Harley-Davidson racing history and glory. The handful of eight-valves with remanufactured cylinders are a problem. What are they, restored period pieces or retro bikes? But even a home-grown eight-valve is a four-star, to me.

1916–1924 Four-Valve Singles

Collectibility	
Usually	★★★★☆
With documented championship history	★★★★★
Other factors	N/A

These models had less charisma than companion twins; the singles were used mainly used for half-mile dirt-track races of lesser stature than one-mile dirt-track and road-race courses.

1917–1929 Miscellaneous Racers—Non-Two Cam F-Head Racers/Hillclimbers, with Factory Racing Frame or "Dealer's" Racing Frame

Collectibility	★★★★☆
Other factors	N/A

More local-interest races were won by these models than by the glamorous Two Cams, because Joe Rider could buy a "one-cam" but couldn't buy a Two Cam until 1928. Factory or dealer's racing frames are distinguished by a shorter-than-stock wheelbase, and either no countershaft provision or provision for a simple countershaft but no transmission mountings. The bikes either ran with a rear-wheel clutch or with no clutch.

Also in 1923 came new eight-valve and four-valve cylinders. Each cylinder still was combined with its head in one casting. Instead of two moderately elongated, somewhat-triangular open exhaust ports, each head had two very wide, oblong open ports.

In late 1924, the Two Cam valve gear received another update. The right crankcase top was changed so that the lifter blocks (tappets) were

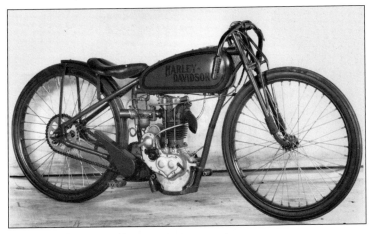

1925 Peashooter Racer
Because Harley-Davidson and Indian were launching 21.35-cubic inch (350-cc) road model singles for the 1926 model year, the companies used their clout to set up a racing class for these types. These Harley single-cylinder racers were known as "Peashooters," a term that is now applied to both road and racing versions. © H-D Michigan, Inc.

1927 Eight-valve
From 1916 through 1927, and possibly later, Harley-Davidson built a few eight-valve overheads for factory team use. These came in several varieties, including models with the "banjo" cam case cover and models with the later "peanut" cam case cover shown here. Also, there were different exhaust setups; some earlier models had traditional exhaust stacks instead of open ports. All Harley eight-valves and their four-valve single-cylinder counterparts had hemispherical combustion chambers. © H-D Michigan, Inc.

contained in removable housings. Also, the pivoted valve lifters (cam followers) were eliminated. Instead, the valves were directly moved by the cam lobes through the lifter blocks (tappets). Two Cam enthusiasts referred to motors with this valve gear as "direct-action" Two Cams.

When Harley-Davidson brought out its 21-cubic inch (350-cc) side-valve economy single in 1925, racing of these lightweights was surely in the cards. That's because Indian also had a new 21-cubic inch single, and both firms wanted to show off their new babies. These new Harley single-cylinder racers took on the nickname "Peashooter." Originally, all 21-cubic inch racers used a conventional two-valve cylinder head.

In 1927, due to the popularity of hillclimbing, Harley-Davidson began building special hillclimbers. These had a longer wheelbase, reinforced upper frame structure, and additional struts on the frame rear section.

By 1928, some Peashooters were fitted with two exhaust ports, but there was still only one exhaust valve (some pre-1928 Peashooters may have used the two-port head). Detail changes were made over the years, including, by 1928, a new cylinder head with larger cooling fins and a cast-in inlet manifold. Most of the Peashooters were delivered without brakes for dirt-track racing, but by 1928 (and perhaps earlier) some Peashooters had front and rear brakes for so-called TT racing, the forerunner of motocross. One of these TT Peashooters had motor number

1927 F-head
The engine number of this factory F-head hillclimber is 27FHAD50? (last digit illegible, correction to American Racing Motorcycles). Extra frame bracing is on the rear end. All three American factories built special Class A (unrestricted) hillclimbers. The public yearned for the V-twin sound, something they didn't get from watching single-cylinder bikes race. © H-D Michigan, Inc.

1929/30 Overhead Valve 45
The popularity of 45-cubic inch (750-cc) road models made a 45-cubic inch class obligatory in racing and hillclimbing. However, by the time Harley made a handful of 45-cubic inch specials, the only form of Class A (unrestricted) 45-cubic inch competition was hillclimbing. © H-D Michigan, Inc.

28SA531, the "SA" signifying a Schebler barrel carburetor. Incidentally, although it had been some years since the term "500 motors," Harley-Davidson still had the habit of numbering its competition jobs in the 500 series.

In 1928, the factory built two experimental V-twin hillclimber models, which copied the cylinder and cylinder-head design of the Peashooter overhead-valve singles. These were unsuccessful. Two are known to have survived.

For the 1928 and 1929 seasons, Harley-Davidson offered road-model Two Cams. Both the road-model and racing Two Cams had new removable lifter-block (tappet) housings on the top of the right crankcase. The new lifter-block housings had a raised section for oil return to the crankcase.

In 1929, Harley-Davidson introduced a 45-cubic inch (750-cc) overhead-valve hillclimber to compete with Indian 45-cubic inch overheads. Each cylinder head had two conventional round exhaust ports fitted with short exhaust pipes, but only one exhaust valve. The new hillclimber featured a stubby fuel/oil tank and a new frame with a single large curved front down tube. In 1930, the Forty-five overhead was fitted with a trailing-link front fork, still with standard Harley-Davidson upper coil springs. One of these Forty-five overhead hillclimbers with the stubby tank and trailing-link fork had motor number 30DAH507. Later, a different small but conventionally shaped fuel/oil tank was used, and this version had a different frame. The late frame featured a shorter steering head and twin small-diameter curved front down tubes.

In either 1929 or 1930, the company debuted a 30.50-cubic inch (500-cc) single-cylinder motor for hillclimbing in this class. At least one of these new motors, number 30DAB521, was placed in a road racing frame, but its ultimate use is unknown. The new two-valve twin-port motor underwent testing as a possible new road model, but the management decided not to make the overhead-valve single because it would mainly rob sales from the Forty-five side-valve

1934 Speedway Racer
This 30.50-cubic inch (500-cc) model was designed for the newly popular "short track" racing (now termed speedway racing). Speedway was the rage from 1933 through the outbreak of World War II, but didn't catch on again after the war. © H-D Michigan, Inc.

twin. At least two different cylinders and cylinder heads were built, the later version having larger cooling fins.

Another 1930 competition experiment was a Forty-five overhead-valve V-twin road-racer with twin exhaust ports. Three archival photos document this attractive motorcycle, which apparently was built for European racing.

In 1931, speedway racing became popular in the United States. For "short-track racing" as the game was then called, Harley-Davidson built one or more experimental 30.50-cubic inch (500-cc) single-cylinder motorcycles, possibly as early as 1932.

For Harley-Davidson and Indian, the Great Depression reached its bottom in 1933. Both factories were operating at less than 10 percent of their production capacities. Spectator interest in the racing of Peashooters and Peashooter derivatives had dwindled, not only because of the poor economy but also because single-cylinder racing didn't have the right magic for a nation of V-twin enthusiasts. This was all the more so because only a handful of racing stars had a real chance of winning the important races, and because factory support of these stars and their motorcycles was keeping local dealers out of the game.

To save money, the frightened factories invented a new form of racing, featuring the Harley-Davidson Forty-five side-valve versus the Indian Scout side-valve. All motorcycles had to be stock and had to be owned by their riders. No factory support was to be provided. The new game was called "Class C," as there already existed Class A for all-out factory special motorcycles and team support, and Class B for professional riders using stock motorcycles.

In 1934, the company brought out the limited-production 30.50-cubic inch (500-cc) single-cylinder CAC short-track (speedway) racer. The CAC strongly resembled JAP-powered racers of the era.

The CAC failed to win a strong following in speedway racing, which was dominated first by the English-built Rudge and then by JAP-powered specials.

The new Class C format steadily gained ground at the expense of Class A racing. In late 1936, the American Motorcycle Association (AMA) banned pre-1930 motorcycles from competition, ostensibly for safety reasons but largely because the old Two Cam F-heads were winning some races at the expense of newer Harleys. In 1938, the last Class A national championship races were conducted.

From 1933 through 1940 Harley-Davidson battled in the Class C racing wars with stripped-down versions of the road-going WL series. The specifications of the top-of-the-line Forty-fives became progressively less suitable for street and touring use, as these hopped-up, so-called road models were fitted with larger and larger inlet ports and carburetors. In reality, the top-of-the-line designation applied to racing motorcycles that went through the formality of being sold with full road equipment in order to comply with the rules of the AMA. The unofficial racers were known in 1937 and 1938 as the WLDR, in 1939 as the WLD Special, and in 1940 again as the WLDR. These street-legal Forty-fives are discussed in Chapter 3.

The 1941 WR, a brakeless flat-tracker, and WRTT, a brake-equipped road and TT racer, were milestone motorcycles. Neither

1941 WRTT
The 1941 WRTT for road races and TTs and the WR for flat-track races were the first Harley-Davidsons sold directly for Class C (stock) racing. All previous Class C racing was done with stripped-down road models. © H-D Michigan, Inc.

1941 WRTT
This WRTT road racer is outfitted with special over-sized tanks used for the Daytona Beach 200-mile race.

machine had a battery, lights, or full fenders. Thus, for the first time Harley-Davidson offered these Forty-fives as race-ready motorcycles without the trouble and expense of removing road equipment. The Harley racers were fitted with larger crankpins, new connecting rods, special inlet and exhaust cam gears, a 1-1/2-inch carburetor, and 25 percent stronger valve springs. Also, the inlet ports, manifold, and combustion chamber were polished. Additionally, the racers had lighter flat tappets (valve lifters) instead of roller tappets.

After World War II, changes to the WR and WRTT Class C racers and hillclimbers were in the details. Meanwhile, stripped-down Sixty-one and Seventy-four overhead-valve models continued to be used in TT racing.

In 1952, the K-derived KR and KRTT flat-trackers and TT road-racers debuted. The KR retained a rigid frame, but the KRTT had the new swinging arm rear suspension. These models continued in production with continuous refinements through 1969. Through the years, Harley-Davidson offered a wide range of sprockets, wheels, tires, tanks, and so forth.

Offered as an off-road model was the fully sprung 1953 KRM with no lights, bobbed front and rear fenders, a pillion pad on the rear fender, a short muffler, and a skid pan under the engine. In 1954, the KH-derived 55-cubic-inch (900 cc) KHRTT and KHRM were in the lineup as TT and off-road models, respectively. The KH engine wasn't permitted in Class C road racing, which stuck to the 45-cubic-inch (750 cc) limit for side-valve designs. According to Harley-Davidson's official publication *The Legend Begins*, the KHRM was listed only for 1954, but according to the 1955 competition sales brochure, the KHRM was still alive. Whether around for one or two seasons, the KHRM's 50-pound weight disadvantage (compared to British vertical twins) proved decisive. The overhead-valve KHRTT was sold through 1957.

In 1958, the Sportster-derived XLRTT replaced the KHRTT as a TT model. In 1964, the KRTT road racer was offered with a fairing in response to the AMA's decision to permit this equipment. Substantial KR and KRTT development occurred after 1965, which is beyond the scope of this book. Later major changes included rear suspension on the KR flat-trackers and twin carburetors on the KRTT road racers. A detailed history of the KR and KRTT models is provided by Alan Girdler's *Harley Racers*, published by Motorbooks International.

The Aermacchi built 250-cc (15-cubic inch) Sprints were built in flat-track, TT, and road-racing trim from 1961 through the end of this book's 1965 closure, and beyond. Road-racing Sprints were briefly successful at the top level of expert-class racing, where factory-sponsored riders won several road races including the 1963 and 1964 Daytona events. But by 1965, two-strokes ruled, and the road-racing Sprints quickly faded from the picture.

The Sprint's most prominent racing role was in quarter-mile short-track racing. Sprint short-trackers were prominent throughout the 1960s and were the motorcycle of choice for many dealers interested in

1917–1929 Miscellaneous Racers—Non-Two Cam F-Head Racers/Hillclimbers and Stripped-Down Stock Machines with Road-Model Frames

Collectibility	★★★★☆
Other factors	N/A

These were either poor-boy racers (three-star rating) or they are merely quick-and-dirty restorations of road models—incomplete road models, in other words (two-and-a-half-star rating).

1919–1929 Two Cam F-Head Racers

Collectibility	
Usually	★★★★☆
With documented	
championship history	★★★★★
Other factors	N/A

From 1919 through 1927 you could buy a Two Cam only if you had factory connections. Their distribution was limited to favored dealers and riders. Model years 1928 and 1929 offered these to Joe Rider. If you find a pre-1928 Two Cam, it's probably got some interesting history, but racing documentation is poor. Vital records were lost years ago.

1920 to Circa 1925 E-Motor Racers

Collectibility	★★★★☆
Other factors	N/A

These models were not the top-of-the-line racers, but they were important.

1920 to Circa 1925 Racers with Dealer Racing Frames

Collectibility	★★★★☆
Other factors	N/A

These models were not the top-of-the-line equipment, but they were important.

Racing oil tank
Harley-Davidson built a few cast-aluminum oil tanks for favored riders. Racing was supposed to have been a stock machine game. Harley-Davidson and Indian complied with the rules by cataloging racing equipment and offering it for sale.

1950 WR
From 1946 through 1949, the WR flat-trackers won most of the top flight races. Around 1950 competition from British bikes intensified. On the 1950 model the magneto could either be mounted vertically as shown here or horizontally as on earlier versions. © H-D Michigan, Inc.

sponsoring a local hot-shot rider. Sprint short-trackers put on many an impressive display. I recall watching a missing Sprint during the Daytona-week short-track program that featured the nation's top racing stars. The sputtering Sprint passed every smooth-running rival—like they were parked! Two-strokes eventually took over short-track racing as they had taken over road racing. Too bad.

Johnny Racer, Peter Philanthropist

Pick your era and your image. They're both for sale. An old racer or hillclimber won't be ridden much, outside of your garage. They're excellent for garage use, by the way. I recommend pajamas and bathrobe, and be sure your wife has already gone to bed. Even if your old iron is actually raced in today's old-bike circuit, the amount of running time isn't going to be much. Besides, another guy younger than you will probably do the riding, as your jockey. Impractical? Hell, yes! After all, for the money, you could've gotten Delaware—not the board game, the actual state. But the old competition bikes include the cream of the cream. To own one is to own a piece of history, a work of art. As good as an old battle axe is for you, there's a big multiplier effect because of all the timid souls like me who get to admire it for a few minutes when your treasure is on display. In other words, you too can be a philanthropist. Remember, decades from now, your widow will be so grateful when she trades your eight-valve for New York.

1952 KRTT
This 1952 KRTT is equipped for TT racing, in which brakes were permitted. © H-D Michigan, Inc.

1954 KRM
The KRM was an off-road model built to compete with British singles and vertical twins in enduro events. The KRM and follow-on KHRM weren't successful because they were about 50 pounds heavier than the Union Jack rivals. © H-D Michigan, Inc.

1925 and Later Peashooters

Collectibility	★★★★☆
Other factors	N/A

The Peashooters divided honors with their Indian counterparts in a lackluster era. This form of racing came along after the days of multi-brand competition and salaried factory racing teams.

1927 and Later Special Hillclimbers

Collectibility	
Usually	★★★★☆
With documented championship history	★★★★★
Other factors	N/A

These models won many victories and much publicity in the 1920s and 1930s, when hillclimbing was at its zenith.

1930 and Later Forty-Five Overhead-Valve V-Twin Racers

Collectibility	★★★★☆
Other factors	N/A

Unfortunately, there are no known survivors and the racing history is insignificant.

1960s action
The essence of Harley-Davidson's motorcycle racing heritage is captured in this 1960s photo of George Roeder in brakeless half-mile dirt-track action. Long beautiful slides on half- and quarter-mile tracks are a mere memory, undone by a crazy rule change that allowed brakes. Even today's 100-plus-mile-an-hour mile-trackers never get as sideways as the mile-trackers of the 1900–1969 no-brakes era. © *H-D Michigan, Inc.*

1961 Sprint Road Racer
Road racing versions of the Sprint enjoyed much success in 1963 and 1964 but were then eclipsed by Japanese two-strokes. © *H-D Michigan, Inc.*

1931–1932 Experimental Speedway Racers

Collectibility	★★★★☆
Other factors	N/A

There are no known survivors of these models. Unfortunately, they have no notable racing history.

1934 and Later CAC Limited-Production Speedway Racers

Collectibility	★★★★☆
Other factors	N/A

Rare but not big winners.

1937–1938 WLDR and 1939 WLD Special

Collectibility	
Usually	★★★★☆
With documented championship history	★★★★★
Other factors	N/A

These were the first models designed with Class C (stock machines) racing in mind, still equipped with road equipment. Showable in racing trim. Added value with factory racing accessories.

1941 WR and WRTT

Collectibility	
Usually	★★★★⧸
With documented championship history	★★★★★
Other factors	N/A

These were sires of the series that was Harley-Davidson's racing stable through 1951; many victories and championships. Added value with factory racing accessories.

1946–1951 WR and WRTT

Collectibility	
Usually	★★★★
With documented championship history	★★★★★
Other factors	N/A

These were important, but were increasingly challenged by foreign bikes in their day.

1952–1965 KR and KRTT

Collectibility

Usually ★★★★☆

With documented
championship history ★★★★★

Other factors N/A

These were the last side-valve two-wheeled American motorcycles built in quantity. The genre dominated American racing during this period—and even beyond.

1952–1956 KRM and KHRM

Collectibility ★★★☆☆

Other factors N/A

These racers were not successful.

1958 and Later XLRTT

Collectibility

Usually ★★★☆☆

With documented
championship history ★★★★★

Other factors N/A

These racers were used only infrequently (TTs only).

1961–1965 Sprint CRTT Road Racers

Collectibility

Usually ★★★★☆

With documented
championship history ★★★★★

Other factors N/A

The Sprint road racers brought lots of good publicity to Harley-Davidson in the early 1960s, but 250-cc racing was a sideshow. Big wins at Daytona and elsewhere didn't translate into big sales for the road models.

1961–1965 Sprint Short-Trackers

Collectibility

Usually ★★★☆☆

Special frames (Sonic,
Trackmaster, etc.) ★★★★☆

With documented
star-rider history ★★★★★

Other factors N/A

These were used in lesser-stature races, but some were ridden in these races by rising-star riders.

Appendix A: Pricing Guide, Points to Consider, Dealers Listing

Asking Prices

Most classic and collectible Harley-Davidsons are sold in one-on-one deals. Listed here are some typical asking prices and price ranges of antique Harley-Davidsons offered for direct sale by owners. You will have to provide your own interpretation as to what these figures mean in your shopping situation. About all we know is that most old Harleys change hands for less than the asking price. Unless the seller is particularly adamant in advertising and in direct communication, always make a counteroffer. Sometimes the seller's expected price is shown in the asking price. For example, a price that's a few hundred dollars above a round figure like $20,000 probably means the seller is really after $20,000. So, counter with $19,000 and see what happens. When a seller who emphasizes a firm selling price, and you think the price is too high, follow up with a letter and enclosed stamped self-addressed envelope; firmness can fade after the seller gets tired of the process.

Authenticity is a major factor in the value of a classic and collectible Harley-Davidson. An authentic example is outfitted correctly when it includes only those parts and accessories that were correct at the time of original sale. For the ultimate in detailed descriptions and photos of post-1935 twins, consult Bruce Palmer's *How to Restore Your Harley-Davidson* (Motorbooks International). For all pre-1946 models, consult my *Inside Harley-Davidson* (Motorbooks International). Be particularly careful about overrestoration. Lacquer looks different from enamel and lacquer wasn't used back then. Chrome plating wasn't around prior to 1930; shiny stuff was nickel plated in those days. Harley was big on Parkerizing small parts such as brake pedals, so examine any bike carefully for correct finish details.

Eighty-three issues of *Old Bike* spanning the years 1989–1997 were reviewed—thanks to their kindness in selling all available back issues at cost. (You can subscribe to *Old Bike* by calling 815-734-1101.) After sorting through the data, I realized asking prices have gone up a lot during the period. For this reason, I decided to limit my reporting to advertised prices for the immediate two years prior to publication. Also, I limited my database to motorcycles offered for sale in the United States or Canada.

Californian Dean Rigsby (209-599-2165) is a sales agent dealing with large numbers of on-hand classic and collectible motorcycles, which range from rideable to top-quality restorations. I included his motorcycles in the database:

- Pre-1920s: no restored or rideable machines listed. Note: three years prior to publication, the oldest known Harley on the free market, a 1905 model, sold for $140,000; five years before publication, eight-valve racers went for about $30,000.
- 1920s V-twin F-heads: top quality, $25,000; rideable, $12,500.
- 1920s Peashooters: near-top quality, $14,900; no lower-quality machines listed.
- 1930s V-twin side-valves: top quality, $25,000; rideable, $12,500.
- 1936 Knuckleheads: top quality, $59,900; no lower-quality machines listed.
- Other 1930s Knuckleheads: top quality, $28,900–$35,000; no lower-quality machines listed.
- 1940s V-twin side-valves: top quality, $25,000; rideable, $9,000.
- 1940s 125s: no restored or rideable machines listed.
- 1940s Panheads: top quality, $18,500; rideable, $12,500.
- 1950s WLs and 74-cubic-inch side-valves: no restored or rideable machines listed.
- 1950s Ks and KHs: no restored machines listed; unrestored and rideable, $4,800–$6,000.
- 1950s Panheads: top quality, $13,500–$19,500; rideable, $11,500.
- 1950s 125s, 165s, and Hummers: top quality, $5,500; rideable, $3,500.
- 1950s Sportsters: no restored machines listed; rideable, $5,800.
- 1960s Panheads: top quality, $9,500–$19,500; rideable, $8,500–$16,000.
- 1960s 165s and 175s: top quality, $5,500–$6,000; no lower-quality machines listed.
- 1960s Toppers: no restored machines listed; rideable, $1,500.
- 1960 Sportsters: no restored machines listed; rideable, $6,500.

Points to Consider

Here are some points passed along by JR Harleys & Classics and by Harley-Davidson 45" Restoration Company. Forty-fives are plentiful, feasible, and cheap. Not many civilian models were exported after World War II because there were large numbers of Army Forty-fives available overseas. Avoid pre-1941 Forty-fives because of transmission problems. The main problem with all Forty-fives is the transmission because there's no drain plug; therefore, most transmissions collect moisture over the years, which means a transmission rebuild. Scarcity of parts is another problem with pre-1941 Forty-fives. Most 1941–1973 parts are interchangeable. If you want a

Servi-Car, pick 1951 and later examples because they have hydraulic brakes.

The frames for all the American-built Harleys of the era don't have "weep" holes to release trapped moisture, so frames require a careful examination and, often, repair of corroded sections. Side-valve 74 and 80 parts are plentiful, except for sheet metal. Restored two-strokes aren't a good investment because you don't get enough of a price break to justify the huge performance gap that separates these from the all other Harleys. (Remember, though, that the name of the game is fun; investment value is only one consideration.) Presently, in the United States, there's not much interest in Sprints; but Aermacchi-branded road-racers go for big bucks in Europe.

Dealers

Twin-Cylinder Parts

Advanced Cycle Machining, 1711 Winter St., Superior, WI 54880, ph. (715) 392-5795, fax (715) 392-7073. Does just about any machining work imaginable. Items repaired include crankcases, cylinders, cylinder heads, and forks. Does specialty work such as no-lead valve seats and guides, two-plug heads, and plumber-nut-to-O-Ring manifold conversions.

Antique Cycle Supply, Inc., P.O. Box 600, Rockford, MI 49341, ph. (616) 636- 8200, fax (616) 636-8669. Parts for Forty-five, K/KH, Seventy-four SV, Eighty SV, Knuckleheads, Panheads. Harley-Davidson parts books, Harley-Davidson service literature, new models' editions (photo copies) of *The Enthusiast*. Catalog published.

Norm Baril, (904) 756-1981. V-twin parts.

Bollenbach Engineering, 296 Williams Place, East Dundee, IL 60118, ph. (847) 428-2800, fax (847) 428-0774. Complete restorations and smaller restoration and repair jobs. Numerous award-winning restorations.

Brandt's Harley-Davidson, 1617 So. Wabash St., Wabash, IN 46992, (219) 563-6443. Some NOS parts, complete restorations, especially 1950s, and lots of Knucklehead parts.

Charleston Custom Cycle, 211 Washington, Charleston, IL 61920, (217) 345-2577. More than one million parts, including more than 800,000 Italian Harley-Davidson parts. World's largest stock of 1945–1978 single-cylinder (mostly Italian) parts. Some K-Model parts. They still buy old parts inventories from dealers and have a large inventory of NOS parts for the Big Twins, XL models, and Forty-five models, Harley snowmobiles, and early golf carts. They do not have used parts, only NOS or reproduction.

Chris' Harley-Davidson Restoration and Parts, 9716 Lemona Ave. #36, North Hills, CA 91343-2422, (818) 894-2113. Specialist in Knucklehead parts; also handle other V-twin parts.

Classic Restorations, P.O. Box 1508, Oshkosh, WI 54902, (414) 233-7461.

Dean's Harley-Davidson, (215) 723-2907.

Mike Egan's Vintage Motorcycle, 136 No. Ojai St., P.O. Box 430, Santa Paula, CA 93060-0430, (805) 933-1557, send SASE. Specializing in the rebuilding and restoration service of Harley-Davidson overhead-valve and flat-head Big Twins, and Forty-five engines and transmissions dating back to the 1910s. Restoration and replacement parts, accessories, original service- and parts-manual reprints and tools for Harley-Davidsons from the mid-1930s to 1965. Mail order vintage parts and accessories catalog for your convenience.

Flathead Power, Fredrikfors 820 60, Delsbo, Sweden. For U-model flatheads: aluminum heads, 14- or 18-mm plugs; cam sets, stock and up; tappet guides; pinion gears; bushing kits; stronger cases are coming, with cam covers. For Knuckleheads: rocker housings 356-T6, rocker covers cast in aluminum, higher lids for use of Shovelhead valves; rocker arms cast in steel and hardened; and tappet guides. More parts to come, including U-model frames and stronger crankcases.

Graves Harley-Davidson, 5702 58th St., Lubbock, TX 79424-1120, telephone (806) 791-4597, fax (806) 791-0218.

Harbor Vintage Cycle, Rt. 2, Box 248, Jonesville, VT 05466, ph. (802) 434-4040, fax (802) 434-5635.

Harley-Davidson of Crete, 1048 Main St., Crete, IL 60417, ph. (708) 672-6601, fax (708) 672-6654. Parts for Panheads and some Shovelheads.

Harley-Davidson Sales, 404 23rd St., Columbus, NE 68601, (402) 564-8732. Lots of Panhead and Forty-five parts, some Knucklehead parts, a few VL parts, no Italian parts, no American-made two-stroke parts. Machine work on Panhead cylinder heads and miscellaneous fabrication, especially on Panheads.

Harley-Davidson Sales, Inc., 14550 Lorain Ave., Cleveland, OH 44111. Letters and faxes only; fax (216) 252-4447.

45" Restoration Company, P.O. Box 12843, Albany, NY 12212, (518) 459-5012. More than 1,400 Forty-five parts stocked including more than 200 remanufactured parts. Catalog published.

Harley Shop, 321-B MacDonald Crescent, Ft. McMurray, Alberta, Canada T9H 4B7, ph./fax (403) 791-0187.

Have Wrench Will Travel Harley-Davidson, 2315 South Avenue West, Missoula, MT 59801, (406) 721-2154.

Indian Joe Martin's, P.O. Box 3156, Chatanooga, TN 37404, (423) 698-1787. "Indian" Joe Martin's Antique Motorcycle Parts carries thousands of NOS, military surplus, and quality reproductions for Harley-Davidson motorcycles. The majority of the original parts are for the Harley Forty-five models, but they also carry parts for the Big Twins. For their latest mail-order parts catalog send $3 ($6 for foreign orders) check or money order.

Jeff's American Classics, 270 No. Highway 99W, Dundee, OR 97115, (503) 538-7028. New, used, and NOS parts for 1936-and-later twins. Over 30 tons of parts. Jeff is an AMCA judge and guarantees the authenticity of all parts shipped; nationwide shipping. Many rare accessories and other items in stock, such as seats, speedometers, 1939 accessory stainless steel fender trim, finned D-ring covers, air cleaners, winged-bird front fender ornament, and so on. Sidecar, package truck, Forty-five, and Servi-Car parts. Lots of Knucklehead and Panhead parts; some K-model parts; no Italian parts; no American-made two-stroke parts.

Jim's Harley-Davidson, P.O. Box 166 State Rt. 707, Mendon, OH 45862, (419) 795-4185. Lots of parts for 1936-and-up twins; some pre-1936 parts. No K-Model parts. Parts for lightweights; see listing for lightweights.

JR Harleys & Classics, Rt. 5, Box 124K, (formerly Rt. 4), Greenville, AL 36037, (334) 382-2547. Complete restorations. Showroom. Can supply *anything* for 1936–1965.

Kesko/Hoover, 603 East Carson Ave., Cushing, OK 74203, (918) 225-1818. Specializes in parts for Italian-made Harley-Davidson lightweights, but they also have some parts for American-made two-strokes, plus XLs and FLs. They offer complete machine-shop services, including very specialized valve jobs for Sprints. Racing and performance work and parts are offered. Service manuals are available for the Italian models and manual purchasers are entitled to free diagnostic help by their experienced and professional staff. Some service tools are currently available and others are forthcoming.

Kick-Start Motorcycle Parts, Inc. (Charles Wesholski), P.O. Box 9347, Wyoming, MI 49509, (616) 245-8991. Parts for 1936–1947 Knuckleheads, including remanufactured cylinder heads. Parts for 1930–1948 Flatheads. Currently building an inventory of Panhead parts. Publishes a catalog.

Lancaster Harley-Davidson, Inc., 308 Beaver Valley Pike, Willow Street, PA 17584, (717) 464-2703. Parts for 1936 and later twins, side-valve and overhead-valve.

Molenar's, 5617 Calumet Ave., Hammond, IN 46320, (219) 563-6443. Mostly big-twin; some 125-cc parts recently found.

David Sarafan, Rt. 16, P.O. Box 338, Santa Fe, NM 87505, (603) 332-4280. Parts for Forty-fives, including WLAs and WRs. Some Knucklehead and JD parts.

The 74 Shop (Peggy Barber), P.O. Box 62, Saugerties, NY 12477, (914) 246-0432.

Sports Motors Harley-Davidson, 1814 Oxford Ave., Eau Claire, WI 54701, ph. (715) 834-0451, fax (715) 832-0076.

Stan's Harley-Davidson, State Street Road, Batavia, NY 14020, (716) 343-9598.

Suburban Motors Harley-Davidson, 139 No. Main, Thiensville, WI 53092, ph. (414) 242-2464, fax (414) 242-7700. Complete restorations, early 1900s and later. Lots of early Sportster, Panhead, and Shovelhead parts; a few VL parts; no Italian parts; no American-made two-stroke parts.

Ted's V-twins, (800) 833-8946.

Throttle Masters M/C Salvage, 3921 So. Archer Ave., Chicago, IL 60632, ph. (773) 247-6114, fax (773) 247-7194. Twenty-five years established as an independent shop with parts, accessories, and repair for Harley-Davidsons. Also, on-going salvage operation with used parts from the 1930s to 1980s for Big Twins, Sportsters, Forty-fives, and Servi-Cars. Has literally tons of used Servi-Car parts, with many from the Chicago Police Department. Many "impossible" parts remanufactured.

Vince's Antique & Modern Cycle Supply, 1031 California Dr., Burlingame, CA 94010, ph. (415) 548-9175, fax (415) 548-9176. Lots of Knucklehead parts and complete Knucklehead motorcycles, some VL parts, very few K-Model parts. Complete restorations, usually built to customer order but sometimes in stock for sale.

Vintage Classics Motorcycle Restorations (Paul Pfaffle), 1332 E. Main St., Waukesha, WI 53186.

VL Heaven, P.O. Box 28, Ware, Herts., SG11 1AG, ENGLAND, ph./fax +44.1920.463383. Steve Slocombe, the person behind this company, is the author of *Buying and Restoring a 1930–36 Harley-Davidson Big Twin*. This 230-page book ($40) contains more than 50 parts diagrams, as well as parts finish and paint-striping details. A 2,000-item VL parts and price list is $10, both prices include air mail costs. VL Heaven claims a range of NOS, used, and quality repro parts covering about 90 percent of the 1930–1936 big-twin model range. Visa/MC/money orders OK.

V-Twin Mfg., Box 473, Valls Gate, NY 12584. Parts for 1939 and later Big Twins (side-valve, Knucklehead, Panhead), and some for 1936–1938, plus parts for Sportster and Model K. Crank cases, timing-case covers, and all engine internals for 1939–1965 Big Twins. Knucklehead, Panhead, and Sportster oil pumps. Transmission cases, tops, kick covers, and all internals for Big Twins and Sportster. Reproduction (replica) frames: 1940 to early 1946, wishbone for 1948 Big Twins, wishbone for 1949–1951 Panhead, 1954–1957 straight-leg Panhead, 1958–1964 Duo-Glide. The 790-page catalog is printed on glossy paper, with more than 5,000 illustrations.

Walkem's, R.R. 1, Norval, ONT., LOP 1KO. Established in 1979. Services mainly older model Harley-Davidsons. Complete motorcycle restorations or any repairs required, including frame straightening, case repair, gas-tank repair/restoration, cylinders resleeved. In-house cad and chrome plating, and in-house painting. Complete machine shop, factory-trained mechanics, and extensive parts inventory.

American-Made Two-Strokes and Italian-Made Models
(Note: the term "Hummer" in these advertisements refers to all American-made two-strokes.)

Antique Cycle Supply, Inc., P.O. Box 600, Rockford, MI 49341, (616)874-6817.

Bayliss & Son, 97 Mistly Lane, Stafford, VA 22554, (540) 752-2663.

Jerry Barbour, P.O. Box 242, Lizella, GA 31052-0242, (912) 935-8638. Specializing in Aermacchi/Harley-Davidson lightweights, 1961–1978 50 cc to 350 cc (Sprint, M-50, M-65, Rapido, Leggero, SX/SS 175/250). Buy, sell, trade, NOS, reconditioned, or used parts. Restoration and service. Also, parts for 1948–1966 American-made two-strokes.

Charleston Custom Cycle, 211 Washington, Charleston, IL 61920, (217) 345-2577. More than one million parts, including more than 800,000 Italian Harley-Davidson parts. World's largest stock of 1945–1978 single-cylinder (mostly Italian) parts. Some K-Model parts.

Chosa's Harley-Davidson, 922 So. Country Club Dr., Mesa, AZ 85210, (602) 844-2818. Lots of small parts for Italian models, such as pistons and piston rings. No large body items like tanks and fenders.

Dale's Modern Harley-Davidson, 225 E. Baseline, San Bernadino, CA 92410, ph. (909) 884-6464, fax (909) 381-4700.

Jim's Harley-Davidson, P.O. Box 166 State Rt. 707, Mendon, OH 45862, (419) 795-4185. Lots of parts for American-made two-strokes. Reproduction parts such as seat pans, Model 165 carburetor cover, chain guards, gaskets, carburetor parts, pistons, clutches, and exhaust systems. Complete restorations. Reproduction parts for Topper motorscooters, such as foot rests, foot boards, seats, clutch parts, gaskets, and pistons. Also have Big Twin parts.

Kesko/Hoover, 603 East Carson Ave., Cushing, OK 74203, (918) 225-1818. They specialize in parts for Italian-made Harley-Davidson lightweights and offer a complete machine shop, including specialized valve jobs for Sprints. Racing and performance work and parts are offered. Service manuals are available for the Italian models, and manual purchasers are entitled to free diagnostic help by their experienced and professional staff. Some service tools are currently available and others are forthcoming.

Lancaster Harley-Davidson, Inc., 308 Beaver Valley Pike, Willow Street, PA 17584, (717) 464-2703. Fairly good supply of parts for Italian-made models. A few parts for American-made two-strokes. Complete restorations. Some Big Twin parts.

Lange's, 19916 Old Owen Road, Monroe, WA 98272, (360) 794-7934. Specializing in Harley-Davidson 125-, 165-, and 175-cc American-made two-stroke models, Lee Lange is bringing Hummers back to life. Full engine and transmission rebuilds and mechanical and electrical service. Rolling basket cases to museum-grade restorations for sale. Original and authentic reproduction parts from the Lange fabrication shop. Reasonable and responsive.

The Harley Hummer Nut, Travis Scott, 6800 Doe Valley Rd., Guffey, CO 80820. NOS parts, used parts, and everything that is being reproduced for these bikes. Some new items include hubcaps, seat pans and complete seats, exhaust pipe clamps, seat springs, jiffy-stand springs, 1948–1950 cables, crash bars, and much more. Send $2 for a 17-page list of parts for sale or trade. Also, project bikes to fit any budget.

Moto Italia, 13960 Highway 9, Boulder Creek, CA 95006, ph./fax (408) 338-3340. On the internet at http://www.aa.net/~garage/motoital.html. Specializing in parts, tools, and manuals for the Italian-made Aermacchi Harley-Davidson from 1961 and later.

Mike Stamm, 3401 S. 1st, Abilene, TX 79605, (915) 676-8788. NOS, used, and reproduction Hummer parts. NOS Goodyear tires: 3.50x18 A/T Eagles and 16x19 Grasshoppers. Also available: tool boxes, chain guards, seats, seat springs and brackets, and speedometers. NOS mint in-box complete Teleglide windshield assemblies and NOS piston rings. Dealership banners, posters, postcards, NOS owner's manuals, oil cans, catalog rack, parts books and miscellaneous items. Send $3 for memorabilia list with SASE.

Index